Parallel Programming
with OpenACC

Parallel Programming
with OpenACC

Edited By

Rob Farber

AMSTERDAM • BOSTON • HEIDELBERG • LONDON
NEW YORK • OXFORD • PARIS • SAN DIEGO
SAN FRANCISCO • SINGAPORE • SYDNEY • TOKYO

Morgan Kaufmann is an imprint of Elsevier

Library of Congress Cataloging-in-Publication Data
A catalog record for this book is available from the Library of Congress

British Library Cataloguing-in-Publication Data
A catalogue record for this book is available from the British Library

ISBN: 978-0-12-410397-9

For information on all Morgan Kaufmann publications
visit our website at https://www.elsevier.com/

Publisher: Todd Green
Acquisition Editor: Todd Green
Editorial Project Manager: Lindsay Lawrence
Production Project Manager: Priya Kumaraguruparan
Cover Designer: Miles Hitchens

Typeset by SPi Global, India

Contents

Contributors

C. Keith Cassidy
University of Illinois at Urbana-Champaign, United States

Keith is a graduate student in the Department of Physics at the University of Illinois Urbana-Champaign. As part of the Theoretical and Computational Biophysics Group, his research centers on the use of computational methodologies to study molecular signal transduction and information processing within the context of bacterial chemotaxis.

Sunita Chandrasekaran
University of Delaware, United States

Sunita is an Assistant Professor at the Computer & Information Sciences department and an affiliated faculty member with the Center for Bioinformatics & Computational Biology (CBCB) at the University of Delaware. She explores high-level programming abstractions for HPC and embedded systems. She also creates validation suites testing conformance of compiler implementations to programming standard specifications. She is a member of the OpenMP and OpenACC standard communities. She also contributes scientific parallel applications to SPEC HPG, of which she is a member. She has worked with the Multicore Association consortium to design and use open standard APIs for embedded systems. Dr. Chandrasekaran earned her PhD in Computer Science Engineering from Nanyang Technological University, Singapore for creating a high-level software stack for FPGAs.

Barbara Chapman
Stony Brook University, United States

Barbara is a Professor of Applied Mathematics and Statistics, and of Computer Science, at Stony Brook University, where she is affiliated with the Institute for Advanced Computational Science. She has performed research on parallel programming interfaces and the related implementation technology for over 20 years and has been involved in efforts to develop community standards for parallel programming, including OpenMP, OpenACC, and OpenSHMEM. Her group at the University of Houston developed the OpenUH compiler that enabled practical experimentation with proposed extensions and implementation techniques. Dr. Chapman has participated in the work of the Multicore Association and explores the use of accelerators to obtain high performance on a broad variety of applications.

Mathew Colgrove
The Portland Group, United States

Mat is an NVIDIA Dev Tech working with the PGI compiler team. Mat's primary focus is on training, customer support, and programming advice on using the PGI compilers, as well as OpenACC. Mat is also NVIDIA's representative on SPEC's CPU and HPG benchmarking committees.

Janus Juul Eriksen
Aarhus University, Denmark

Janus is a postdoctoral researcher employed at the qLEAP Center for Theoretical Chemistry, Department of Chemistry, Aarhus University, Denmark. His work is concerned in part with new theoretical developments in the area of accurate wave function-based quantum chemistry and in part the HPC adaption of the resulting models.

Robert Dietrich
Technische Universität Dresden, Germany

Robert studied Information Systems Technology at Technische Universitaet Dresden and graduated in 2009. The focus as junior researcher and his diploma thesis was FPGA programmability in the context of high-performance computing. After graduation, he worked on the support of hardware accelerators and coprocessors in known performance analysis tools such as VampirTrace, Score-P, and Vampir. He is an active member in the OpenACC consortium and the OpenMP committee, focusing on the standardization of tools support. He has carried out recent research in automatic analysis techniques for applications on heterogeneous architectures.

Rob Farber
TechEnablement.com, United States

Rob is a scientist and consultant with an extensive background in HPC and a long history of starting companies as well as working with national laboratories and corporations engaged in HPC, real-time, and machine learning. Rob is well published in technical and peer-reviewed literature. He has authored/edited several books and is the CEO/Publisher of TechEnablement.com.

Saber Feki
King Abdullah University of Science and Technology, Saudi Arabia

Saber leads the Computational Scientists Team at the Supercomputing Core Laboratory at King Abdullah University of Science and Technology. He was part of the technical team for the procurement and led the acceptance of the world's top 10 supercomputer, Shaheen XC40. Saber received his MSc and PhD degrees in computer science from the University of Houston in 2008 and 2010, respectively. He then joined the oil and gas company TOTAL in 2011 as HPC Research Scientist. Saber has been with KAUST since 2012. His research interests include parallel programming models and automatic performance tuning of MPI communications and OpenACC accelerated applications such as computational electromagnetics and seismic imaging.

Oliver Fuhrer
MeteoSwiss, Switzerland

Oliver is the team leader of the model development group at the Federal Office of Meteorology and Climatology MeteoSwiss, Zurich. He has over 10 years' experience in the fields of high-performance computing, regional climate simulation, and numerical weather prediction. He has applied and developed parallel software on vector (NEC SX-5) as well as massively parallel (HPC Cluster Brutus, Cray XT-4/5, XE6, XK7, XC30, as well as several experimental heterogeneous cluster solutions) architectures. He studied physics at ETH Zurich, where he also completed his PhD in 2000 at the Institute of Atmospheric and Climate Science (IAC, ETH) on the topic of numerical simulation of convection at very high resolutions. He regularly lectures a course on numerical methods at ETH Zurich.

Wayne Gaudin
AWE plc., United Kingdom

Wayne is a Computational Physicist with over 20 years of experience working on complex codes in an HPC environment. Over the last 3 years, he has concentrated on assessing emerging technologies and programming models in a number of algorithmic areas.

Andy Herdman
AWE plc., United Kingdom

Andy is Head of the High Performance Computing section at AWE plc. He graduated from Newcastle University with a BSc (Hons) in Mathematics and Statistics; he also holds an MSc in Applied Mathematics. He has worked in the HPC applications field for over 20 years. Roles have included Technical Team Leader, responsible for code porting and optimization, and Group Leader of multidisciplined teams, covering engineering codes, data visualization, and advanced technologies. He is currently a Visiting Fellow at the University of Warwick, researching his doctorate in the field of high-performance computing.

Guido Juckeland
Helmholtz-Zentrum Dresden-Rossendorf (HZDR), Germany

Guido runs the Computational Science Group at Helmholtz-Zentrum Dresden-Rossendorf (HZDR) and coordinates the work of the GPU Center of Excellence at Dresden. He and also represents HZDR at the SPEC High Performance Group and OpenACC committee. He received his PhD for his work on performance analysis for hardware accelerators.

Jiri Kraus
NVIDIA GmbH, Germany

Jiri is a senior developer in NVIDIA's European Developer Technology team. As a consultant for GPU HPC applications at the NVIDIA Julich Applications Lab and the Power Acceleration and Design Center (PADC), Jiri collaborates with developers and scientists at the Julich Supercomputing Centre and the Forschungszentrum Julich. Before joining NVIDIA, he worked on the parallelization and optimization of scientific and technical applications for clusters of multicore CPUs and GPUs at Fraunhofer SCAI in St. Augustin. He holds a diploma in mathematics from the University of Cologne, Germany.

Xavier Lapillonne
MeteoSwiss, Switzerland

Xavier is a senior scientist in the model development group at the Federal Office of Meteorology and Climatology MeteoSwiss, Zurich since 2015. He is working in the field of high-performance computing, in particular on hybrid systems, and is currently the project leader of the Performance on Massively Parallel Architectures project for the Consortium for Small-Scale Modeling (COSMO). He received a PhD in physics from EPF Lausanne in 2010, where he worked on massively parallel codes to simulate turbulence in hot plasmas. He has experience in developing and running scientific models on many supercomputers, including hybrid architectures (IBM blue gene, Bull NovaScale, Cray XT-4/5, XE6, XK7, XC30, CS-Storm).

Jeff Larkin
NVIDIA Corp, United States

Jeff is a software engineer in NVIDIA's developer technologies group where he specializes in porting and optimizing high-performance computing applications. He currently lives in Knoxville, TN with his wife and son. Jeff represents NVIDIA to both the OpenACC and OpenMP standards organizations where he works on the future development of both specifications. Prior to joining NVIDIA, Jeff worked in the Cray Supercomputing Center of Excellence at Oak Ridge National Laboratory and has degrees in Computer Science from Furman University (BSc) and the University of Tennessee (MS).

Ty McKercher
NVIDIA Corp, USA

Ty is a Director, and Principal Solution Architect for the Worldwide Field Organization at NVIDIA. He often serves as a technical consultant, helping integrate prerelease hardware and software during customer technology evaluations. He has over 8 years of experience deploying GPUs in demanding HPC production environments. He is a coauthor of *Professional CUDA C Programming*.

Katherine Osterried
MeteoSwiss, Switzerland

Katherine is the regional climate modeling scientific programmer at the Center for Climate Systems Modeling, a competency center based at the Swiss Federal Institute of Technology in Zurich. She works on the development and implementation of regional climate models on high-performance computing systems in the context of numerical weather prediction and regional climate simulations. She has more than 10 years of experience in scientific programming, including contributions to the development of the GPU capable version of the numerical weather prediction code. Katherine holds a BSc in Mathematics and Physics from Southwestern University and a PhD in Geophysical Fluid Dynamics from the Massachusetts Institute of Technology/Woods Hole Oceanographic Institution Joint Program.

Juan R. Perilla
University of Illinois at Urbana-Champaign, United States

Juan received his PhD in Biophysics from the Johns Hopkins University. He is currently a research scientist in the Theoretical and Computational Biophysics Group at the University of Illinois at Urbana-Champaign. His research focuses on the molecular architecture of the HIV-1 capsid, and its interactions with cellular host-factors and drug compounds.

Oliver Perks
AWE plc., United Kingdom

Oliver is an HPC researcher at AWE plc focusing on development of applications for emerging and future hardware. Oliver has a PhD in HPC from Warwick University for developing tools and methods for analyzing performance characteristics of parallel applications.

Klaus Schulten
University of Illinois at Urbana-Champaign,
United States

Prof. Schulten is a leader in the field of computational biophysics, having devoted over 40 years to establishing the physical mechanisms underlying processes and organization in living systems from the atomic to the organism scale. Schulten is a strong proponent of the use of simulations as a "computational microscope," to augment experimental research, and to lead to discoveries that could not be made through experiments so far. The molecular dynamics and structure analysis programs NAMD and VMD, born and continuously developed in his group, are used today by many thousands of researchers across the world.

He holds a Diploma degree in physics from the University of Muenster, Germany (1969), and a PhD in chemical physics from Harvard University (1974). Schulten came to the University of Illinois in 1988, and in 1989 joined the Beckman Institute and founded the Theoretical and Computational Biophysics Group, which operates the NIH Center for Macromolecular Modeling and Bioinformatics.

Since 2008 he has been co-director of the NSF-funded Center for the Physics of Living Cells.

Schulten's awards and honors include: 2015 Biophysical Society National Lecturer, Blue Waters Professorship, National Center for Supercomputing Applications (2014); Professorship, University of Illinois Center for Advanced Study (2013); Distinguished Service Award, Biophysical Society (2013); IEEE Computer Society Sidney Fernbach Award (2012); Fellow of the Biophysical Society (2012); Award in Computational Biology (2008); Humboldt Award of the German Humboldt Foundation (2004); University of Illinois Scholar (1996); Fellow of the American Physical Society (1993); and Nernst Prize of the Physical Chemistry Society of Germany (1981).

Malek Smaoui
King Abdullah University of Science and Technology, Saudi Arabia

Malek is a Lecturer in the Computer, Electrical and Mathematical Sciences & Engineering division at King Abdullah University of Science and Technology, where she offers courses on various topics including programming, data structures and algorithms, parallel programming, and computer architecture. She received her MSc and PhD degrees in computer science from the University of Houston in 2008 and 2011, respectively. Her research interests include nature-inspired optimization algorithms and volunteer computing.

John E. Stone
University of Illinois at Urbana-Champaign, United States

John is a Senior Research Programmer in the Theoretical and Computational Biophysics Group at the University of Illinois at Urbana-Champaign. He is the lead developer of VMD, a high-performance molecular visualization tool used by researchers all over the world.

John also serves as an Associate Director for the GPU Center of Excellence at the University of Illinois at Urbana-Champaign. His research interests include molecular visualization, GPU computing, parallel computing, ray tracing, haptics, virtual environments, and immersive visualization. Mr. Stone was inducted as an NVIDIA CUDA Fellow in 2010. In 2015 Mr. Stone joined the Khronos Group Advisory Panel for the Vulkan Graphics API. Mr. Stone is also a consultant for projects involving high-performance computing, GPUs, and computer graphics. John received his MS in Computer Science from the University of Missouri at Rolla in 1998.

Michael Wolfe
The Portland Group, United States

Michael has over 40 years of experience designing and implementing languages and compilers for high-performance and parallel computers in industry and academia, most recently including PGI OpenACC for multicore and heterogeneous targets. He has written one textbook, "High Performance Compilers for Parallel Computing," and a number of technical papers, and occasionally writes articles for the online newsletter HPCwire.

Dr. Rengan Xu
University of Houston, United States

Rengan is a Systems Staff Engineer (HPC Benchmarking Specialist) in Dell. He earned his PhD degree in Computer Science from the University of Houston in May 2016. His research interests include the programming models for multicore system and accelerators, and the implementation of these programming models in the compiler and runtime. He also has rich experience on application parallelization and optimization using different high-performance programming models.

Foreword by Michael Wolfe

It's all about Performance.

In one short sentence, that sums up this book—*Parallel Programming with OpenACC*. For many readers, that sums up what you want and need, whether you believe it yet or not. From the beginning of digital computing until the turn of the millennium, we expected and received faster computer systems almost every year, due largely to semiconductor technology improvements. For the past 12 years, processor clock rates have not improved. This means that parallelism, in some form, is the only avenue for higher performance.

Parallel computing is not a new topic. For over 50 years, parallelism in computer designs has been exploited in one form or another. Pipelined processors with multiple independent functional units appeared in the 1960s with the Control Data 6600 and 7600 and the IBM 360 model 91. Vector processors appeared in the 1970s with the Control Data STAR, Texas Instruments ASC, and Cray 1. Multiprocessor systems were also designed and built in that time period, and symmetric shared memory multiprocessors became common in the 1980s, particularly with the availability of single-chip 32-bit microprocessors. Highly parallel multi-node computer systems became available in the 1980s as well, such as the nCUBE hypercube, Intel iPSC/1, and many, many more. The various message-passing programming models eventually became standardized in the Message Passing Interface in common use today. For a programmer, today's top supercomputers have many similarities to those early hypercube systems, though the largest current systems have more than 90,000 nodes.

Now we are at another inflection point in the design of high-performance computer systems.

Parallelism is still the performance driver, and these systems will have many message-passing nodes, but the nodes themselves are now becoming highly parallel. Even workstations are much more parallel than in the past. This is due in part to processor microarchitecture adopting the pipelining and multiple functional unit features of early supercomputers. These processors include SIMD instructions, with similar functionality to early vector processors, and incorporate multiple cores, each core acting like an independent processor in the symmetric, shared-memory operating system. Some workstations and supercomputer nodes have multiple processor chips as well, with cache coherence managed by a high speed inter-processor interconnect. The number of cores at each node or in a high-end workstation is increasing dramatically, from single digits to over 20 today and many more in the near future. The Intel Many Integrated Core (MIC) CPUs will have up to 72 cores on a single chip by the time this book is published. Many CPUs have cores that also support multiple hardware threads, delivering higher overall performance by taking advantage of even more application-level parallelism.

Recently, the use of attached accelerators has become common, in particular using GPUs for computing. Attached accelerators appeared as far back as the

1970s, with the Floating Point Systems AP-120B and the IBM 3838. As semiconductor technology has grown more complex and expensive, it has become less economically feasible to design and implement an accelerator customized for high performance computing. However, GPUs have the advantage that their "day job," graphics processing, pays for much of the design and validation cost. GPUs as compute devices thus benefit from the same economic advantages as high-volume CPUs.

GPUs are optimized for the kind of highly parallel, regular computations that appear in the graphics pipeline, which just happens to map well onto many scientific and engineering applications. GPUs are designed with the same kinds of parallelism that appear in current CPUs, including pipelining, many cores, SIMD-style execution, and multithreading, but the numbers and widths for a GPU are much higher. GPUs also give up the large cache, instead opting for more cores and a higher bandwidth memory interface, a design decision we also see in the latest Intel MIC processor.

This all looks like a great deal of new complexity being foisted on the poor application programmer. In fact, all of the advanced computer system designs we see today and foresee in the future take advantage of the same kinds of parallelism commonly used over the past five decades, although with more parallelism on smaller devices. Since applications often live longer than any single computer system, they can and should be written to deliver high performance on future systems that haven't even been designed yet. This book will help you craft your application with the right algorithms and the right data structures, so you can benefit from the highly parallel systems available today, and those coming over the next few decades.

The challenge that you, the reader, must undertake when designing or refactoring your application for the next decade or two is to expose and express enough parallelism in your application to fill all those parallel compute lanes. This includes enough multicore parallelism to keep many tens or hundreds of compute cores busy, and perhaps another factor of 2–10 more to fill the multithreading slots. This also includes enough SIMD parallelism to take advantage of SIMD instructions and high bandwidth memories. You must design scalable algorithms and data structures to take advantage of all the compute parallelism and high bandwidth memory paths. Since you cannot improve what you cannot measure, use the profile and trace tools at your disposal to identify your hot spots. If possible, run your application on two or more very different target systems, to measure its portability and stability.

Along the way, you must choose an appropriate language in which to express your application. There are many good options, but this book focuses on OpenACC directives. As a language, OpenACC has three advantages. First, while parallel programming is never easy, adding directives to a working program is more straightforward than rewriting in a new language. Second, OpenACC was designed for the highly parallel future. It intentionally has fewer ways to insert synchronization into your program, forcing you to design more scalable programs. Third, OpenACC was designed with portability across different accelerated systems as well as CPU-only systems in mind. You can write a single OpenACC program that performs well on very different target systems. You certainly don't want to be in the position of having to refactor or re-tune your application every time a vendor comes out with a new model, or your users move to a new supercomputer.

Remember that the final goal is Performance! There are many aspects of a program that lead to higher performance. Design your program to exploit all of them.

Michael Wolfe,
OpenACC Technical Committee Chair and PGI Compiler Engineer.

Preface

Welcome to our book, a collection of introductory, intermediate, and advanced chapters that provides an OpenACC education from beginner to advanced. The book draws on 23 authors from around the world who have shared their expertise in both teaching and working with highly parallel programming. Their examples are both timely and timeless. Each chapter is written to be self-contained for private study or as a section for classroom study. PowerPoint slides and example codes are available on the github: https://github.com/rmfarber/ParallelProgrammingWithOpenACC.

This book is about parallel programming and not about OpenACC pragmas alone, or providing information that can be gleaned from documentation. It is about acquiring the knowledge to write practical and performant as well as portable parallel programs that can run across a broad spectrum of devices, ranging from CPUs to GPUs. To make this concrete, the authors in this book demonstrate the use of compilers by vendors like PGI, Cray, and PathScale to create working example codes and demonstrate them running on Intel x86 processors, Cavium 96-core 64-bit ARMv8 processor chipsets, and NVIDIA GPUs.

Performance and profiling go hand-in-hand, which is why both open source and PGI profilers are also included.

It is amazing how the OpenACC standard has changed, and compiler technology matured since my first June 11, 2012 OpenACC tutorial on the Dr. Dobbs website: "Easy GPU Parallelism with OpenACC." The past 4 years of intense development mean that OpenACC is now available at most HPC sites and even in the freely available GNU compiler toolset. Access and availability is why real application examples are provided in the intermediate and advanced programming chapters—because programmers need to solve real problems, not just work on classroom problems. Meanwhile, OpenACC is still new enough that we can all benefit from a few good introductory chapters!

Acknowledgments

It has been my good fortune to work with the incredible contributors to this book. I admire their dedication, intelligence, and willingness to share their expertise. Their names are listed at the start of their chapters to which they contributed, and you can learn more about them and see their pictures in the "Contributor" section in this book. I hope you reap the full benefit of the hard work and years of experience they poured into each chapter.

Also never forget that being able to write and speak clearly are essential skills in any field, be it science, technology, or life. If in doubt, write a book! I can recommend an excellent publisher who is named on the book cover.

Thank you to Michael Wolfe for his support and extraordinary contributions to OpenACC, and to offering his thoughts in the Foreword.

Thank you to Todd Green, Julia Levites, Duncan Poole, Pat Brooks, and Nadeem Mohammed without whom this book would not have happened.

I'd like to thank a few of the many others who worked hard behind the scenes on this book: Nikolai Sakharnykh, James Beyer, Ken Hester, Brent Leback, James Norris, Kshitij Mehta, Adrian Jackson, Abid Muslim Malik, Maxime Hughes, Sunita Chandrasekaran, and Kartik Mankad. We have been blessed with the support and encouragement of management at NVIDIA, PGI, PathScale, and Cavium plus the fruits of the labor of those who are working to develop the OpenACC standard and compilers.

I wish to personally thank my son Ryan Farber for his love and the time I spent away from him while working on this project. Ryan is proof that I am the older model. He is growing into a global mover and shaker. I am blessed with a son who will far exceed my accomplishments. I'd also like to thank my friends James Reinders and Bertil Schmidt who have edited (many) books in the past and who provided insight that helped me create this book.

Kudo's to the entire Morgan Kaufmann team including the three people we worked with directly: Todd Green, Lindsay Lawrence and Priya Kumaraguruparan.

So many people offered information, advice, and vision that it simply not possible to name them all. I thank everyone who helped, and I apologize to any who helped and were not mentioned here.

Thank you all,
Rob Farber

From serial to parallel programming using OpenACC

1

Rob Farber

CEO/Publisher of TechEnablement.com

The purpose of this chapter is to introduce the reader to OpenACC® and demonstrate how it can be used to write portable parallel programs that can run on multicore CPUs and accelerators like GPUs. Example programs will show the reader how to compile and run on both CPUs and GPUs.

At the end of this chapter the reader will have a basic understanding of:

- How to create, build and run OpenACC applications
- Three rules of high-performance OpenACC programming
- The basic concepts of data-parallel and task-parallel programming
- An understanding of Big-O notation and Amdahl's law
- Race conditions, atomic operations, and how to avoid them
- The importance of lock-free programming
- How to control parallel resource utilization in OpenACC

A SIMPLE DATA-PARALLEL LOOP

Programming a sequential processor requires writing a program that specifies each of the tasks and data operations needed to compute some end result. OpenACC was created so programmers can insert pragmas to provide information to the compiler about parallelization opportunities and data movement operations to and from accelerators. Programmers use pragmas to work in concert with the compiler to create, tune and optimize parallel codes to achieve high performance.

OpenACC helps programmers write efficient data- and task-parallel software.

Data-parallelism focuses on distributing data operations across multiple concurrent threads of execution. A *thread* in computer science is short for a thread of execution that runs a section of code serially. By using multiple threads of execution, an application can make use of parallel hardware such as multicore processors

Parallel Programming with OpenACC. http://dx.doi.org/10.1016/B978-0-12-410397-9.00001-9

and massively parallel GPUs, which in turn can make the application run faster as multiple threads can be concurrently running—at the same time—meaning more work can be performed per unit time.

Similarly, *task-parallelism* focuses on distributing computational tasks across multiple concurrent threads of execution. Again, the application will run faster as multiple tasks can be performed in parallel at the same time.

The following C++ example, *accFill_ex1.cpp* makes data-parallelism concrete as the program dynamically allocates and then fills an array of values in the byte array **status** (Fig. 1).

```cpp
#include <iostream>
using namespace std;
#include <cstdlib>
#include <cassert>

int main(int argc, char *argv[])
{
  if(argc < 2) {
    cerr << "Use: nCount" << endl;
    return -1;
  }

  int nCount = atoi(argv[1])*1000000;

  if(nCount < 0) {
    cerr << "ERROR: nCount must be greater than zero!" << endl;
    return -1;
  }

  // allocate variables
  char *status = new char[nCount];

  // Here is where we fill the status vector
#pragma acc parallel loop copyout( status[0:nCount] )
  for(int i=0; i < nCount; i++)
    status[i] = 1;

  // Sanity check to see that array is filled with ones
  int sum=0;
  for(int i=0; i < nCount; i++)
    sum += status[i];

  cout << "Final sum is " << (sum/1000000) << " millions" << endl;

  assert(sum == nCount);

  delete [] status;

  return 0; // normal exit
}
```

FIG. 1

A data-parallel example that initializes an array using multiple threads of execution.

This example follows good programming practice by performing checks that the user input makes sense: specifically that the array size is greater than zero. A sanity check is also performed to confirm that the **status** array was indeed correctly filled with ones before the program exits. The actual check is performed via a call to `assert()`, which will generate a core dump if the conditional (`sum == nCount`) is proven false. Also note that assert shouldn't be called within a parallel region on the device as early exits are not allowed.

Using *assert()* while writing code is an excellent way to help verify code correctness as assertions can quickly find coding errors while debugging. Assertions can literally be removed from the code by defining **NDEBUG** during compilation once debugging is finished. As a result, no runtime or memory is consumed by *assert()* once debugging is finished.

Good programming practice dictates that the success of the Application Program Interface (API) calls should be verified. Astute readers will note that the success of the dynamic memory allocation of **status** was not checked. This was omitted for brevity.

The only OpenACC annotation required to convert *accFill_ex1.cpp* from a sequential code to one that can run in parallel using potentially thousands of concurrent threads of execution is the line, "`#pragma acc parallel loop copyout(status[0:nCount])`."

This pragma can be interpreted as follows:

- "`#pragma acc parallel loop`": The "`#pragma acc`" tells the compiler this is an OpenACC pragma. The "`parallel`" keyword tells the compiler to use the rules for a parallel construct (as opposed to a `kernels` construct), which will be discussed in the next section. The "`loop`" clause tells the compiler that we actually want the C++ **for** loop to be parallelized. OpenACC pragmas utilize C++ scoping rules to define the scope of the code block to which this pragma applies. In this example, the code contained in the **for** loop will run in parallel.
- "`copyout(status[0:nCount])`": This clause tells the OpenACC compiler to create an array of **status** values with starting index 0 with **nCount** elements on the OpenACC device(s). The elements will only be copied back from the device at the end of the parallel region so the host version of **status** will contain the same contents as the accelerator version.
  - We used the `copyout()` rather than `copy()` clause in this example to avoid the unnecessary movement of uninitialized data from the host to the accelerator.
  - Compilers are not required perform data movements in the special case when the OpenACC host that runs the sequential code shares the same memory as the parallel device. For example, no data movement occurs when running this OpenACC example on a multicore processor.

The source code can be compiled to run on both the Central Processing Unit (CPU) and Graphical Processing Unit (GPU) using a Portland Group (PGI®) unified binary as shown in Fig. 2. A unified binary contains the executable for multiple devices. The "-Minfo=accel" command-line argument tells the compiler to output accelerator information for various loops. As can be seen in boldface, both Tesla and Multicore kernels were generated. We use "tesla" because the "nvidia" keyword is deprecated. Counterintuitively, "tesla" executables can run on all NVIDIA® GPUs. This chapter uses version 16.5 of the PGI compiler.

```
$ pgc++ -std=c++11 -acc -ta=multicore,tesla -Minfo=accel accFill_ex1.cpp -o accFill_ex1
main:
     21, Generating copyout(status[:nCount])
         Accelerator kernel generated
         Generating Tesla code
         25, #pragma acc loop gang, vector(128) /* blockIdx.x threadIdx.x */
     21, Generating Multicore code
         25, #pragma acc loop gang
```

FIG. 2

Compilation messages for both CPU and GPU devices in a unified binary.

The following shows that the code runs correctly on a multicore ×86 processor as well as an NVIDIA GPU. The PGI OpenACC runtime checks the **ACC_DEVICE_TYPE** environmental variable when running a unified binary to determine which device to use (Fig. 3).

```
$ export ACC_DEVICE_TYPE=host
$ $ ./accFill_ex1 1000
Final sum is 1000 millions
$ export ACC_DEVICE_TYPE=nvidia
$ ./accFill_ex1 1000
Final sum is 1000 millions
```

FIG. 3

Running on both the host and GPU using a PGI unified binary.

THE OpenACC KERNELS CONSTRUCT COMPARED TO THE PARALLEL CONSTRUCT

OpenACC has two parallel computing constructs, the `parallel` construct used in the previous *accFilll_ex1.cpp* example and the `kernels` construct which will be demonstrated next.

Succinctly, a parallel construct in OpenACC tells the compiler that everything in the scope of the following region is a single parallel operation that will run in each thread. Adding a "loop" clause (per the preceding example) tells the compiler to try and parallelize everything inside the loop in each thread, which is the behavior OpenMP® programmers would expect. In CUDA terms, the parallel construct gets translated into a single CUDA kernel.

Safety tip: A common error is to forget to specify the loop directive (e.g., only specify #pragma acc parallel), which mistakenly tells the compiler that everything in the scope of the following code block will run in parallel, which means one **for** loop will run in each parallel thread! Also, it is easy to forget the "acc" in the pragma, in which case the loop will not get parallelized at all. These are but two of a myriad of reasons why it is important to check the compiler messages as well as verify that each parallel region actually runs in parallel on the device(s).

In contrast, a `kernels` construct gives the compiler much more flexibility to generate efficient parallel code for the targeted device(s) including combining loops into a single parallel kernel or creating multiple parallel kernels. It also places the responsibility on the compiler to ensure that it is safe to parallelize the loop, unlike `parallel` where it is told that it is safe to do so. This also means the compiler will tend to be very cautious and sometimes require more information before it will parallelize certain loops. There are three steps to the kernels parallelization process:

1. Identify the loops that can be executed in parallel.
2. Map that abstract loop parallelism onto concrete hardware parallelism (e.g., threads that can run on a multicore processor or into to appropriate parallel configuration for a GPU).
3. Have the compiler generate and optimize the actual code to implement the selected parallelism mapping.

The following example, *accFill_ex2.cpp* utilizes the `kernels` construct to perform both the fill operation and calculation of the sum in parallel on the OpenACC device. Use of the `kernels` construct in this example eliminates the need to transfer the array as all computations will be performed on the device (Fig. 4).

Note that the logic of the C++ code is identical between the two examples, but the OpenACC pragmas are different.

- accTask_ex1.cpp: `#pragma acc parallel loop copyout(status[0:nCount])`
- accTask_ex2.cpp: `#pragma acc kernels create(status[0:nCount])`

In addition, curly brackets, "{" and "}" were added to define the scope of the `kernels` construct. A `create` clause was also used to allocate space for the status array on the OpenACC device.

A vector reduction was specified via the second pragma "`#pragma acc loop vector reduction(+:sum)`."

Very simply, the reduction specified in the code sums all the values of in the **status** array using vector instructions when the target device supports them. More precisely, the `reduction()` clause takes an operator (in this case "+") and one or more scalar variables. Our example uses the variable **sum**. At the end of the OpenACC region the parallel result is combined with the value of the original variable. This is why **sum** must be initialized to some value (in this case zero) before the reduction else undefined behavior will result.

The `vector` clause tells the OpenACC that it can exploit *vector parallelism*.

Succinctly, vector instructions use hardware to effectively (from a software point of view) perform a number of operations at the same time, thus it is another form of parallelism. Each core in a modern multicore ×86 processor can issue vector instructions to a hardware vector units (or multiple per-core vector units) to perform multiple data-parallel operations at the same time. The AVX-512 vector instruction set, for example, is the current longest vector instruction set provided on ×86 processors that can perform up to 16 concurrent single-precision, 32-bit floating-point operations per instruction call. The end result is an up to 16× performance multiplier per vector unit. This can result in a large overall performance gain when all the vector

```cpp
#include <iostream>
using namespace std;
#include <cstdlib>
#include <cassert>

int main(int argc, char *argv[])
{
  if(argc < 2) {
    cerr << "Use: nCount" << endl;
    return -1;
  }

  int nCount = atoi(argv[1])*1000000;

  if(nCount < 0) {
    cerr << "ERROR: nCount must be greater than zero!" << endl;
    return -1;
  }

  // allocate variables
  char *status = new char[nCount];

  // Here is where we fill the status vector
  int sum=0; // Important to zero-initialize sum
#pragma acc kernels create( status[0:nCount] )
  {
    for(int i=0; i < nCount; i++)
      status[i] = 1;
#pragma acc loop vector reduction(+:sum)
    for(int i=0; i < nCount; i++)
      sum += status[i];
  }

  cout << "Final sum is " << (sum/1000000) << " millions" << endl;

  // Sanity check to see that array is filled with ones
  assert(sum == nCount);

  delete [] status;

  return 0; // normal exit
}
```

FIG. 4

A kernels based data-parallel fill example accFill_ex2.cpp.

units on all the cores in a high-end processor are fully utilized. GPUs utilize SIMD (Single Instruction Multiple Data) instructions to achieve a similar performance multiplier effect, except that vectorization naturally occurs in hardware across a group of threads referred to as a warp (CUDA terminology for a set of 32 threads) rather than through the explicit issuance of vector instructions by the programmer or compiler.

A schematic representation showing the performance benefits of vector and parallel programming on multicore processors is shown in Fig. 5.

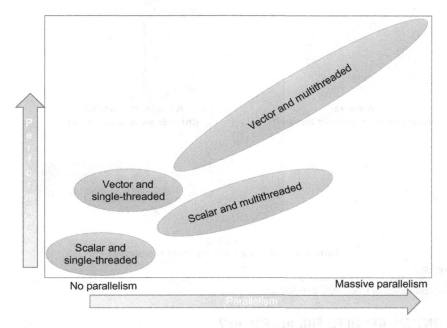

FIG. 5

Multicore parallel and vector performance.

THE VARIOUS FORMS OF OpenACC PARALLELISM

The OpenACC execution model allows users to express three levels of parallelism: gang, worker, and vector.

As illustrated in Fig. 6, starting at the top:

- A thread: The core parallel concept is a single, serial thread of execution that runs any valid C, C++, or Fortran code.
- A worker: Groups of threads that can operate together in a SIMD or vector fashion are called workers. (CUDA programmers will recognize that a worker is just the OpenACC name for a warp.)
- Vectors: Vectors cause worker threads to work in lockstep when running vector or SIMD instruction.
- A gang: Groups of workers are called gangs. (CUDA programmers will recognize a gang is another name for a CUDA threadblock.) Gangs operate independently of each other.

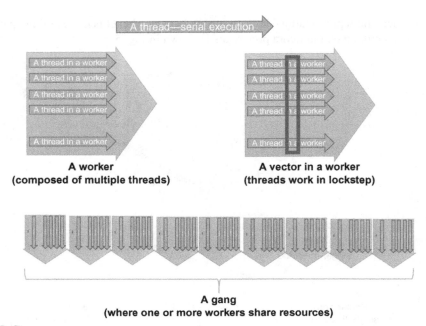

FIG. 6

Various forms of OpenACC parallelism.

RUNTIME RESULTS FOR accFill_ex2

As can be seen in the following PGI compiler report, the source code utilizes the `create()` clause to allocate the data on the device; no copy operation was required. The compiler also decided that both loops in the kernels region were parallelizable on both the GPU and multicore CPU target devices (Fig. 7).

```
$ pgc++ -std=c++11 -acc -ta=multicore,tesla -Minfo=accel accFill_ex2.cpp -o accFill_ex2
main:
    26, Generating create(status[:nCount])
    27, Loop is parallelizable
        Accelerator kernel generated
        Generating Tesla code
        27, #pragma acc loop gang, vector(128) /* blockIdx.x threadIdx.x */
    27, Generating Multicore code
        27, #pragma acc loop gang
    30, Loop is parallelizable
        Accelerator kernel generated
        Generating Tesla code
        30, #pragma acc loop gang, vector(128) /* blockIdx.x threadIdx.x */
            Generating reduction(+:sum)
```

FIG. 7

PGI compiler output for accFill_ex2.cpp.

The following commands show that the code runs correctly on both the CPU and GPU. The **ACC_DEVICE_TYPE** environment variable was used to specify the runtime device (Fig. 8).

```
$ export ACC_DEVICE_TYPE=host
$ ./accFill_ex2 1000
Final sum is 1000 millions
$ export ACC_DEVICE_TYPE=nvidia
$ ./accFill_ex2 1000
Final sum is 1000 millions
```

FIG. 8

Example showing the application running on both the CPU and GPU.

A SIMPLE TASK-PARALLEL EXAMPLE

The following example, *accTask.cpp*, demonstrates how to run a single task in parallel on the OpenACC device.

Care must be taken when using task-based parallelism as the target OpenACC device may have performance constraints that can adversely affect performance. In general, it is best to have all the OpenACC threads running the same task at the same time so the parallel tasks can map efficiently onto the GPU SIMD streaming multiprocessors as well as the vector units of conventional multicore processors. More advanced readers will want to look into the use of the OpenACC *async()* clauses and streams, which give programmers the ability to implement very complex task-based parallelism. In particular, interested readers should look into parallel task decomposition and dependency graphs. One possibility is "Introduction to Parallel Computing" (Grama, Abshul, Karypis, & Kumar, 2003), but there are also many talks and tutorials available on the Internet.

The following *accTask.cpp* driver shown in Fig. 9 assumes that the *task()* function is declared inline or decorated with a pragma that tells the compiler it is an OpenACC routine.

The only new concepts introduced in the main method is the use of the C++ high-resolution clock class, that reports time with the shortest tick period and the call to the task() method.

An example busy-loop method is provided in Fig. 10.

```cpp
#include <iostream>
using namespace std;
#include <cstdlib>
#include <cassert>
#include <chrono>
using namespace std::chrono;

// a sequential task
// place task code here

int main(int argc, char *argv[])
{
  if(argc < 3) {
    cerr << "Use: nCount nLoop" << endl;
    return -1;
  }

  int nCount = atoi(argv[1]);
  int nLoop = atoi(argv[2]);

  if(nCount < 0 || nLoop < 0) {
    cerr << "ERROR: both nCount and nLoop must be greater than zero!" << endl;
    return -1;
  }

  high_resolution_clock::time_point t1 = high_resolution_clock::now();

  // Here is where we evaluate the task(s)
  int sum=0;
#pragma acc parallel loop reduction(+:sum)
  for(int i=0; i < nCount; i++)
    sum += task(i,nLoop);

  high_resolution_clock::time_point t2 = high_resolution_clock::now();
  duration<double> time_span = duration_cast< duration<double> >(t2 - t1);

  cout << "Duration " << time_span.count() << " second" << endl;
  cout << "Final sum is " << sum << endl;

  // Sanity check to see that array is filled with ones
  assert(sum == nCount);

  return 0; // normal exit
}
```

FIG. 9

accTask.cpp.

```
// a task that runs in a thread
#pragma acc routine worker
inline char task(int index, int nLoop)
{
  long counter=0;
  for(long i=0; i < 1000000*nLoop; i++)
      counter += (i>=0)?1:0;

  // return 1 if the counter is correct
  return( ((counter/1000000) == nLoop)?1:0 );
}
```

FIG. 10

An example busy-loop computational task.

This method utilizes the OpenACC `routine` directive. OpenACC 2.0 introduced `#pragma acc routine`, which instructs the compiler to build a device version of the function or subroutine so that it may be called from a device region. The `worker` clause tells the compiler that any code in the routine, and any other routines called within this `task()` will run in a worker. Short tasks can also be included using the C++ **inline** keyword.

AMDAHL'S LAW AND SCALING

We can see the scaling behavior of an application by graphing the time it tasks to run as the parallelism increases. The big deal about parallel programming that it can ideally deliver a factor of N speedup when running on a parallel computer that has N processing elements. In other words, a program can potentially run 10× faster (for a fixed problem size) on a ten core processor, and 1000× faster on a GPU that supports 1000 concurrent threads of execution. People discuss the parallel vs. serial speedup in terms of *Amdahl's Law*.

Amdahl's law is named after the computer architect Gene Amdahl. It is not really a law but rather an approximation that models the ideal speedup that can happen when serial programs are modified to run in parallel. For this approximation to be valid, it is necessary that the problem size remains the same when parallelized, frequently referred to as strong scaling. In other words, assume that a serial program is modified to run in parallel and that the amount of work performed by the program does not change significantly in the parallel version of the code. Obviously, the parallel sections can potentially run much, much faster depending on the hardware capabilities. Thus, the expected speedup, $S(N)$ of the parallel code over the serial code when using N processors is dictated by the proportion of a program that can be made parallel, P, and the portion of that cannot be parallelized, $(1-P)$. This relationship is shown in Eq. (1):

$$S(N) = \frac{1}{(1-P) + P/N} \qquad (1)$$

Equation 1: Amdahl's law

Amdahl's law tells us that inventive OpenACC developers have two goals when parallelizing an application:

1. Express the parallel sections of code so they run as fast as possible. Ideally they should run N times faster when using N processors.
2. Utilize whatever techniques or inventiveness they have to minimize the $(1-P)$ serial time.

It is possible that the parallel sections can run so fast that the program's runtime can become dominated by the serial section(s) of code. This is one of the reasons why computer architects pair powerful sequential processors (e.g., CPUs) with parallel accelerators and coprocessors.

It is expected that the *accTask.cpp* example busy-work task of incrementing a counter in-place will run at full speed on all OpenACC devices because it is designed to be 100% compute bound, meaning the processor is the system component that limits performance. Real-applications are generally much more complex where performance can be affected by other factors such as memory and network bandwidth. Many parallel applications become performance limited as the amount of parallelism increases because they rely heavily on accessing data in memory. Thus adding more processing elements does not help performance—and may actually decrease performance—as the processing elements become starved for data. Both the parallel *accFill_ex1.cpp* and kernels *accFill_ex2.cpp* examples are memory bound, meaning the performance of the memory subsystem is what limits performance.

Cache based computer architectures can help, as frequently accessed, or *hot* data, can be prefetched and kept in much faster cache memory. This is the reason why parallel programmers are so interested in *locality* and *streaming* behavior. Programs that can exploit high data locality generally run much faster because they can run out of register or cache memory. The *accTask.cpp* program is one example as it uses only one register and does not perform any memory fetches in the busy loop. Programs that stream data out of memory also tend to run faster because the data can be prefetched into faster cache memory. In the ideal case, streaming applications can appear to be completely free of memory subsystem limitations and exhibit wonderful scalability. They key is to perform enough computations per data item fetched so the cost of the memory transactions can be hidden. This remains true when data is fetched from memory, across a network, from storage, or across the PCIe bus.

BIG-O CONSIDERATIONS AND DATA TRANSFERS

Big-O notation is a convenient way to describe how the size of problem affects the consumption by an algorithm of some resource such as processor time or memory as a function of its input. In this way, computer scientists can describe the worst and average case runtime behavior of an algorithm. These Big-O descriptions can be used to compare algorithms, which can help us understand the types of parallel algorithms that might exhibit a high computation per data item fetched and identify those of interest for OpenACC offload programming.

Some common Big-O growth rates are as follows:

- $O(1)$: These are constant time (or space) algorithms that always consume the same resources regardless of the size of the input set. For example, indexing a single element in a vector does not vary in time or with the size of the data set and thus exhibits $O(1)$ runtime growth.
- $O(N)$: Resource consumption with these algorithms increases linearly with the size, represented by N, of the input. This is common for algorithms that loop over a data set (of size N) where the work inside the loop requires constant time.
- $O(N^2)$: Performance is directly proportional the square of the size of the input data set. Typical examples are algorithms that use nested loops over an input data set exhibit $O(N^2)$ runtime. Deeper nested iterations commonly show greater runtime (e.g., three nested loops result in $O(N^3)$, $O(N^4)$ when four loops are nested, etc.

There are many excellent texts on algorithm analysis that provide a more precise and comprehensive description of Big-O notation. One popular text is "Introduction to Algorithms" (Cormen, Leiserson, & Rivest, 2009). There are also numerous resources on the Internet discussing and teaching Big-O notation and algorithm analysis.

Most computationally oriented scientists and programmers are familiar with BLAS (the Basic Linear Algebra Subprograms) library. BLAS is the *de facto* programming interface for basic linear algebra. To remain competitive, most processor vendors provide highly optimized BLAS libraries. Powerful heterogeneous high-performance dense linear algebra libraries such as the MAGMA project at the University of Tennessee Innovative Computing Laboratory are also available. Heterogeneous computation can utilize the computational capabilities of both the host processor (CPU) and several types of OpenACC devices. MAGMA in particular can attain high performance by exploiting all the system computational capabilities. It is available for free download.

BLAS is structured according to three different levels with increasing data and runtime requirements.

- Level-1: Vector-vector operations that require $O(N)$ data and $O(N)$ work. Examples include taking the inner product of two vectors, or scaling a vector by a constant multiplier.

- Level-2: Matrix-vector operations that require $O(N^2)$ data and $O(N^2)$ work. Examples include matrix-vector multiplication or a single right-hand-side triangular solve.
- Level-3: Matrix-vector operations that require $O(N^2)$ data and $O(N^3)$ work. Examples include dense matrix-matrix multiplication.

The following table illustrates the amount of work that is performed by each BLAS level assuming that N floating-point values are transferred from the host to an OpenACC device that requires data movement (Table 1).

Table 1 Work Per Datum by BLAS Level

BLAS Level	Data	Work	Work Per Datum
1	$O(N)$	$O(N)$	$O(1)$
2	$O(N^2)$	$O(N^2)$	$O(1)$
3	$O(N^2)$	$O(N^3)$	$O(N)$

We see that Level-3 BLAS operations should run efficiently because they perform $O(N)$ work for every floating-point value transferred to the OpenACC parallel device. The same work-per-datum analysis applies to nonBLAS related computational problems as well.

It should be clear that achieving good performance requires keeping as much data as possible on the OpenACC device and in cache memory close to the processor. After that, attaining high performance requires performing as many calculations per datum like the level-3 BLAS operations. Creating a pipeline of many lower arithmetic density computations can help, but this will only increase performance when each operation can keep the OpenACC device busy long enough to overcome any offload startup latencies. Alternatively, it is possible to increase performance—sometime significantly—by combining multiple low-density operations like BLAS level-2 and level-2 operation. The `kernel` pragma clause can help do exactly that.

The preceding discussion can be summarized into three rules of offload mode programming:

1. *Get the data on the OpenACC device(s) and keep it there.*
   This will reduce or eliminate data transfer overhead as much as possible. In particular, OpenACC programmers should learn to use the `present()` clause and conditional data movement clauses like `present_or_copy()`. OpenACC runtimes are permitted to eliminate data transfers when running on a shared memory device, such as a multicore CPU.
2. *Give the OpenACC device(s) enough work to do.*
   A challenge with quick-to-run parallel sections of code is that startup time on the OpenACC device can match or exceed the runtime. Remember that most modern OpenACC devices are capable of multiple TF/s (Teraflop/s) performance. Essentially the application must perform 1 million operations for

every microsecond (millionths of a second) to match the overhead of starting a parallel section of code on one of these devices.

3. *Focus on data reuse to avoid memory bandwidth limitations.*

   As discussed, programming for a high locality of data reuse means the compiler and hardware can work on your behalf to keep data in the highest performing register and cache memory. The OpenACC compiler can also help with optimizing register reuse and prefetching. Similarly, the present_and_* OpenACC clauses can reuse data that has already been transferred to the device.

THE SCALABILITY OF THE accTask.cpp CODE

As mentioned, the *accTask.cpp* code was designed to have extremely high locality of reference. In fact, it should only use one register variable and exhibit no significant memory performance dependencies.

The following output shows the runtime of a single-threaded version of *accTask. cpp* on an x86 CPU (Fig. 11):

```
$ pgc++ -Ofast -std=c++11 accTask.cpp -o accTask.single
$ ./accTask.single 1 10000
Duration 14.5115 second
Final sum is 1
rmfarber@bd:~/OpenACC_book/myChapter$ ./accTask.single 4 10000
Duration 57.4627 second
Final sum is 4
```

FIG. 11

Compiling and running accTask sequentially.

Notice that the single-threaded task takes approximately 4× longer on an Intel quad-core E5630 system running at 2.53 GHz when it had to run four tasks sequentially (e.g., 57.4627/14.5115 = 3.95). The ratio is approximate as there is some granularity in the time measurement.

A bash script (shown in Fig. 12) was used to generate a list of runtimes that can then be graphed to see how the runtime scales with number of cores (e.g., parallel processing elements).

```
export ACC_DEVICE_TYPE=host
#!/bin/bash
for j in $(seq 1 1 40)
do
    ./accTask $j 1000
done
```

FIG. 12

Script to test scalability.

The resulting graph shown in Fig. 13 illustrates a stair-step pattern in the runtime relative to the single-threaded value based on the number of cores. In other words, the runtime is the same depending on if we oversubscribe the same number of tasks per core. For example, we get a 2× the runtime of a single thread when we oversubscribe the hardware cores by 2×. This behavior can be clearly seen as we continue oversubscribing the processor cores.

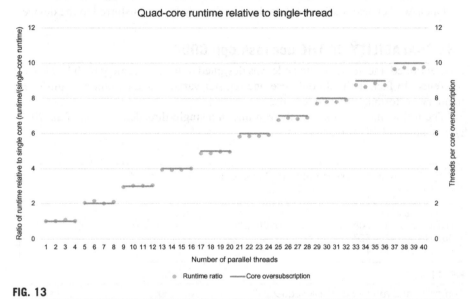

FIG. 13

Runtime relative to single-threaded version on quad-core CPU.

We see similar scaling when using the PathScale Enzo OpenACC compiler to build an executable that runs on a 96-core Cavium ThunderX® ARM64 system (Fig. 14).

PARALLEL EXECUTION AND RACE CONDITIONS

OpenACC parallelizes **for** loops (and **DO** loops in Fortran) so the code in the body of the loop can run in parallel using concurrent hardware threads of execution.

This can be somewhat confusing, as the variable **i** in the following for loop appears to be incremented sequentially, but in reality threads using many values of **i** in this **for** loop variable may be running in parallel at the same time. It is very important to note that OpenACC makes no guarantees about the order in which threads will run. In fact, it is not even possible to even assume monotonicity. For example, it is possible that the **nCount**-1 iteration of this loop may actually complete before the zeroth loop iteration!

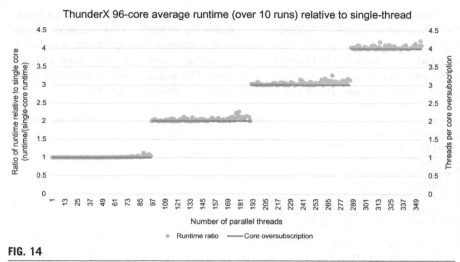

FIG. 14

Speedup over single-thread on 96-core Cavium ThunderX® system (results courtesy PathScale and Cavium).

It is very important to note that OpenACC makes no guarantees about the order in which threads will run.

In short, OpenACC programmers cannot and should not make any assumptions about the order that threads will run (Fig. 15).

```
#pragma acc parallel loop
  for(unsigned int i=0; i < nCount; i++) {
    // do something in each thread
  }
```

FIG. 15

An OpenACC parallel loop.

RACE CONDITIONS

Data dependencies across threads in the parallel loop can pose a problem to OpenACC programmers, especially as OpenACC does not provide any locking mechanism aside from atomic operations to protect against race conditions. A *race condition* occurs when multiple threads race to perform some operation on a shared data item. The result can be undefined unless the operation, such as a write or read-modify-write operation can occur atomically, meaning the operation starts and runs to completion before another thread can access the shared data item. (Note: There is no race condition on read-only data items.)

An obvious example of a shared data dependency occurs when updating a counter in parallel as shown in boldface in the following example. This example utilizes a #pragma acc atomic update to protect the **counter** variable when it is being updated via counter++. In OpenACC, it is possible to protect an individual variable using an atomic read, write, or update pragma. This example uses conditional compilation so we can see what happens if the atomic is omitted (Fig. 16).

```cpp
#include <iostream>
using namespace std;
#include <cstdlib>
#include <cassert>
#include <chrono>
using namespace std::chrono;

int main(int argc, char *argv[])
{
   if(argc < 2) {
      cerr << "Use: nCount" << endl;
      return 1;
      }
    int nCount = atoi(argv[1]);

   if(nCount <= 0) {
      cerr << "ERROR: nCount must be greater than zero!" << endl;
      return 1;
   }

   high_resolution_clock::time_point t1 = high_resolution_clock::now();

   // Here is where we define and increment the counter.
    int counter=0;
#pragma acc parallel loop
   for( int i=0; i < nCount; i++) {
#ifdef USE_ATOMIC
      #pragma acc atomic update
#endif
      counter++;
   }

   high_resolution_clock::time_point t2 = high_resolution_clock::now();
   duration<double> time_span = duration_cast<duration<double>>(t2 - t1);

   cout << "counter " << counter
        << " Duration " << time_span.count() << " second" << endl;
   assert(counter == nCount);

   return 0; // normal exit
}
```

FIG. 16

accCounter.cpp: an example containing a race condition.

Failure to include an atomic pragma is a common error that will result in a race condition that can cause garbage and nondeterministic results as the programmer has no control over the order of execution of the threads. The nondeterministic behavior is particularly dangerous as the program might report seemingly correct results when debugging and then fail in production. Also, the application may run correctly on one platform and fail on another, or run correctly with a particular software release and then fail when the software is updated.

The PGI OpenACC compiler is smart enough to detect the error in this example when the atomic is omitted. As can be seen in boldface in Fig. 17, the compiler decided to generate serial code using only one thread to ensure correctness. The reason is given in the following information line that the variable **counter** is *live-out* from the loop. Stated simply: a variable is *live* if it holds a value that may be needed in the future and it is *live-out* when the compiler dataflow analysis determines it is potentially needed by other statements on exit from a code block. There are many excellent texts and presentations available on compiler data flow analysis that can provide the precise *live-out* mathematical definition, which is beyond the scope of this chapter.

```
$ pgc++ -std=c++11 -acc -ta=multicore,tesla:cc35 -Minfo=accel accCounter.cpp -o accCounter_no_atomic
main:
        24, Accelerator kernel generated
            Generating Tesla code
            26, #pragma acc loop seq
        24, Generating Single core code
        30, Accelerator restriction: induction variable live-out from loop: counter
```

FIG. 17

PGI output when the atomic is omitted.

Defining **USE_ATOMIC** during compilation includes the OpenACC atomic pragma. In this example the PGI compiler reports it can generate a parallel kernel for the GPU and a multicore loop for the CPU. The command-line argument *"nvidia:cc35"* tells the compiler to target an NVIDIA 3.5 compute capability. This was done to see the effect of the more efficient modern GPU atomic operations on the runtime as compute capability 2.x (e.g., Fermi) and later generation GPUs have much more efficient atomic operations.

While atomic operations are convenient, it is important to avoid using them as they can force serialization during the runtime as only one thread can access the atomic variable at a time. The *accCounter.cpp* example is an admittedly worst case scenario as every thread must queue up to perform the counter++ operation.

As seen in Fig. 18, the compiler reports the generation of parallel code. As expected contention over the **counter** variable caused the parallel code to scale linearly. Shown in Fig. 19, the parallel runtime can be significantly worse than the serial code due to the thread and atomic operation overheads.

```
$ pgc++ -DUSE_ATOMIC -std=c++11 -acc -ta=multicore,tesla:cc35 -Minfo=accel accCounter.cpp -o accCounter_w_atomic
main:
     24, Accelerator kernel generated
         Generating Tesla code
         26, #pragma acc loop gang, vector(128) /* blockIdx.x threadIdx.x */
     24, Generating copy(counter)
         Generating Multicore code
         26, #pragma acc loop gang
```

FIG. 18

PGI output when atomic is included.

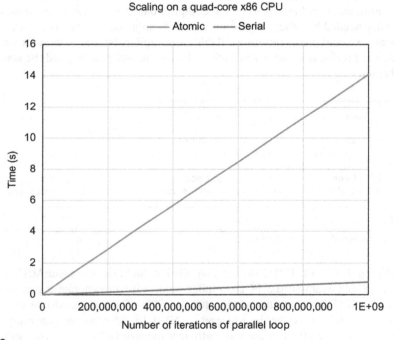

FIG. 19

Scaling on a quad-core ×86 system.

The runtime on an NVIDIA Tesla® K40 (Compute Capability 3.5) GPU shows that the serial version still scales linearly. Counterintuitively, the parallel version exhibits constant runtime (lower line). This is caused by optimizations NVIDIA has made in hardware that allow some atomic operations to scale in a massively parallel computing environment. For more information, we recommend reading "Massive Atomics for Massive Parallelism on GPUs" (Egielski, Huang, & Zhang, 2014) and the "NVIDIA's Fermi: The First Complete GPU Computing Architecture" (Glaskowsky, 2009) (Fig. 20).

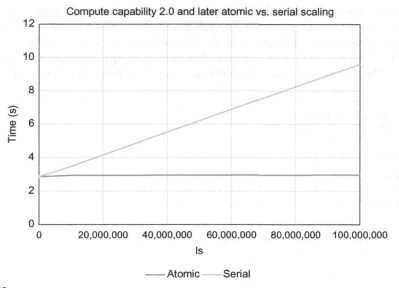

FIG. 20

Scaling on an NVIDA K40 GPU using an atomic increment in place.

LOCK-FREE PROGRAMMING

Mutual exclusion locks are a commonly used mechanism for synchronizing processes or threads that need access to some shared resource in parallel programs. They work as their name suggests: if a thread "locks" a resource, another thread that wishes to access it will need to wait till the first thread unlocks it. Once that happens, the second one would then proceed to lock it till it is processing it. The program's threads must be disciplined to unlock it as soon as they are done using the shared resource to keep the program execution flowing smoothly.

Due to the absence of locks in OpenACC, programmers need to become acquainted with the concept of *lock-free* programming and data structures.

A *lock-free* method guarantees progress of at least one of the threads executing the method. There may be circumstances where some threads can be delayed, but it is guaranteed that at least one thread of makes progress at each step. Statistically, all threads will make progress in a lock-free method over time. According to Blechmann (2016) a data structure is considered to be lock-free if some concurrent operations are guaranteed to be finished in a finite number of steps.

Readers are highly encouraged to delve deeper into lock-free programming and lock-free data structures. An excellent source of further information is "The Art of Multiprocessor Programming" (Herlihy & Shavit, 2012).

Lock-free programming is more challenging than simply using a lock to protect a critical region (say with OpenMP #pragma omp critical). However, lock-*based* programs can't provide any of the performance guarantees of a lock-free method. In practice, locks are a common culprit that limits or prevents scaling. Deadlock is also a problem that is avoided in lock-free programming. *Deadlock* can occur when two threads get stuck waiting for the other thread to release a lock on a shared resource.

A simple solution to increase the scalability our contrived counter problem is to reduce the probability that one or more threads need to queue up to perform the atomic operation. This is done with a pair of nested loops in *accParaCounter.cpp* shown in Fig. 21.

```cpp
#include <iostream>
using namespace std;
#include <cstdlib>
#include <cassert>
#include <chrono>
using namespace std::chrono;

int main(int argc, char *argv[])
{
    if(argc < 3) {
       cerr << "Use: nCount nPartial" << endl;
       return 1;
       }
     int nCount = atoi(argv[1]);
     int nPartial = atoi(argv[2]);

     if(nCount <= 0 || nPartial <= 0) {
        cerr << "ERROR: nCount and nPartial must be greater than zero!" << endl;
        return 1;
     }

     high_resolution_clock::time_point t1 = high_resolution_clock::now();

     // Here is where we define and increment the counter.
      int counter=0;
#pragma acc parallel loop
     for( int i=0; i < nCount; i += nPartial) {
       int partialSum=0;
       int n = (i+nPartial < nCount)?i+nPartial:nCount;
#pragma acc loop worker reduction(+:partialSum)
       for( int j=i; j < n; j++) {
         partialSum += 1;
       }
#pragma acc atomic update
       counter += partialSum;
     }

     high_resolution_clock::time_point t2 = high_resolution_clock::now();
     duration<double> time_span = duration_cast<duration<double>>(t2 - t1);

     cout << "counter " << counter
          << " Duration " << time_span.count() << " second" << endl;
     assert(counter == nCount);

     return 0; // normal exit
}
```

FIG. 21

A faster version, accParaCounter.cpp that reduces contention on the shared resource.

While trivial, the *accParaCounter.cpp* source code will be used in the next section to implement a more interesting parallel random number generator (PRNG) code. PRNGs are key to Monte Carlo methods that are an important part of scientific (Newman & Barkema, 1999) and financial computing (Glasserman, 2003). Readers are encouraged to investigate PRNGs and Monte Carlo methods further.

As can be seen in the *accParaCounter.cpp* source code, the parallel **for** loop has been broken into two nested loops: (1) an outer parallel loop with an **nPartial** increment, and (2) an inner loop that exploits worker parallelism to increment a local variable **nPartial** times.

Following is a revised scaling graph showing the performance of *accParaCounter. cpp* using 1000 for the number iterations of the nested inner vector loop. Note the parallel performance is much better and now exceeds that of the serial version (Fig. 22).

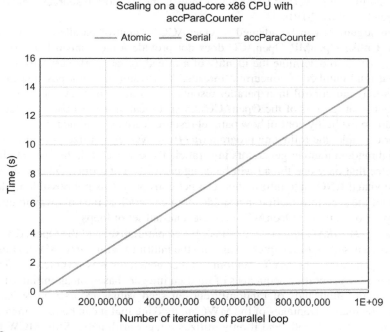

FIG. 22

Scaling behavior of the reduced-contention parallel version.

CONTROLLING PARALLEL RESOURCES

This same nested loop structure use in *accParaCounter.cpp* can be used to control the parallelism of the loop and hence the parallel resource consumption.

Most parallel programmers follow the approach of exploiting the greatest amount of parallelism in the system to achieve the highest performance.

The idea behind large numbers of threads is to give the parallel scheduler as many threads as possible to choose from to maximize the chances that all the computing resources will be fully utilized. GPU programmers like to speak in terms of *occupancy* as a measure of thread level parallelism. A high occupancy implies that the scheduler has more active threads to choose from, and hence the opportunity to achieve higher performance.

High occupancy does not necessarily translate into the fastest application performance. *Instruction level parallelism (ILP)* can be equally effective in hiding thread latency by keeping the processor (or GPU) busy with fewer threads that consume fewer resources and introduce less overhead. However, the programmer has to arrange the computation to ensure best use of the parallel hardware. The reasoning for ILP is simple yet powerful: Using fewer threads means more resources can be used per thread (Volkov, 2010).

This argument can be adapted to OpenACC to control parallel resource utilization. Unlike OpenMP, OpenACC does not provide a mechanism like `omp_get_thread_num()` to determine the identity of a thread, or `omp_get_num_threads()` to find out total number of concurrent threads. As a result, it is not possible to write classes that can control their parallel resource utilization. Instead, OpenACC programmers—at least as of the OpenACC 2.5 specification—must use a nested loop structure to explicitly control how parallel resources are used in their programs.

For example, the following program (*accParaRNG.cpp*) utilizes a number of sequential random number generators in parallel. To be successful, the program has to guarantee that only one thread will be using each RNG at a time. Otherwise, internally updated RNG state information can get corrupted. It is not possible to do the update of the seed information in a single atomic operation, the only way to guarantee correct operation in OpenACC is to use a nested set of loops.

The *accParaRNG.cpp* code uses task-based parallelism and the OpenACC constructs discussed in this chapter along with the multiply-with-carry (MWC) random number generator. The MWC random number generator was invented by George Marsaglia for generating sequences of random integers based on an initial set from two to many thousands of randomly chosen seed values (Marsaglia & Zaman, 1991). The main advantages of the MWC method are that it can be implemented in a few lines of C++ code and it only utilizes integer arithmetic. Still, MCW leads to the very fast generation of decent sequences of random numbers. The reader can substitute more elaborate random number generators in *accParaRNG.cpp* such as the widely used Mersenne Twister (Matsumoto & Nishimura, 1998) and test them with a suite like the Dieharder random number test suite (Brown, 2016; Figs. 23 and 24).

Join the top and bottom half of the program and place in *accParaRNG.cpp*. The example can then be compiled into a PGI unified binary and tested on both the CPU and GPU as follows (Fig. 25):

```
#include <iostream>
using namespace std;
#include <cstdlib>
#include <cassert>
#include <chrono>
using namespace std::chrono;
// A mask to strip off the lower bits. Use currently uses lowest bit
#define MASK 0x1

// Simple Multiply-with-Carry RNG (George Marsaglia)
typedef struct SimpleMWC_RNG {
  uint32_t m_z, m_w;

  SimpleMWC_RNG() { m_z = random(); m_w = random();}
#pragma acc routine worker
  inline uint32_t rand() {
    m_z = 36969 * (m_z & 65535) + (m_z >> 16);
    m_w = 18000 * (m_w & 65535) + (m_w >> 16);
    return (m_z << 16) + (m_w & 65535);
  }
} SimpleMWC_RNG_t;


int testGolden(SimpleMWC_RNG_t *gold_rng, int nRNG, int nCount)
{
    int sequentialSum=0;
    for( int i=0; i < nCount; i += nRNG) {
      int n = ((i+nRNG < nCount)?nRNG:nCount - i);
      int index = i/nRNG;
      int partialSum=0;
      for( int j=0; j < n; j++) {
        partialSum += gold_rng[index].rand()%MASK;
      }
      sequentialSum += partialSum;
    }
    return sequentialSum;
}
```

FIG. 23

Top half of accParaRNG.cpp.

MAKE YOUR LIFE SIMPLE

Pragmas and high-level APIs are designed to provide convenient software functionality. They hide many details of the underlying implementation to free a programmer's attention for other tasks. A colleague humorously refers to pragma-based programming as a negotiation that occurs between the developer and the compiler as pragmas are only informational statements provided by the programmer to the assist the compiler. This means that pragmas are not subject to the same level of syntax, type, and sanity checking as the rest of the source code. The compiler is

```
int main(int argc, char *argv[])
{
  if(argc < 4) {
    cerr << "Use: nCount nRNG doGolden" << endl;
    return 1;
  }
  int nCount = atoi(argv[1]);
  int nRNG = atoi(argv[2]);
  int doGolden = atoi(argv[3]);

  if(nCount <= 0 || nRNG <= 0) {
    cerr << "ERROR: nCount and nRNG must be greater than zero!" << endl;
    return 1;
  }

  srandom(0); // set a seed for the host random number generator
  SimpleMWC_RNG_t *rng=new SimpleMWC_RNG_t[nRNG];
  SimpleMWC_RNG_t *gold_rng=new SimpleMWC_RNG_t[nRNG];

  for(int j=0; j < nRNG; j++) gold_rng[j] = rng[j]; // copy the rng initial conditions

  high_resolution_clock::time_point t1 = high_resolution_clock::now();

  // Here is where we define the parallelism over the random number generators
  int parallelSum=0;
#pragma acc parallel loop pcopyin(rng[0:nRNG])
  for( int i=0; i < nCount; i += nRNG) {
    int n = ((i+nRNG < nCount)?nRNG:nCount - i);
    int index = i/nRNG;
    int partialSum=0;
#pragma acc loop worker reduction(+:partialSum)
    for( int j=0; j < n; j++) {
      partialSum += rng[index].rand()%MASK;
    }
#pragma acc atomic update
    parallelSum += partialSum;
  }

  high_resolution_clock::time_point t2 = high_resolution_clock::now();
  duration<double> time_span = duration_cast<duration<double>>(t2 - t1);

  cout << "nCount " << nCount
       << " Duration " << time_span.count() << " second" << endl;

  if(doGolden) {
    assert(testGolden(gold_rng, nRNG, nCount) == parallelSum);
    cout << "\tSuccess!" << endl;
  }
  delete [] rng; delete [] gold_rng;

  return 0; // normal exit
}
```

FIG. 24

Bottom half of accParaRNG.cpp.

free to ignore any pragma for any reason including: it does not support the pragma, syntax errors, code complexity, unresolved (or potentially unresolved) dependencies, edge cases where the compiler cannot guarantee that data structures (like vectors or arrays) do not overlap and a huge number of other reasons. For this reason, it is essential to use profiling tools and closely examine informational messages from the compiler to ensure that the pragmas have the intended effect and achieve high performance.

```
$ pgc++ -std=c++11 -acc -fast -ta=multicore,tesla:cc35 -Minfo=accel accParaRNG.cpp -o accParaRNG
main:
     63, Generating copyin(rng[:nRNG])
         Accelerator kernel generated
         Generating Tesla code
         65, #pragma acc loop gang /* blockIdx.x */
         70, #pragma acc loop worker(128) /* threadIdx.y */
             Generating reduction(+:partialSum)
     63, Generating copy(parallelSum)
         Generating Multicore code
         65, #pragma acc loop gang
     70, Loop is parallelizable
SimpleMWC_RNG::rand():
     16, Generating acc routine worker
         Generating Tesla code

$ export ACC_DEVICE_TYPE=host
$ ./accParaRNG 100000000 16384 1
nCount 100000000 Duration 0.0315882 second
       Success!

$ export ACC_DEVICE_TYPE=nvidia
$ ./accParaRNG 100000000 16384 1
nCount 100000000 Duration 2.83268 second
       Success!
```

FIG. 25

Compilation and successful execution of accParaRNG.cpp on both a CPU and GPU.

REFERENCES

Blechmann, T. (2016). *Boost.Lockfree*. Retrieved from boost.org http://www.boost.org/doc/libs/1_60_0/doc/html/lockfree.html.

Brown, R. G. (2016). *Dieharder: a random number test suite*. Retrieved from Duke University https://www.phy.duke.edu/~rgb/General/dieharder.php.

Cormen, T. H., Leiserson, C. E., & Rivest, R. L. (2009). *Introduction to algorithms* (3rd ed.). Cambridge, MA: The MIT Press. https://mitpress.mit.edu/books/introduction-algorithms.

Egielski, I., Huang, J., & Zhang, E. Z. (2014). Massive atomics for massive parallelism on GPUs. *SIGPLAN Not*, *49*(11), 93–103. http://dx.doi.org/10.1145/2775049.2602993.

Glaskowsky, P. N. (2009). *NVIDIA's Fermi: The first complete GPU computing architecture*. NVIDIA. Retrieved from, http://www.nvidia.com/content/PDF/fermi_white_papers/P.Glaskowsky_NVIDIAFermi-TheFirstCompleteGPUComputingArchitecture.pdf.

Glasserman, P. (2003). *Monte Carlo methods in financial engineering*. New York, NY: Springer-Verlag.

Grama, A., Abshul, G., Karypis, G., & Kumar, V. (2003). *Introduction to parallel computing* (2nd ed.). Boston, MA: Addison Wesley.

Herlihy, M., & Shavit, N. (2012). *The art of multiprocessor programming*. Burlington, MA: Morgan Kaufmann.

Marsaglia, G., & Zaman, A. (1991). A new class of random number generators. *The Annals of Applied Probability*, *1*(3), 426–480.

Matsumoto, M., & Nishimura, T. (1998). Mersenne twister: A 623-dimensionally equidis-tributed uniform pseudo-random number generator. *ACM Transactions on Modeling and Computer Simulation*, 8(1), 3–30. http://dx.doi.org/10.1145/272991.272995.

Newman, M. E., & Barkema, G. T. (1999). *Monte Carlo methods in statistical physics*. Oxford: Clarendon Press.

Volkov, V. (2010). *volkov 10-PMAA*. Retrieved April 2011, from, http://eech.berkeley.edu http://www.eecs.berkeley.edu/~volkov/volkov10-PMAA.pdf.

Profile-guided development with OpenACC

2

Jeff Larkin
NVIDIA, Santa Clara, CA, United States

The purpose of this chapter is to introduce OpenACC programming by accelerating a real benchmark application. Readers will learn to profile the code and incrementally improve the application by adding OpenACC directives. By the end of the chapter the example application will be transformed from a serial code to one that can run in parallel on both offloaded accelerators, such as Graphic Processing Units (GPUs), and multicore targets, such as multicore Central Processing Units (CPUs).

At the end of this chapter the reader will have a basic understanding of:

- The OpenACC kernels directive
- OpenACC data directives and clauses
- The PGProf profiler
- OpenACC's three levels of parallelism
- Data dependencies

Compiler directives, such as OpenACC, provide developers with a means of expressing information to the compiler that is above and beyond what is available in the standard programming languages. For instance, OpenACC provides mechanisms for expressing parallelism of loops and the movement of data between distinct physical memories, neither of which is directly available in C, C++, or Fortran, the base languages supported by OpenACC. As such, programmers typically add directives to existing codes incrementally, applying the directives first to high-impact functions and loops and then address other parts of the code as they becoming increasingly important. Profile-guided development is a technique that uses performance analysis tools to inform the programmer at each step which parts of the application will deliver the greatest impact once accelerated. In this chapter we will use The Portland Group (PGI) compiler and PGPROF performance analysis tool to accelerate a benchmark code through incremental improvements. By the end of this chapter we will have taken a serial benchmark and parallelized it completely with OpenACC.

Prerequisites for completing this chapter: a working OpenACC compiler and make executable (the NVIDIA OpenACC Toolkit will be used in the examples); the ability to read, understand, and compile a C or Fortran code; the ability to run the executable produced by the OpenACC compiler.

BENCHMARK CODE: CONJUGATE GRADIENT

Throughout this chapter we will be working with a simple benchmark code that implements the conjugate gradient method. The conjugate gradient method is an iterative method to approximate the solution to a sparse system of linear equations that is too large to be solved directly. It is not necessary to understand the mathematics of this method to complete this chapter; a benchmark implementing this method has been provided in both C and Fortran. For brevity, only the C code samples will be shown in this chapter, but the steps can be applied in the same way to the Fortran version. The code used in this chapter is licensed under the Apache License, Version 2.0, please read the included license for more details.

The example code has two data structures of interest. The first is a Vector structure, which contains a pointer to an array and an integer storing the length of the array. The second structure is a Matrix, which stores a sparse 2D Matrix in compressed sparse row format, meaning that only the non-zero elements of each row are stored, along with metadata representing where the elements would reside in the full matrix if it were stored with both zero and non-zero elements. These two data structures, along with several functions for creating, destroying, and manipulating these data structures are found in vector.h and matrix.h respectively.

The first step to profile-guided development is simply to build the code and obtain a baseline profile. We'll use this profile to inform our first steps in accelerating the code and also as a point of comparison for each successive step, both in terms of correctness and performance. A makefile has been provided with the benchmark code, which is preconfigured to build with the PGI compiler. If you are using a different OpenACC compiler, it will be necessary to modify the Makefile to use this compiler.

BUILDING THE CODE

The provided makefile will build the serial code for the CPU using the PGI compiler without modification simply by running the `make` command. In order to obtain some additional information to help with our initial performance study, we'll modify the compiler flags to add several profiling options.

- -Minfo=all,ccff: This compiler flag instructs the compiler to print information about how it optimizes the code and additionally embed this information in the executable for use by tools that support the common compiler feedback format.

The modified makefile is shown in Fig. 1.

At this point we have an executable (cg.x) that will serially execute the CG benchmark. The expected output is found in Fig. 2. The exact time required to run the executable will vary depending on CPU performance, but the total iterations and tolerance values should always match the values shown.

```
 1 CXX=pgc++
 2 CXXFLAGS=-fast -Minfo=all,ccff
 3 LDFLAGS=${CXXFLAGS}
 4
 5 cg.x: main.o
 6         ${CXX} $^ -o $@ ${LDFLAGS}
 7
 8 main.o: main.cpp matrix.h matrix_functions.h vector.h
vector_functions.h
 9
10 .SUFFIXES: .o .cpp .h
11
12 .PHONY: clean
13 clean:
14         rm -Rf cg.x pgprof* *.o core
```

FIG. 1

Makefile contents for initial performance analysis.

```
Rows: 8120601, nnz: 218535025
Iteration: 0, Tolerance: 4.0067e+08
Iteration: 10, Tolerance: 1.8772e+07
Iteration: 20, Tolerance: 6.4359e+05
Iteration: 30, Tolerance: 2.3202e+04
Iteration: 40, Tolerance: 8.3565e+02
Iteration: 50, Tolerance: 3.0039e+01
Iteration: 60, Tolerance: 1.0764e+00
Iteration: 70, Tolerance: 3.8360e-02
Iteration: 80, Tolerance: 1.3515e-03
Iteration: 90, Tolerance: 4.6209e-05
Total Iterations: 100 Total Time: 20.690567s
```

FIG. 2

Example output for CG benchmark code.

INITIAL BENCHMARKING

We will now use the PGProf profiler to obtain a baseline CPU profile for the code. This will help us to understand where the executable is spending its time so that we can focus our efforts on the functions and loops that will deliver the greatest performance speed-up. The PGProf profiler is installed with the PGI Compiler and OpenACC Toolkit. To open it, use the pgprof command from your command terminal. Once the profiler window is open, select *New Session* from the *File* menu, opening the *Create New Session* dialog box. By the box labeled *File*, press the *Browse* button and browse to and select your executable, which will be called cg.x. Once you have selected your executable, press the *Next* button and then the *Finish* button. At this point the profiler will run the executable, sampling the state of the program at a regular frequency to gather performance information. When complete, choose the CPU Details tab in the bottom part of the window to display a table of the most important functions in the executable. The window will look similar to what is shown in Fig. 3.

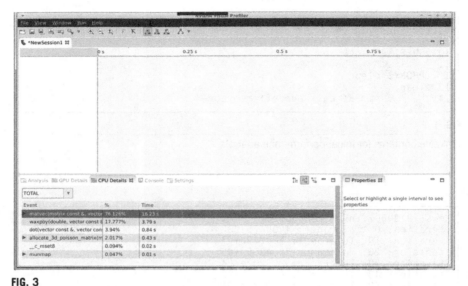

FIG. 3

PGProf profiler showing the CPU details tab.

At this point, double-clicking on the most time-consuming function, matvec, will bring up a dialog to choose the location of your source files. Once you have selected the directory containing your sources, a new tab will be opened to the matvec routine in matrix_functions.h. The loop on line 33 will have a symbol in the margin to the left indicating that the profiler is able to read compiler feedback about this loop. Hovering over the graph symbol will bring up a box showing information about what optimizations the compiler was able to perform on the loop and the computational intensity of the loop. See Fig. 4 for an example.

Reading compiler feedback is the only way to understand what information the compiler is able to determine about your code and what actions it takes based on this information. The compiler may choose to rearrange the loops in your code, break them into more manageable chunks, parallelize the code to run using vector instructions such as SSE or AVX, or maybe not do anything at all because it is unable to determine what optimizations will be safe and profitable. Frequently the programmer will know information about the code that the compiler is not able to learn on its own, resulting in the compiler missing optimization and parallelization opportunities. Throughout this chapter we will be providing the compiler with more

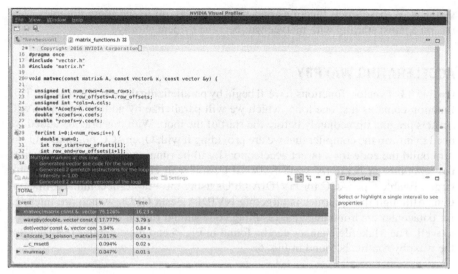

FIG. 4

PGProf profiler displaying compiler feedback information about an important loop.

information to improve the actions it takes to optimize and parallelize this code. This is, in many ways, the primary goal of OpenACC programming: providing the compiler with enough additional information about the code that it can made good decisions on how to parallelize it to any hardware.

Exploring the CPU performance table we see that there's three functions of interest: matvec, waxpy, and dot. The fourth most time-consuming routine is allocate_3d_poisson_matrix, which is an initialization routine that is only run once, so it will be ignored. Examining the code shows that the matvec routine contains a doubly nested loop that performance a sparse matrix/vector product and the other two routines both contain a single loop that perform two common vector operations ($aX + bY$ and dot product). These are the three loop nests where we will focus our efforts to parallelize the benchmark.

DESCRIBE PARALLELISM

Now that we know where the code is spending its time, let's begin to parallelize the important loops. It is generally a best practice to start at the top of the time-consuming routines and work your way down, since speeding up a routine that takes up 75% of the execution time will have a much greater impact on the performance of the code than speeding up one that only takes up 15%. That would mean that we should focus our effort first on the matvec routine and then move on to waxpby and dot. Since this may be your first ever OpenACC code, however, let's start with the simplest of these three functions and work our way up to the more complex. The reason against starting with matvec will become evident shortly.

ACCELERATING WAXPBY

On line 33 of vector_functions.h we'll begin by parallelizing the waxpby routine. This function contains just one loop, which we will parallelize by adding the OpenACC kernels pragma immediately before the start of the loop. With this pragma added we need to inform the compiler that we are providing it with OpenACC pragmas and ask it to build the code for a target accelerator. I will be running the code on a machine that contains an NVIDIA Tesla K20c GPU, so I will choose the *tesla* accelerator target. Enable OpenACC for NVIDIA GPUs using the −ta=tesla command-line option. Although the compiler is targeting NVIDIA Tesla GPUs, which are intended for datacenter environments, the resulting code should run on other NVIDIA GPUs as well. The Makefile changes can be found in Fig. 5 and the compiler feedback for the waxpby routine is found in Fig. 6.

```
2 CXXFLAGS=-fast -ta=tesla:lineinfo -Minfo=all,ccff
```

FIG. 5

Makefile changes to enable OpenACC support.

```
waxpby(double, const vector &, double, const vector &, const vector
&):
     21, include "vector_functions.h"
        40, Generating copyout(wcoefs[:n])
            Generating copyin(xcoefs[:n],ycoefs[:n])
        41, Complex loop carried dependence of ycoefs->,xcoefs->
prevents parallelization
            Loop carried dependence of wcoefs-> prevents
parallelization
            Loop carried backward dependence of wcoefs-> prevents
vectorization
            Accelerator scalar kernel generated
            Accelerator kernel generated
            41, #pragma acc loop seq
```

FIG. 6

Initial compiler feedback for OpenACC version of waxpby function.

We see from the compiler feedback that although it generated a GPU kernel, something went wrong when it tried to parallelize the loop. Specifically, the compiler believes that a data dependency could exist between iterations of the loop. A data dependency occurs when one loop iteration depends upon data from another loop iteration. Close examination of the loop body reveals that each iteration of the loop is completely data-independent of each other iteration, meaning that the results calculated in one iteration will not be used by any other. So why does the compiler believe that the loop has a data dependency? The problem lies in the low-level nature of the C and C++ programming languages, which represent arrays simply as pointers into memory; pointers which can potentially point to the *same* memory. The problem is that the compile cannot prove that the three arrays used in the loop do not *alias*, or overlap, with each other, so it has to assume that parallelizing the loop would be unsafe. We can provide the compiler with more information in one of two ways. One possibility is to give the compiler more information about the pointers by promising that they will never alias. This can be done by adding the C99 `restrict` keyword. While this is not a C++ keyword, the PGI compiler will accept this keyword in C++ codes.[1] We could also give the compiler more information about the loop itself using the OpenACC `loop` directive. The loop directive gives an OpenACC compiler additional information about the very next loop. We can use the loop independent clause to inform the OpenACC compiler that all iterations of the loop are independent, meaning that no two iterations depend up the data of the other, thus overriding the compiler's dependency analysis of the loop. Both solutions are promises that the programmer makes to the compiler about the code. If the promise is broken then unpredictable results can occur. In this code, we cannot make the guarantee that our vectors will not alias, since at times the function is called with y and w being the same vector, so we will use loop `independent` instead. The final code for waxpby appears in Fig. 7 along with compiler feedback in Fig. 8. Notice from the compiler feedback that the compiler has now determined that the loop at line 41 is parallelizable.

```
33 void waxpby(double alpha, const vector &x, double beta, const
vector &y, const vector& w) {
34   unsigned int n=x.n;
35   double *restrict xcoefs=x.coefs;
36   double *ycoefs=y.coefs;
37   double *wcoefs=w.coefs;
38
39 #pragma acc kernels
40   {
41 #pragma acc loop independent
42     for(int i=0;i<n;i++) {
43       wcoefs[i]=alpha*xcoefs[i]+beta*ycoefs[i];
44     }
45   }
46 }
```

FIG. 7

Final waxpby code with OpenACC.

[1] Some C++ compilers will not accept the restrict keyword, but will accept __restrict instead.

```
waxpby(double, const vector &, double, const vector &, const vector
&):
     21, include "vector_functions.h"
        40, Generating copyout(wcoefs[:n])
            Generating copyin(xcoefs[:n],ycoefs[:n])
        42, Loop is parallelizable
        Accelerator kernel generated
        Generating Tesla code
            42, #pragma acc loop gang, vector(128) /* blockIdx.x
threadIdx.x */
```

FIG. 8

Compiler feedback for corrected waxpby OpenACC code.

Looking more closely at the compiler feedback, notice that the compiler did more than just parallelize the loop for my GPU. The compiler understands that my target accelerator has a physically distinct memory from my host CPU, so it will be necessary to relocate my input arrays to the GPU for processing and my output array back for use later. The output for line 40 tells us that it recognizes that xcoefs and ycoefs are input arrays, so it generates a *copy in* to the GPU, and wcoefs is an output array, so it generates a *copy out* of the GPU. What the feedback is actually showing are *data clauses*, additional information about how the data within our compute region is used. In this case, the compiler was able to correctly determine the size, shape, and usage of our three arrays, so it generated implicit data clauses for those arrays. Sometimes the compiler will be overly cautious about data movement, so it is necessary for the programmer to override its decisions by adding explicit data clauses to the kernels directive. Other times the compiler cannot actually determine the size or shape of the arrays used within a region, so it will abort and ask for more information, as you will see when we work on the matvec routine.

Before moving on, it is always important to recompile and rerun the code to check for any errors that we may have introduced. It is much simpler to find and correct errors after making small changes than waiting until after we've made a lot of changes. After rerunning the code you should see that you're still getting the same answers, but the code has now slowed down. If we rerun the executable within the PGProf profiler now, we'll see the reason for the slowdown. Fig. 9 shows the GPU timeline that the profile gathered when I reran the executable, zoomed in a bit for clarity. What we see across the timeline are individual GPU operations (kernels) and associated data transfers. Notice that for each call to waxpby we now copy two arrays to the device and one array back for use by other function. This is really inefficient. Ideally we'll want to leave our data in GPU memory for as long as possible and avoid these intermediate data transfers. The only way to do that is to accelerate the remaining functions so that the data transfers become unnecessary.

ACCELERATING DOT

Let's quickly look at the dot routine as well, because the compiler will help us in other was when we use the OpenACC kernels pragma. Just as before, we will add a kernels pragma around the interesting loop and recompile the code. Fig. 10 shows the OpenACC version of the function and Fig. 11 shows the compiler feedback.

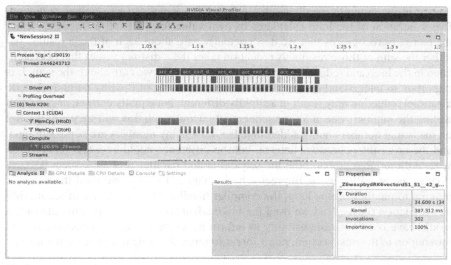

FIG. 9

Profile of accelerated WAXPBY showing excess data movement.

```
21  double dot(const vector& x, const vector& y) {
22    double sum=0;
23    unsigned int n=x.n;
24    double *xcoefs=x.coefs;
25    double *ycoefs=y.coefs;
26
27  #pragma acc kernels
28    for(int i=0;i<n;i++) {
29      sum+=xcoefs[i]*ycoefs[i];
30    }
31    return sum;
32  }
```

FIG. 10

OpenACC version of dot function.

```
dot(const vector &, const vector &):
    21, include "vector_functions.h"
        25, Generating copyin(xcoefs[:n],ycoefs[:n])
        28, Loop is parallelizable
            Accelerator kernel generated
            Generating Tesla code
            28, #pragma acc loop gang, vector(128) /* blockIdx.x
threadIdx.x *
            29, Generating implicit reduction(+:sum)
```

FIG. 11

Compiler feedback for OpenACC dot function.

Notice in the compiler feedback that at line 29 it generated an implicit *reduction*. Every iteration of the loop calculates its own value for `xcoefs[i]*ycoefs[i]`, but the compiler recognizes that we don't actually care about each of those results, but rather the sum of those results. A reduction takes the *n* distinct values that get calculated in the loop and reduces them down to the one value we care about: the sum. It is important to understand that due to the imprecise nature of floating point arithmetic a parallel reduction may result in a slightly different, but equally correct, answer than adding the numbers one at a time sequentially. How much this will vary will depend on the actual numbers being added together, how many numbers are being summed, and the order the operations happen, but the difference could be a few bits or even several digits. Remember, both the sequential and parallel sum are correct because floating point arithmetic is imprecise by its nature. Because we used the `kernels` pragma to parallelize this loop, the compiler handled the complexity of identifying this reduction for us. Had we used the more advanced `parallel` pragma instead, it would have been our responsibility to inform the compiler of the reduction. Before moving on to the next section, don't forget to rerun the code to check for mistakes.

ACCELERATING MATVEC

The final routine that needs to be accelerated is the matvec routine. As was said earlier, were this more than a teaching exercise this routine would have been the correct place to start our effort, since it is the most dominant routine by far, but this routine has some interesting complexities that require us to take additional steps when expressing the parallelism contained within. Let's start by taking the same approach as the other two routines: add the restrict keyword to our arrays and wrap our loop nest with a kernels pragma. When we attempt to build this routine, however, the compiler issues an error message, as shown in Fig. 12.

```
PGCC-S-0155-Compiler failed to translate accelerator region (see -
Minfo messages): Could not find allocated-variable index for symbol
(main.cpp: 27)
matvec(const matrix &, const vector &, const vector &):
     23, include "matrix_functions.h"
          30, Loop is parallelizable
               Accelerator kernel generated
               Generating Tesla code
               30, #pragma acc loop gang, vector(128) /* blockIdx.x
threadIdx.x */
               34, #pragma acc loop seq
          34, Accelerator restriction: size of the GPU copy of
xcoefs,Acoefs,cols is unknown
               Loop is parallelizable
PGCC/x86 Linux 16.4-0: compilation completed with severe errors
```

FIG. 12

Compiler output from initial attempt to accelerate matvec function.

The most important part of the compiler output here is the accelerator restriction at line 34, which states that it doesn't know how to calculate the size of the arrays used inside the kernels region, specifically the three arrays used within the innermost loop. In the previous two examples, the compiler could determine based on the number of loop iterations how much data needed to be relocated to the accelerator, but because the loop bounds inside of matvec are hidden within our matrix data structure, it is impossible for the compiler to determine how to relocate the key arrays. This is a case where we will need to add explicit data clauses to our kernels pragma to give the compiler more information about our data structures. Table 1 lists the five most common data clauses and their meanings. We've already seen the copyin and copyout clauses implicitly used by the compiler in the previous functions.

Table 1 Data Clauses and Their Meanings

Clause	Behavior
copyin	Check whether the listed variables are already present on the device, if not create space and copy the current data in to the device copy
copyout	Check whether the listed variables are already present on the device, if not create space on the device and copy the resulting data out of the device copy after the last use
copy	Behaves like the variables appeared in both a copyin and copyout data clause
create	Check whether the listed variables are already present on the device, if not create empty space on the device
present	Assume that the listed variables are already present on the device

In order for the compiler to parallelize the loop nest in matvec for my GPU, which requires the offloading of data, we'll need to tell the compiler the shape of at least the three arrays used within the inner loop. All three of these arrays are used only for reading, so we can use a copyin data clause, but we'll need to tell the compiler the *shape* of the arrays, which we can learn by looking at how they are allocated in the allocate_3d_poisson_matrix function, located in matrix.h. The data clauses accept a list of variables with information about the size and shape of the variables. In C and C++ the size and shape of the arrays are provided using square brackets ([and]) containing the starting index and number of elements to transfer, e.g., [0:100] to start copying at index 0 and copy 100 elements of the array. In Fortran the syntax uses parentheses and used the first and last index to copy, for instance (1:100) to start at index 1 and copy all elements up to element 100 in the array. The difference in syntax between these programming languages is intentional to fit with the conventions of the base programming languages. Since Fortran variables are self-describing, the size and shape information can be left off if the entire variable needs to be moved to the device.

Fig. 13 shows the modified code for the matvec function. Notice the addition of a copy data clause to the kernels direction, which informs the compiler both how to allocate space for the affected variables on the accelerator, but also that the data is only needed as input to the loops. With this change, we're now able to run the full CG calculation in parallel on the accelerator and get correct answers, but notice in Fig. 14 that the runtime is now longer than our original code.

```
29 #pragma acc kernels
copyin(cols[0:A.nnz],Acoefs[0:A.nnz],xcoefs[0:x.n])
30    for(int i=0;i<num_rows;i++) {
31       double sum=0;
32       int row_start=row_offsets[i];
33       int row_end=row_offsets[i+1];
34       for(int j=row_start;j<row_end;j++) {
35          unsigned int Acol=cols[j];
36          double Acoef=Acoefs[j];
37          double xcoef=xcoefs[Acol];
38          sum+=Acoef*xcoef;
39       }
40       ycoefs[i]=sum;
41    }
```

FIG. 13

Modified matvec loops with data clause.

```
Rows: 8120601, nnz: 218535025
Iteration: 0, Tolerance: 4.0067e+08
Iteration: 10, Tolerance: 1.8772e+07
Iteration: 20, Tolerance: 6.4359e+05
Iteration: 30, Tolerance: 2.3202e+04
Iteration: 40, Tolerance: 8.3565e+02
Iteration: 50, Tolerance: 3.0039e+01
Iteration: 60, Tolerance: 1.0764e+00
Iteration: 70, Tolerance: 3.8360e-02
Iteration: 80, Tolerance: 1.3515e-03
Iteration: 90, Tolerance: 4.6209e-05
Total Iterations: 100 Total Time: 77.121338s
Final Tolerance: 1.9934e-06
```

FIG. 14

CG benchmark output after accelerating all three major functions.

Let's rerun the executable using the PGProf profiler to see if we can determine why the code is so much slower than it was before, even though it is now running in parallel on our GPU. Fig. 15 shows the GPU timeline returned from PGProf, zoomed in for clarity.

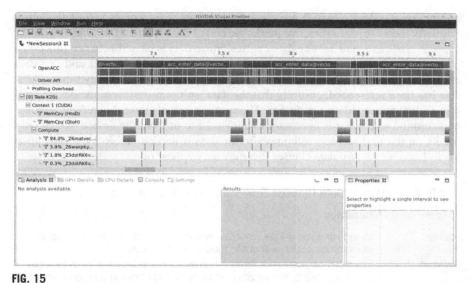

FIG. 15

Profile timeline after accelerating matvec function.

DESCRIBE DATA MOVEMENT

In order to ensure that our three accelerated routines share the device arrays and remove the necessity to copy data to and from the device in each function, we will introduce OpenACC data directives to express the desired data motion at a higher level in the program call tree. By taking control of the data motion from the compiler we are able to express our knowledge about how the data is actually used by the program as a whole, rather than requiring the compiler to make cautious decisions based only on how the data is used inside individual functions.

OpenACC has two different types of directives for managing the allocation of device memory: structured and unstructured. The structured approach has a defined beginning and end within the same program scope, for instance a function, which limits its ability to express data motion to programs where the data motion can be neatly represented in a structured way. Unstructured data directives provide the programmer more flexibility in where data management occurs, allowing the allocation and deletion of device data to happen in different places in the program. While this is especially useful in C++ classes, where data is frequently allocated in a constructor and deleted in the destructor, it also provides the programmer with a clean way to manage the device memory alongside of the management of host memory. For this reason we'll use the unstructured data directives to manage the device data in the existing data management routines.

The `enter data` and `exit data` directives are used for unstructured data management. As the names imply, `enter data` specifies the beginning of a variable's lifetime on the device, which are controlled by the `create` or `copyin` data clause. Similarly the `exit data` directive marks the end of the lifetime of a variable with the `copyout`, `release`, and `delete` data clauses. Since data is passed between functions, it is actually possible that the same variable may have multiple enter and exit data directives that refer to it, so the runtime will keep a count of how many times a variable has been referenced, ensuring that the data isn't removed from the device until it is no longer needed on the device. The runtime will also use this reference count to determine whether it is necessary to copy data to or from the device, which only occurs on the first and last references to the data if needed. Table 2 expands upon Table 1 adding the two data clauses that may only appear on `exit data` directives.

Table 2 Additional Data Clauses Only Valid on Exit Data Directives

Clause	Behavior
delete	Listed variables will be immediately removed from the device, regardless of reference count, without triggering any data copy
release	The reference count for listed variables will be reduced. If the reference count reaches 0, the variable will be removed from the device without triggering any data copy

DESCRIBING DATA MOVEMENT OF MATRIX AND VECTOR

To avoid unnecessary data movement in each of the three functions we've parallelized we will add unstructured data directives to the functions that manage the data in our Matrix and Vector structures. It is important to remember that OpenACC's data model is host-first, meaning that data directives that allocate data on the device must appear *after* host allocations (malloc, allocate, new, etc.) and data directives that deallocate device data must appear *before* host deallocations (free, deallocate, delete, etc.). Given this, let's add enter data directives to the allocate_3d_poisson_ matrix and allocate_vector functions, in matrix.h and vector.h respectively. Since allocate_3d_poisson_matrix does some additional initialization, it is simplest to add the directives to the end of the routine so that the device copy of the data structure will contain the initialized data.

Fig. 16 shows an abbreviated listing of the allocate_3d_poisson_matrix function with the `enter data` directives added. It may seem strange at first to copy A to the device and then all of the member arrays inside A. The A structure contains two scalar numbers, plus 3 pointers that are used on the device. The *copyin* of A at line 71 copies the structure, with the 5 elements that I just described. When the 3 pointers are copied, however, they will contain pointers back to the host memory, since the pointers were simply copied to the device. It is then necessary to copy the data pointed to by those pointers, which is what the pragma at line 72 achieves. Line 72 gives the three arrays contained in A shapes and copies their data to the device. When removing the data from the device in the free_matrix function, these operations should be done in the reverse order, as shown in Fig. 17.

```
29 void allocate_3d_poisson_matrix(matrix &A, int N) {
30    int num_rows=(N+1)*(N+1)*(N+1);
31    int nnz=27*num_rows;
32    A.num_rows=num_rows;
33    A.row_offsets=(unsigned
int*)malloc((num_rows+1)*sizeof(unsigned int));
34    A.cols=(unsigned int*)malloc(nnz*sizeof(unsigned int));
35    A.coefs=(double*)malloc(nnz*sizeof(double));
36
37    int offsets[27];
38    double coefs[27];
39    int zstride=N*N;
40    int ystride=N;
41
<Shortened for space>
68
69    A.row_offsets[num_rows]=nnz;
70    A.nnz=nnz;
71 #pragma acc enter data copyin(A)
72 #pragma acc enter data
copyin(A.row_offsets[0:num_rows+1],A.cols[0:nnz],A.coefs[0:nnz])
73 }
```

FIG. 16

Modified matrix allocation function.

```
75 void free_matrix(matrix &A) {
76    unsigned int *row_offsets=A.row_offsets;
77    unsigned int * cols=A.cols;
78    double * coefs=A.coefs;
79
80 #pragma acc exit data delete(A.row_offsets,A.cols,A.coefs)
81
82    free(row_offsets);
83    free(cols);
84    free(coefs);
85 }
```

FIG. 17

Modified matrix free function.

The allocate_vector and free_vector functions can be similarly modified to relocate Vector structures to the accelerator as well. Since allocate_vector does not initialize the vector with any data, the create data clause can be used to allocate space without causing any data copies to occur, as shown in Fig. 18.

At this point the benchmark will run with all Matrix and Vector data structures residing on the device for the entire calculation, but it will give incorrect results because the code fails to initialize the vector data structures on the accelerator. To fix this, it is necessary to modify the initialize_vector function to update the device data with the initialized host data. This can be done with the OpenACC update directive.

```
24 void allocate_vector(vector &v, unsigned int n) {
25   v.n=n;
26   v.coefs=(double*)malloc(n*sizeof(double));
27 #pragma acc enter data create(v)
28 #pragma acc enter data create(v.coefs[0:n])
29 }
30
31 void free_vector(vector &v) {
32 #pragma acc exit data delete(v.coefs)
33 #pragma acc exit data delete(v)
34   free(v.coefs);
35   v.n=0;
36 }
```

FIG. 18

Modified allocate_vector and free_vector functions.

The update directive causes the data in the host and device copies of a variable to be made consistent, either by copying the data from the device copy to the host, or vice versa. On architectures with a unified memory for both the host and accelerator devices update operations are ignored.

The update directive accepts a device or self clause to declare which copy of the data should be modified. Since we want to update the device's data using the data from the host, the device clause is used, specifying that the device's copy of the coefficients array should updated. An update directive can be used in the initialize_vector function to copy the data in the initialized host vector to the device, as shown in Fig. 19. When using the update directive, the amount of data to update is specified in the same way as the data clauses, as shown earlier. In the case of Fortran arrays, if the entire array needs to be updated then the bounds can be left off.

```
38 void initialize_vector(vector &v,double val) {
39
40   for(int i=0;i<v.n;i++)
41     v.coefs[i]=val;
42 #pragma acc update device(v.coefs[0:v.n])
43 }
```

FIG. 19

Updated initialize_vector function.

One point of confusion for new OpenACC programmers is why the clause for updating the host's arrays is called self. OpenACC 1.0 used the host keyword to specify that the host array should be updated with the data from the device array, but since OpenACC 2.0 opened up the possibility of nesting OpenACC regions within other OpenACC compute regions, it is possible that the thread performing the update isn't on the host, but rather is on a different accelerator. Fig. 20 shows a pseudo-code example of a kernels region nested within another kernels region. When the update

```
1 #pragma acc kernels
2 for (int i = 0; i < N; i++)
3 {
4    #pragma acc update device(A[0:N])
5    #pragma acc kernels
6    for (int j = 0; j < N; j++)
7      A[j] = j;
8    #pragma acc update self(A[0:N])
9 }
```

FIG. 20

Example of update directive in nested OpenACC regions.

on line 4 occurs, the device running the outer `kernels` region will copy the values from its copy of A to the device that will run the `kernels` region on line 5. At line 8 the device running the outer kernels region needs to copy back the results from the inner region. Saying *update the host copy* is not correct, since the kernels region at line 1 might not be running on the host, so OpenACC 2.0 introduced the idea of update *self*, as-in *update **my** copy of the data with the device data*. The `host` keyword still exists in OpenACC 2.0 and beyond, but it has been defined to always mean self instead.

At this point building and running the benchmark code results in a large performance improvement on the example system. Examining the PGProf timeline (Fig. 21) shows that the data is copied to the device at the very beginning of the execution and only the resulting norm is copied back periodically. This is because we've expressed to the compiler that it should generate our data structures directly on the accelerator and the compute regions that were added in the previous section

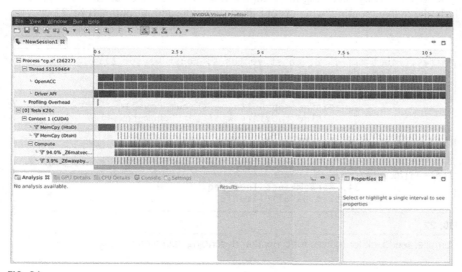

FIG. 21

Profile timeline after expressing data motion.

check for the presence of the data and, upon finding the data on the device, reuse the existing device data. On accelerators with discrete memory, such as the GPU used in this example, expressing data motion is often the step where programmers will see the greatest speed-up, since the significant bottleneck of copying data over the PCIe bus is removed. It is tempting to think that because this step creates such a large speed-up it should be done first. Doing so is often error prone, however, since it would be necessary to introduce update directives each time an unaccelerated loop is encountered. It is simpler instead to first put all of the loops on the device, at least within a significant portion of the code, and then eliminate unnecessary data transfers. Forgetting to eliminate an unneeded data transfer is simply a performance bug, which is simple to identify with the profiler, while forgetting an update directive because data directives were added to the program too soon is a correctness bug that is often much more difficult to find.

OPTIMIZE LOOPS

At this point the benchmark code is now running 2× faster than the original serial code on the testbed machine, but is this the fastest the code can be? Up to this point all of the pragmas we've added to the code should improve the performance of the benchmark on any parallel processor, but to achieve the best performance on the testbed machine, we'll need to start applying target-specific optimizations. Fortunately OpenACC provides a means for specifying a device_type for optimizations so that the additional clauses will only apply when built for the specified device type. Let's start by accessing the compiler feedback from the current code, particularly the matvec routine, which is our most time-consuming routine (Fig. 22).

```
matvec(const matrix &, const vector &, const vector &):
      23, include "matrix_functions.h"
          27, Generating copyin(cols[:A->nnz],Acoefs[:A-
>nnz],xcoefs[:x->n])
              Generating copyout(ycoefs[:num_rows])
              Generating copyin(row_offsets[:num_rows+1])
          30, Loop is parallelizable
              Accelerator kernel generated
              Generating Tesla code
              30, #pragma acc loop gang, vector(128) /* blockIdx.x
threadIdx.x */
              34, #pragma acc loop seq
          34, Loop is parallelizable
```

FIG. 22

Compiler feedback for matvec function after describing data motion step.

The compiler is providing information about how it is parallelizing the two matvec loops at lines 30 and 24, but in order to understand what it is telling us, we need to understand OpenACC's three levels of parallelism: gangs, workers, and vectors. Starting at the bottom of the levels, *vector* parallelism is very tight-grained parallelism where multiple data elements are operated on with the same instruction. For instance, if I have two arrays of numbers that need to be added together, some hardware has special instructions that are able to operate on groups of numbers from each array and add them all together at the same time. How many numbers get added together by the same instruction is referred to as the *vector length*, and varies from machine to machine. At the top of the levels of parallelism are *gangs*. Gangs operate completely independently of each other, with no opportunity to synchronize with each other and no guarantees about when each gang will run in relation to other gangs. Because gang parallelism is very coarse-grained, it is very scalable. Worker parallelism falls in between gang and vector. A gang is comprised of one or more workers, each of which operate on a vector. The workers within a vector have the ability to synchronize and may share a common cache of very fast memory. Every loop parallelized by an OpenACC compiler will be mapped to at least one of these levels of parallelism, or it will be run sequentially (abbreviated *seq*). Fig. 23 shows the three levels of OpenACC parallelism.

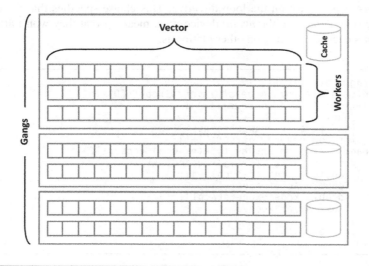

FIG. 23

OpenACC's three levels of parallelism.

With that background, we can see how the OpenACC compiler has mapped our two loops to the levels of parallelism. It has mapped the loop at line 30 to gang and vector parallelism, implicitly creating just one worker per gang, and assigned a vector length of 128. The loop at line 34 is run sequentially. Given this information we can now begin to give the compiler additional information to guide how it maps the loops to the levels of parallelism.

REDUCE VECTOR LENGTH

Since I'm running this benchmark on an NVIDIA GPU, I'll use my understanding of NVIDIA GPUs and the application to make better decisions about how to parallelize the loop. For instance, I know that NVIDIA GPUs perform best when the vector loop accesses data in a *stride-1* manner, meaning each successive loop iteration accesses a successive array element. Although the outer loop accesses the row_offsets array stride-1, the inner loop accesses the Acols, Acoefs, and xcoefs arrays in stride-1, making it a better target for vectorization. Adding a loop pragma above the inner loop allows us to specify what level of parallelism to use on that loop. Additionally we can specify the vector length that should be used. The compiler appears to prefer vector lengths of 128, but our inner loop always operates on 27 non-zero elements, which results in wasting 101 *vector lanes* each time we operate on that loop. It'd be better to reduce the vector length, given what we know about the loop count, to reduce wasted resources. Ideally we'd just reduce the vector length to 27, since we know this is the exact number of loop iterations, but this NVIDIA GPU has a hardware vector length, referred to by NVIDIA as the *warp size*, of 32, so let's reduce the vector length to 32, thus wasting only 5 vector lanes rather than 101. Fig. 24 shows the matvec loops with the inner loop mapped to vector parallelism and a vector length of 32. Notice the *device_type* clause on the loop directive. This clause specifies that the clauses I list are only applied to the *nvidia* device type, meaning that they won't affect the compiler's decision making on other platforms.

```
29 #pragma acc kernels
copyin(cols[0:A.nnz],Acoefs[0:A.nnz],xcoefs[0:x.n])
30    for(int i=0;i<num_rows;i++) {
31       double sum=0;
32       int row_start=row_offsets[i];
33       int row_end=row_offsets[i+1];
34 #pragma acc loop device_type(nvidia) vector(32)
35       for(int j=row_start;j<row_end;j++) {
36          unsigned int Acol=cols[j];
37          double Acoef=Acoefs[j];
38          double xcoef=xcoefs[Acol];
39          sum+=Acoef*xcoef;
40       }
41       ycoefs[i]=sum;
42    }
```

FIG. 24

Matvec function with reduced vector length.

As we see from the output in Fig. 25, this change actually negatively affected the overall performance. It is tempting to reverse this change to the code, since it didn't help our runtime, but I feel quite confident that the decision to vectorize the innermost loop is the right decision, so instead I will turn to the profiler to better understand why I didn't get the speed-up I expected.

```
Rows: 8120601, nnz: 218535025
Iteration: 0, Tolerance: 4.0067e+08
Iteration: 10, Tolerance: 1.8772e+07
Iteration: 20, Tolerance: 6.4359e+05
Iteration: 30, Tolerance: 2.3202e+04
Iteration: 40, Tolerance: 8.3565e+02
Iteration: 50, Tolerance: 3.0039e+01
Iteration: 60, Tolerance: 1.0764e+00
Iteration: 70, Tolerance: 3.8360e-02
Iteration: 80, Tolerance: 1.3515e-03
Iteration: 90, Tolerance: 4.6209e-05
Total Iterations: 100 Total Time: 14.946493s
Final Tolerance: 1.9934e-06
```

FIG. 25

Program output after adjusting vector parallelism.

INCREASE PARALLELISM

In order to determine why customizing the vector length didn't have the desired effect, we'll use the PGProf guided analysis mode to help determine the performance limiter. Guided analysis should be enabled by default, so after starting a new session with the current executable, select the Analysis tab and follow the suggestions provided. The analysis should eventually point toward GPU *occupancy* as the limiting factor, as shown in Fig. 26. Occupancy is a term used by NVIDIA to describe how

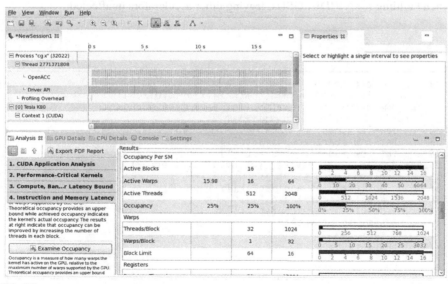

FIG. 26

PGProf profiler showing low GPU occupancy.

well the GPU is saturated compared to how much work it could theoretically run. NVIDIA GPUs are comprised of 1 or more *streaming multiprocessors*, commonly referred to as *SMs*. An SM can manage up to 2048 concurrent threads, although not all of these threads will be actively running at the same time. The profiler output is showing that of the possible 2048 active threads, the SM only has 512 threads, resulting in 25% occupancy. The red line in Fig. 26 shows why this is: the SM can manage at most 16 *threadblocks*, which equate to OpenACC gangs, but it would require 64 to achieve full occupancy due to the size of the gang, which we can see from the "Threads/Block" line only has 32 threads. What all of this is showing is that by reducing the vector length to 32, the total threads per GPU threadblock is reduced to 32 too, so we need to introduce more parallelism in order to better fill the GPU.

We can increase the parallelism within the gang in one of two ways: increase the vector length or increase the workers. We know from the previous section that increasing the vector length doesn't make any sense, since there's not enough work in the inner loop to support a longer vector length, so we'll try increasing the number of workers. The total work within the GPU threadblock can be thought of as *the number of workers × the vector length,* so the most workers we could use is 32, because $32 \times 32 = 1024$ GPU threads. Fig. 27 shows the final matvec loop code and Fig. 28 shows the speed-up from changing the number of workers within each gang.

On this particular test system 8 workers of 32 threads appears to be the optimal gang size. Since the device_type clause is used, these optimizations will only apply when building for NVIDIA GPUs, leaving other accelerators unaffected.

```
29 #pragma acc kernels
copyin(cols[0:A.nnz],Acoefs[0:A.nnz],xcoefs[0:x.n])
30 #pragma acc loop device_type(nvidia) gang worker(8)
31   for(int i=0;i<num_rows;i++) {
32     double sum=0;
33     int row_start=row_offsets[i];
34     int row_end=row_offsets[i+1];
35 #pragma acc loop device_type(nvidia)vector(32)
36     for(int j=row_start;j<row_end;j++) {
37       unsigned int Acol=cols[j];
38       double Acoef=Acoefs[j];
39       double xcoef=xcoefs[Acol];
40       sum+=Acoef*xcoef;
41     }
42     ycoefs[i]=sum;
43   }
44 }
```

FIG. 27

Final matvec loop code.

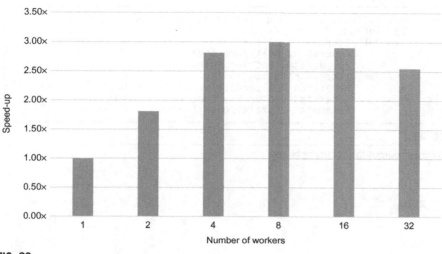

FIG. 28

Speed-up from increasing the number of workers in matvec function.

RUNNING IN PARALLEL ON MULTICORE

It's important to understand that although an NVIDIA GPU was used in this chapter, OpenACC is not a GPU programming model, but rather a general model for parallel programming. Although the loop optimizations we applied in the Optimize Loops section apply only to the GPU on which the code was running, the description of parallelism and data motion are applicable to any parallel architecture. The PGI compiler used throughout this section supports multiple accelerator targets, including GPUs from NVIDIA and AMD and multicore ×86 CPUs. So what happens if we take the code we've written and rerun it on a multicore CPU? Let's start by rebuilding the code for the *multicore* target, instead of the *tesla* target (Figs. 29 and 30).

If we now run the resulting executable it will parallelize the loops on the CPU cores of the benchmark machine, rather than the GPU. It is possible to adjust the number of CPU cores used by setting the ACC_NUM_CORES environment variable to the number of CPU cores to use. Fig. 31 shows the speed-up from adjusting the number of cores from 1 to 12, the maximum number of cores on the benchmark machine. The performance plateau beyond 4 CPU cores is due to the benchmark performance becoming limited by the available CPU bandwidth.

```
1 CXX=pgc++
2 CXXFLAGS=-fast -ta=multicore -Minfo=all -Mneginfo
```

FIG. 29

Makefile changes to target a multicore accelerator.

```
matvec(const matrix &, const vector &, const vector &):
    23, include "matrix_functions.h"
        31, Loop is parallelizable
            Generating Multicore code
            31, #pragma acc loop gang
        36, Loop is parallelizable
            Generated 2 alternate versions of the loop
            Generated vector sse code for the loop
            Generated 2 prefetch instructions for the loop
```

FIG. 30

Compiler output for multicore target.

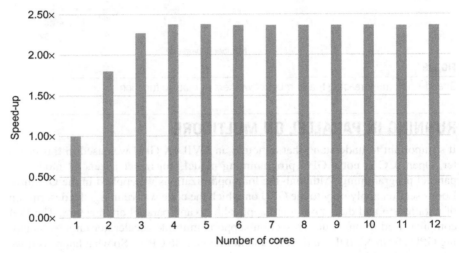

FIG. 31

Performance improvement from multicore acceleration.

SUMMARY

OpenACC is a descriptive model for parallel programming and in this chapter we used several OpenACC features to describe the parallelism and data use of a benchmark application and then optimized it for a particular platform. Although the Portland Group compiler and PGProf profiler were used in this chapter, the same process could be applied to any application using a variety of OpenACC-aware tools.

1. Obtain a profile of the application to identify unexploited parallelism in the code.
2. Incrementally describe the available parallelism to the compiler. When performing this step on architectures with distinct host and accelerator memories, it is common for the code to slow down during this step.

3. Describe the data motion of the application. Compilers must always be cautious with data movement to ensure correctness, but developers are able to see the bigger picture and understand how data is shared between OpenACC regions in different functions. After describing the data and data motion to the compiler, performance will improve significantly on architectures with distinct memories.

4. Finally, use your knowledge of the application and target architecture to optimize the loops. Frequently loop optimizations will provide only small performance gains, but it is sometimes possible to give the compiler more information about the loop than it would see otherwise to obtain even larger performance gains.

Fig. 32 shows the final performance at each step in terms of speed-up over the original serial code. Notice that the final code achieves a 4× speed-up over the original, serial code, and the multicore version achieves nearly 2.5×. Although the code did slow down at times during the process, it is easy to see why particular steps resulted in a slowdown and make corrections to further improve performance. The final result of this process is a code that has can be run on a variety of parallel architectures and has been tuned for one in particular, without negatively affecting the performance of others. This is OpenACC programming in a nutshell, providing the compiler with sufficient information to run effectively on any modern machine.

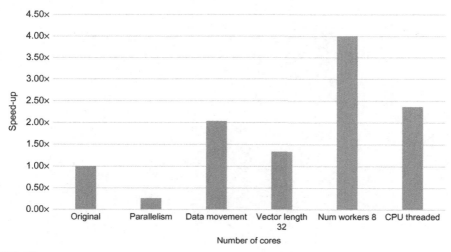

FIG. 32

Final performance results for each step.

Profiling performance of hybrid applications with Score-P and Vampir

3

Guido Juckeland*, Robert Dietrich†

Department of Information Services and Computing, Helmholtz-Zentrum Dresden-Rossendorf (HZDR), Dresden, DEU, Germany* Technische Universität Dresden, Dresden, Germany†

The purpose of this chapter is to familiarize the reader with the concept of evolutionary performance improvement and the tools involved when adding other parallelization paradigms to OpenACC applications. Such hybrid applications can suffer from a number of performance bottlenecks and a holistic picture of all activities during the application run can shed light on how to improve the overall performance.

At the end of this chapter the reader will have a basic understanding of:

- Terminology and methods for performance analysis of hybrid applications (e.g., MPI + OpenACC)
- How to modify hybrid applications to generate and record performance data
- How to visualize and analyze the performance data to make educated choices on application improvement
- Common pitfalls when extending an existing parallel application to include another parallelization paradigm

OpenACC aims at providing a relatively easy and straightforward way to describe parallelism on platforms with hardware accelerators. By design, it is also an approach for porting legacy High Performance Computing (HPC) applications to novel architectures. Legacy and new applications that exceed the capabilities of a single node can use Message Passing Interface (MPI) for internode communication and coarse work distribution. The combined OpenACC and MPI applications are referred to as hybrid applications. It is also possible to combine OpenACC with OpenMP on the host side to utilize all resources of a compute node or to even use all three levels of parallelism (MPI, OpenACC, and OpenMP) concurrently. Tuning application performance for one parallelization paradigm is challenging, adding the second or third level of parallelism introduces a whole new layer of potential performance challenges due to the interaction of all parallelization paradigms. Profile-guided development can also cover these hybrid computation scenarios when using the right profiling tools.

Parallel Programming with OpenACC. http://dx.doi.org/10.1016/B978-0-12-410397-9.00003-2

Profiling tools from compiler or accelerator vendors are usually limited to the scheme the product addresses, e.g., only OpenACC and/or CUDA/OpenCL activity. Nearly all vendor tools are unable to record MPI activity leaving the programmer in the dark how well hybrid applications perform over all aspects of the application parallelism. Research-based performance tools cover this gap. HPCtoolkit, Tau, and Score-P are the most prominent third-party profiling tools that also offer hardware accelerator support. Out of the three Score-P is the one that covers the most parallelization paradigms, can record the most concurrent activity and, as a result, can provide the most complete performance picture even for very complex applications. Therefore, Score-P will be used as the example performance recording tool for this chapter. Vampir will be used for visualizing the performance data since it is by far the most capable trace visualizer and profile generator.

You can get Score-P at http://www.score-p.org and Vampir at http://www.vampir.eu.

PERFORMANCE ANALYSIS TECHNIQUES AND TERMINOLOGY

While the term "profiling" is commonly used to describe application performance analysis as a whole, it technically only refers to a subset of the performance measurement and analysis techniques. A formal comparison of the techniques is shown in Fig. 1.

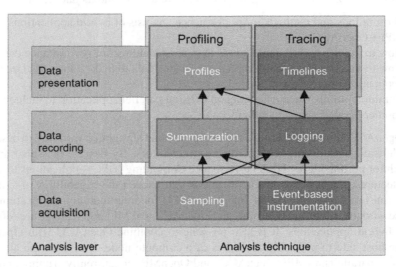

FIG. 1

Formal categorization of performance analysis techniques and their relation (Ilsche, Schuchart, Schöne, & Hackenberg, 2014).

Performance measurement and visualization is composed of three steps: data acquisition, recording, and presentation. The performance monitor wants to analyze the behavior of the application. To do so it can either interrupt the unmodified application and "pull" out information as to what the application was doing when it was interrupted (sampling) or the application can be modified itself to "push" information about its activity to the performance monitor (event based instrumentation). Data recording can either immediately summarize all data or fully log all activity as time-stamped entries. The full log file can be presented as a timeline or a profile for any arbitrary time interval while the summarized data can only be presented as a profile of the whole application run.

All analysis techniques have advantages and disadvantages. For example, *sampling*, which interrupts the application at a fixed sampling rate, e.g., has a constant perturbation of the run time of the application that is measured. However, the measurement accuracy is depending on the sampling frequency. *Event based instrumentation* will record all targeted activity, i.e., all functions or code segments that have been augmented either manually or via the compiler with event triggers, but the run time perturbation depends on the event rate which is not known at compile time and can be of orders of magnitude in a worst-case scenario. Immediate *summarization* maintains a low memory footprint for the performance monitor and does not lead to additional input/ouput (I/O) but it drops the temporal context of the recorded activity, whereas for *logging* it is vice-versa. *Profiles* immediately show activities according to their impact on the application (typically run time distribution over the functions) while they omit the temporal context. *Timelines* again are just the opposite; they show the temporal evolution of a program while making it harder to isolate the most time consuming activity right away.

Event based tracing is able to record the "full picture" of all activity during an application run, albeit at the price of a potentially very high run time perturbation. Fortunately, a compromise between the introduced techniques can be used to generate as much information as necessary at the lowest possible overhead. Score-P offers the—even concurrent—usage of all the presented performance analysis techniques and as such is unique in its capabilities as a performance monitor.

EVOLUTIONARY PERFORMANCE IMPROVEMENT

Examples in this book show that profile-driven development can be used to constantly improve an application's performance using OpenACC by offloading more and more activity and optimizing data transfers. Optimizing hybrid applications follows a similar pattern as illustrated in Fig. 2.

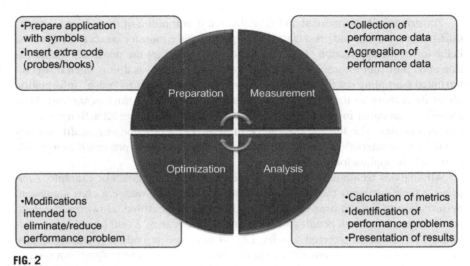

FIG. 2

The evolutionary application performance improvement cycle.

The performance optimization cycle starts with preparation of the application, followed by the actual measurement, and the analysis of the performance data. Based on this data the programmer will try to mitigate performance issues and start the whole process over again.

The remainder of the chapter explains how the first three steps of the performance optimization cycle are carried out with Score-P and Vampir using a particle-in-cell simulation accelerated with CUDA where the CUDA part could easily be substituted with an OpenACC implementation yielding the same results. Furthermore, various optimization steps are introduced which also highlight more generally applicable performance tuning options.

A PARTICLE-IN-CELL SIMULATION OF A LASER DRIVEN ELECTRON BEAM

Particle-in-cell codes simulate the movement of particles in electromagnetic fields by partitioning the simulation domain into a grid (the cells) while maintaining the particles as freely moving entities. The specific simulation (Burau et al., 2010) used for the performance study in this chapter describes how a very high energy laser pulse enters a hydrogen gas and in its wake field accelerates electrons to generate an electron beam traveling at almost the speed of light without the need for a considerably larger conventional particle accelerator.

The actual simulation runs through discrete time steps where each step involves four phases as shown in Fig. 3. First the Lorentz force ($\vec{F}$) on all particles as a result of the electric ($\vec{E}$) and magnetic ($\vec{B}$) fields are computed. Next the particles are moved along those computed forces. Since moving charged particles represent an electric current ($\vec{J}$), those currents are computed next. Lastly the computed current will influence the electric and magnetic fields which need to be updated before the cycle starts over. The duration of a simulated time step is chosen such that no particle can travel further than one cell in one time step.

PIConGPU originates from a proof-of-concept by a high school student during an internship at HZDR. It was a single Graphic Processing Unit (GPU) CUDA implementation that ran orders of magnitude faster than any other PIC code. Since then this application has been ported to multiple GPUs and the code has moved from CUDA C to C++11. Using the steps described in this chapter, the overall performance has been improved even further. Functionality of PIConGPU that can be reused for other applications has been extracted into external libraries, so that other particle-mesh-simulations can benefit from the key components that make PIConGPU so fast. The source code of PIConGPU is available at https://github.com/ComputationalRadiationPhysics/picongpu/.

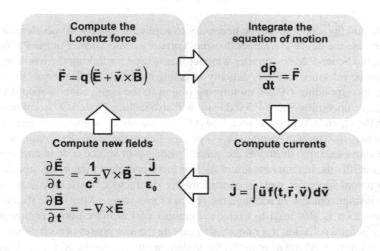

FIG. 3

Phases of the PIConGPU algorithm for a single time step.

PREPARING THE MEASUREMENT THROUGH CODE INSTRUMENTATION

In order to acquire very detailed performance data, the source code of the application under test needs to be modified to push events to a performance monitor. This process is called instrumentation. Score-P typically uses compiler instrumentation, which means the compiler is invoked with additional options to generate callbacks for all function entries and exits which will be handled by Score-P. These callbacks are the events that were introduced previously. This of course requires that the compiler supports the injection of such callbacks which, however, most current compilers do.

All parallelization paradigms (MPI, OpenMP, Pthreads, OpenACC, CUDA, OpenCL, OpenSHMEM, or any combination) are instrumented automatically using provided performance tool interfaces, wrapper libraries, or source-to-source transformation. As a result, Score-P can record all activity directly without manual changes to the source code of the application under test.

In order to invoke the compiler instrumentation, Score-P provides compiler wrappers for most of the common compilers. These wrappers will add the correct flags to insert the necessary callbacks through the compiler. A generic wrapper script called `scorep` provides access to these wrappers. It is used as shown in Fig. 4.

```
# compiler definitions
NVCC = nvcc
CXX = g++
MPICXX = mpic++
```

```
# compiler definitions with Score-P
NVCC = scorep nvcc
CXX = scorep g++
MPICXX = scorep--cuda mpic++
```

FIG. 4

Makefile modification to enable the Score-P compiler wrappers.

In the linking step it might be necessary to explicitly specify the accelerator paradigms in case the Score-P wrapper does not correctly detect them. For the PIConGPU example the Score-P MPI compiler wrapper that is used for linking the whole application must be informed that it is actually targeting a CUDA application so that it will link the corresponding CUDA monitoring plugin to the application to record CUDA activity. The upcoming Score-P 3.0 release will also include OpenACC event recording through the OpenACC performance tool API. It requires a compiler that supports this API and may also require passing the `--openacc` flag to the Score-P compiler wrapper.

The above example illustrates the general principle of source code instrumentation. For PIConGPU the instrumentation is slightly more complex. First of all, one does not want to record functions such as constructors or destructors. Thus, they are compiled without instrumentation. In addition, the option of providing a filter list to the compiler instrumentation is also used to exclude a number of functions from instrumentation. From the general behavior, it is important to capture the four phases of each iteration with as little run time overhead as possible; the underlying details can be added on demand.

Score-P 2.0 introduced the capability of data acquisition of the application activity through sampling. In order to use that feature the application still needs to be instrumented so that the parallelization library activity is still recorded using events and external tools are required for acquiring the call stack.

RECORDING PERFORMANCE INFORMATION DURING THE APPLICATION RUN

An application will launch the Score-P performance monitor automatically with the first instrumented events in the application. The performance monitor is configured through a number of environment variables. In order to minimize the run time perturbation, the default settings of Score-P produce an event based profile that will not include any accelerator activity. To set up Score-P to record all relevant activity for the PIConGPU example, the environment variable as shown in Fig. 5 are used. In order to enable tracing of OpenACC API activity using the upcoming Score-P 3.0 release, the environment variable `SCOREP_OPENACC_ENABLE` needs to be set to "yes." The available options are described in the Score-P documentation.

```
SCOREP_ENABLE_TRACING=yes
SCOREP_CUDA_ENABLE=yes
```

FIG. 5

Score-P environment variables to enable MPI+CUDA tracing.

After the program is executed the current working directory contains a new subdirectory named scorep-<timestamp_of_program_run>. Inside the subdirectory you find both the profile (profile.cubex) as well as the trace file (traces.otf2) as shown in Fig. 6.

```
user@gpunode:~/scorep-20160612_2007_13576532418004250$ ls
profile.cubex  scorep.cfg  traces/  traces.def  traces.otf2
```

FIG. 6

Contents of the scorep-* subdirectory after a successful combined profile and trace run.

The generated profile is a very valuable first approach to understanding the overall application behavior. For applications where the event rate is unknown or expected to be very large, it is generally recommended to only generate a profile first and extend the tracing to only cover the needed levels of information, either through limited instrumentation or through record filtering. The profiles (profile.cubex) can be visualized with the viewer "cube." An example view is shown in Fig. 7.

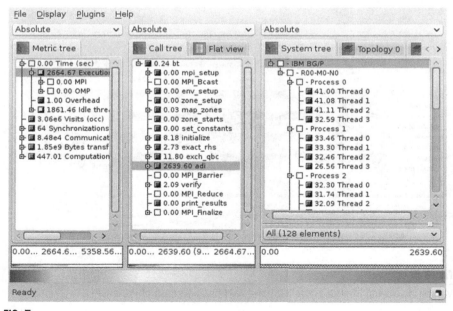

FIG. 7

Screenshot of the cube profile viewer (Geimer et al., 2010).

The cube profile viewer shows the analysis of the application run with respect to multiple metrics (left-most column). In the middle the currently selected metric is split up amongst the functions of the program. In the right column the selected metric for the selected function is split up among all processes and threads of the application run.

The trace file allows for an in-depth analysis of both the profile data as well as the temporal context. How this can be used to optimize our PIConGPU application is shown in the following section. A more detailed explanation of all Score-P settings can be found in the manual that is part of the installation.

LOOKING AT A FIRST PARALLEL PIConGPU IMPLEMENTATION

As a next step, the trace file, traces.otf2, is opened with Vampir, as shown in Fig. 8. The trace thumbnail (top right) shows that only 0.2 s out of the whole application run are selected, and the repetitive pattern suggests that about 2.5 iteration steps of the simulation are shown. In the middle with the color coded activities is the master timeline which shows both the MPI and host processes (Process 1–4) and the corresponding CUDA contexts (Thread 1/1–4). The legend in the lower right shows the meaning of the colors. The black lines between processes represent MPI messages that are exchanged, the ones between a process and a thread are CUDA memory copies. It can be seen that the MPI activity is dominating the program execution while the actual CUDA activity is rather time limited.

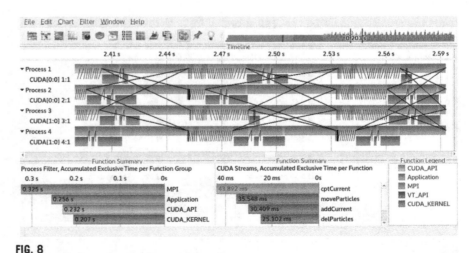

FIG. 8

Vampir displaying the trace of a first naive MPI parallelization of PIConGPU.

The various displays for the performance data can be selected through the toolbar icons on the top left. There are two groups of displays, the timeline displays and statistical displays. The time displays show the activity along the temporal evolution in the horizontal direction. In this group is the master timeline, which shows the color coded activity of all event *streams* (which can be processes, threads, or CUDA streams).

The color code is by default based on the function groups as shown in the function legend display in the lower right. The process timeline shows the calling context over time for one event stream. The counter timeline displays the values of a performance counter associated with one event stream. This can be e.g., a PAPI counter, but also derived counters such as memory allocations or anything that was created with the Vampir metric editor. The temporal context of a counter for all event streams is shown in the performance radar.

The second display group contains the statistics displays which present various profile data. The function summary shows the distribution of run time or number of invocations among functions or function groups. The message summary provides statistics about all data transfers (between host and device or between MPI processes). The other displays are the process summary, the message matrix, the I/O summary and the call tree. A detailed explanation of all Vampir features can be found in its manual which is part of the installation.

The most important feature of Vampir, which sets it apart from standard profiling tools is the ability to zoom into any arbitrary time interval in the program execution timeline. Only an excerpt of the trace is shown in Fig. 8 as indicated in the thumbnail view in the *upper right* (the selected interval is depicted by the two *black bars*). All displays including the statistics are always updated to the currently displayed time interval. As a result, Vampir enables profiling of applications for any phase of the application and at extremely high temporal resolutions. All displays of Vampir can be configured with respect to how they display the information by right-clicking into the display. Left-clicking on anything in any display will bring up a context view that will show details about the selected item (such as start/end time, duration, function name, file name, line number, message size, etc.).

The trace file shown in Fig. 8 depicts the run of a first attempt of parallelizing the single GPU PIConGPU code using MPI to increase the simulation area (weak scaling). The trace shows a typical problem of such a first parallelization attempt: Sequential task execution. In this case one can see that both the MPI activity and the CUDA memory copies dominate the host execution time while GPU utilization is rather low.

The high portion of MPI activity is due to very long message transfer times for rather small messages (which can be analyzed using the message summary). It turns out that PIConGPU computes so fast on the GPU that the MPI transfers cannot be hidden. In order to reduce transfer times the only option is to reduce the transfer latency. In this case the 1 GB Ethernet in the development cluster was augmented with an Infiniband network to provide significantly faster MPI communication.

Another issue is the rather long phase of synchronous CUDA memory copies (the bar of the host processes right before a set of kernels is started on the device). Here, better interleaving of compute and data transfer will increase the overall throughput.

The very low GPU utilization is not an issue by itself, but rather an effect of the host not being able to supply enough work to the GPU as it is waiting for data from others or busy with other work.

FREEING UP THE HOST PROCESS

The next improved version of PIConGPU addresses the identified issues and introduces an additional Pthread into which all MPI communication activity is offloaded (Thread 1–4:2). As shown in Fig. 9 this frees up the host process to launch work to the GPU as soon as all required data are available and to retrieve data for communication with neighboring processes as soon as possible as well. The overall GPU utilization has improved, also due to the reduced message latency of the Infiniband fabric.

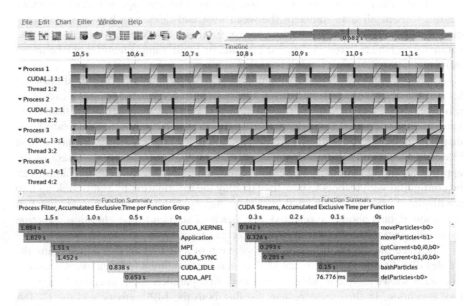

FIG. 9

A first improved version of PIConGPU.

OPTIMIZING GPU KERNELS

Now that the GPU is busy most of the time, the question arises if the GPU computing time can be reduced. Using the function summary to display only the functions of the CUDA group as shown in Fig. 9, it can be seen that the dominating kernel is called "moveParticles" followed by "cptCurrent."

The common part in both kernels have is that they need to traverse the particle list to first accumulate the contribution to the aggregate electrical current of a cell (cptCurrent) and then to update the positions of the particle (moveParticles). It turns out that the used data structure—a linked list of a C struct representing the particles (storing position, velocity, and charge) which was taken over from the originating PIC Central Processing Unit (CPU) implementation—does not work well on a GPU which requires coalesced memory accesses by neighboring CUDA threads. The particle data structure was changed to a list of structs of arrays of 256 floats and the performance improved dramatically as shown in Fig. 10. This is also due to changing the used MPI communication routines from synchronous to asynchronous MPI.

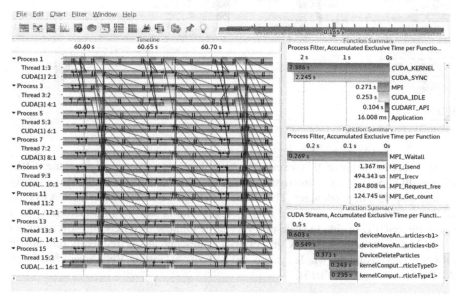

FIG. 10

PIConGPU using the optimized particle data structure and asynchronous MPI communication.

ADDING GPU TASK PARALLELISM

When zooming into a host-device-pair in Fig. 10, it turns out that there is quite some lag between some kernel launches and their start of execution. Furthermore, there are still times when the GPU is idle due to synchronous CUDA memory copies. The introduction of asynchronous GPU activity using CUDA streams enables PIConGPU to push more work to the GPU and let the GPU figure out the best way to process it. The result can be seen in Fig. 11. Each host process now uses CUDA streams (in this case five streams per GPU); one as a target for CUDA memory copies, the remainder to offload concurrent work.

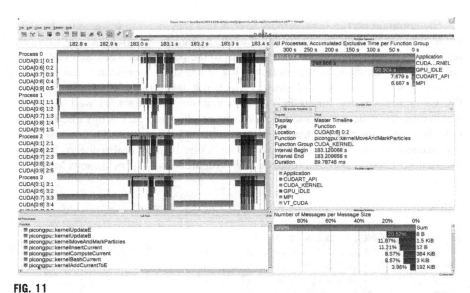

FIG. 11

PIConGPU at large scale, running on 512 nodes of OLCF's Titan.

In order to achieve this extremely high level of concurrency on the GPU, PIConGPU implements an internal event system that can automatically trigger activity and map data dependencies. This event system gets translated into CUDA events, so that a kernel can be launched even if input data is still being transferred. As a result PIConGPU is able to scale to a very large number of GPUs and still maintain a very high GPU utilization. PIConGPU and its descendants is frequently running on OLCF's Titan using the whole system and has been a Gordon-Bell-Award finalist in 2013 (Bussmann et al., 2013).

INVESTIGATING OpenACC RUN TIME EVENTS WITH SCORE-P AND VAMPIR

Compilers and run times have a certain freedom in implementing OpenACC directives. Therefore, it is important to review their conversion and execution. For example, a *kernels* directive can trigger the device initialization, device memory allocations, and data transfers without explicitly specifying respective operations. The profiling interface introduced with OpenACC 2.5 defines a set of events that unveil details on the implementation and execution of OpenACC directives. It enables tools such as Score-P to measure the duration of OpenACC regions, expose waiting time and offloading overhead on the host, and track memory allocations on the accelerator. More accelerator events such as the begin and end of GPU kernels and CPU-GPU data transfers can be gathered with the CUPTI interface for CUDA targets or via OpenCL library wrapping (Dietrich & Tschüter, 2015). OpenACC events relate low-level accelerator events with the application's source code. They are marked as implicit or explicit and, depending on their type, they can also provide information on the variable name of a data transfer or the kernel name of kernel launch operations.

Fig. 12 shows the Vampir visualization for an execution interval of an application that uses MPI, OpenMP, and OpenACC. In the selected interval two MPI processes execute the same program regions, each running two OpenMP threads and one GPU with two CUDA streams. Accelerator activities are triggered asynchronously, but the host is waiting most of the time for their completion. For example, the call tree on the right shows that the update construct triggers a data download from the accelerator to the host and a wait operation. OpenACC and OpenMP regions are annotated with the file name and line number to correlate with the source code.

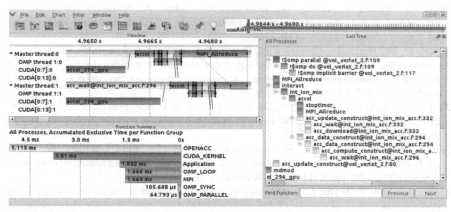

FIG. 12

OpenACC run time events expose the execution of OpenACC directives and relate accelerator activities with the program's source code (Dietrich, Juckeland, & Wolfe, 2015).

SUMMARY

While the PIConGPU example is a specific example, the identified performance bottlenecks are genuine and the presented solutions can be applied to other applications as well. Whether the accelerator is programmed using CUDA (as done with PIConGPU) or OpenACC makes no difference; the utilized improvements are available in both paradigms or refer to the underlying MPI activity.

Lessons learned:

- Performance analysis needs to be an integral part of every (parallel and especially hybrid) program development in order to utilize the available resources as efficient as possible.

- Sample-based profiling offers a first glimpse at potential hot spots in the program execution with very low run time overhead.
- Event based tracing provides the full picture of all concurrent activity during the program execution. The log level should be selected carefully in order to not overload the I/O subsystem.
- Interactive navigation through a trace file with the possibility for intermittent profiling of various application phases provides the application developer with a better understanding of what the program is actually doing at any point in time.
- Asynchronous activity for both MPI and accelerator activity is the key to high performance.

REFERENCES

Burau, H., Widera, R., Hönig, W., Juckeland, G., Debus, A., Kluge, T., et al. (2010). PIConGPU: A fully relativistic particle-in-cell code for a GPU cluster. *IEEE Transactions on Plasma Science*, *38*(10), 2831–2839.

Bussmann, M., Burau, H., Cowan, T. E., Debus, A., Huebl, A., Juckeland, G., et al. (2013). Radiative signatures of the relativistic Kelvin-Helmholtz instability. In *Proceedings of SC13: International conference for high performance computing, networking, storage and analysis (S. 5:1–5:12)*. Denver, CO: ACM.

Dietrich, R., Juckeland, G., & Wolfe, M. (2015). Open ACC programs examined: A performance analysis approach. In *44th international conference on parallel processing (ICPP)* (pp. S310–S319). Beijing: IEEE.

Dietrich, R., & Tschüter, R. (2015). A generic infrastructure for OpenCL performance analysis. In *8th International conference on intelligent data acquisition and advanced computing systems (IDAACS)* (pp. S334–S341). Warsaw: IEEE.

Geimer, M., Wolf, F., Wylie, B. J., Abraham, E., Beckert, D., & Mohr, B. (2010). The Scalasca performance toolset architecture. *Concurrency and Computation: Practice and Experience*, *22*(6), 702–719.

Ilsche, T., Schuchart, J., Schöne, R., & Hackenberg, D. (2014). Combining instrumentation and sampling for trace-based application performance analysis. In *Proceedings of the 8th international workshop on parallel tools for high performance computing* (pp. 123–136). Stuttgart: Springer International Publishing.

Pipelining data transfers with OpenACC

4

Jeff Larkin
NVIDIA, Santa Clara, CA, United States

The purpose of this chapter is to introduce asynchronous programming with OpenACC, particularly in regards to a technique known as pipelining. This chapter will accelerate an existing OpenACC code by enabling the overlap of computation and data transfers.

At the end of this chapter the reader will have an understanding of:

- Asynchronous execution within OpenACC
- Pipelining as a technique to overlap data transfers with computation
- How to use the OpenACC routine directive

To date (Nov. 2016), OpenACC has primarily been used on systems with co-processor accelerators, such as discrete Graphic Processing Unit (GPU), Many-Integrated Core (MIC or Intel Xeon Phi), Field Programmable Gate Array (FPGA), or Digital Signal Processing (DSP) devices. One challenge when dealing with co-processor accelerators is that as the computation is sped up the cost of transferring data between the host and accelerator memory spaces can limit performance improvements. Unfortunately, by the very nature of co-processors, the movement of data between the host and device memory is necessary and can never be fully eliminated. Once data movement is reduced as much as possible the only way to further reduce the effect of the data movement on performance is to overlap data movement with computation. For instance, on an NVIDIA Tesla GPU connected to the host Central Processing Unit (CPU) via PCI Express (PCIe) it is possible to be copying data to the GPU, from the GPU, computing on the GPU, and computing on the CPU all at the same time. Of course, with many operations happening simultaneously the programmer must carefully choreograph and synchronize the independent operations to ensure that the program still produces correct results. This chapter focuses on one particular technique for overlapping data movement with computation using OpenACC asynchronous capabilities: pipelining.

INTRODUCTION TO PIPELINING

Synchronous operations require that one operation must wait for another to complete before it can begin. As an example, consider a grocery checkout line: before the

Parallel Programming with OpenACC. http://dx.doi.org/10.1016/B978-0-12-410397-9.00004-4

customer can pay for their groceries the checkout clerk must finish scanning all of the groceries. Scanning and paying are two distinct operations, but the operation of paying cannot proceed until the operation of scanning the products is complete. This operation is fairly inefficient, since neither the buyer nor payer can do their part of the transaction until the other has completed. To service more customers, it can be tempting to think that the solution is to open more lanes, when in fact a better solution is to optimize what happens within each checkout lane. For instance, a bagger can be busy bagging groceries while the customer is paying, the customer can be preparing the payment while the groceries are being scanned, and the clerk can be scanning one customer's groceries while the next customer begins loading their groceries onto the conveyor belt. Each of these operations are independent and can, at times, be carried out at the same time, provided they occur in the right order. These are the stages in the grocery checkout pipeline: unload the cart onto the belt, scan the groceries, bag the groceries, and pay. By allowing each person in the process to work asynchronously from each other the checkout line is able to process multiple customers in a more efficient manner than simply opening more checkout lanes.

Another example of a pipeline is an automobile assembly line. While Henry Ford did not invent the automobile, he optimized the way automobiles were produced by recognizing that certain steps in the process could be completed at the same time on different cars, provided the steps always occur in a specific order. For example, one worker welds together the frame, another worker adds wheels to a completed frame, and yet another worker adds the body around the completed frame with wheels. By ensuring that each step in the assembly takes a comparable amount of time, assembly lines are an effective way to keep every worker productive while building an automobile in a predictable amount of time.

We can apply this same concept to an OpenACC program. By default, OpenACC directives operate synchronously between the host CPU and the accelerator, meaning that the host CPU waits (blocks) until the accelerator operation completes before moving forward. By making OpenACC regions asynchronous, however, the CPU can immediately do other things, such as enqueue additional work, perform data transfers, or perform other compute operations on the host. Asynchronous operations enable all parts of the system to be productive: the host CPU, the accelerator, and the PCIe bus, when present, for data transfers. In the case study that follows we use a technique known as pipelining to reduce execution time by overlapping operations that can be done simultaneously to keep the parts of the system busy, much like the assembly line discussed previously.

Fig. 1 shows an idealized pipeline that one might build to overlap accelerator computation fully with data transfers, where H2D represents *host to device* copies and D2H represents *device to host* copies. The image is idealized because in reality the time taken by each step does not line up as nicely as shown in the picture. Notice that by pipelining the operations four full operations complete in the time two operations would require to execute in serial. Additionally, pipelining limits the full cost (time) of data transfers to only the first and last transfers; all other transfers are essentially free.

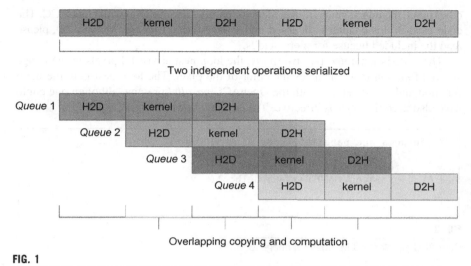

FIG. 1

Serialize execution versus pipelined execution.

EXAMPLE CODE: MANDELBROT GENERATOR

The example code used in this chapter generates a Mandelbrot set like the one shown in Fig. 2. Mandelbrot sets apply a specific formula to each pixel to determine the pixel's color density. Since each pixel of the image can calculate its color independent of each

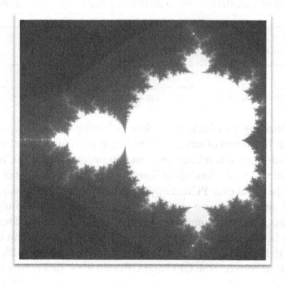

FIG. 2

Sample Mandelbrot set image.

other pixel, the image generation is ideal for parallel acceleration with OpenACC. The code used in this chapter is licensed under the Apache License, Version 2.0, please read the included license for more details.

The code is separated into two parts: the loop nest across all pixels in the image and the function that calculates the color of the pixel. The loop nest is in the main function and is accelerated with the OpenACC *parallel* pragma, although one could have also used the *kernels* directive. The code is shown in Fig. 3.

```
22  #pragma acc parallel loop
23    for(int y=0;y<HEIGHT;y++) {
24      for(int x=0;x<WIDTH;x++) {
25        image[y*WIDTH+x]=mandelbrot(x,y);
26      }
27    }
```

FIG. 3

OpenACC-accelerated Mandelbrot image loop.

Since this requires that the *mandelbrot* function be called from within an OpenACC region, it is necessary to use the *acc routine* pragma, as demonstrated in Fig. 4. Notice that this function is called from each and every loop iteration, and it has been declared acc routine seq. This means that the computations within the function are sequential. OpenACC requires that the programmer reserve the parallelism used within routines so that the compiler knows the levels of parallelism that are available for use parallelizing the rest of the code. By declaring the function as sequential, all types of parallelism are available for the loops that call it.

```
1  #pragma acc routine seq
2  unsigned char mandelbrot(int Px, int Py);
```

FIG. 4

Mandelbrot header file with OpenACC routine directive.

The key to building an effective pipeline is having enough steps, each taking a roughly comparable amount of time, such that each step can be overlapped with other steps. I will be running this test code on a machine with an NVIDIA Tesla K40 GPU. On such a machine there are four operations that can be carried out at the same time: copying data to the GPU over PCIe, copying data from the GPU over PCIe, computing on the GPU, and computing on the CPU. This case study is only able to carry out two operations, however, computing on the GPU and copying data from the GPU memory. This is because the image generation doesn't require input data, so we can ignore the copy to the GPU. Additionally, in this case study it is difficult to load balance the calculation between the CPU and GPU, so we'll just ignore the CPU. Fig. 5 shows the Visual Profiler timeline for the current code, notice the PCIe copies before and after the compute kernel.

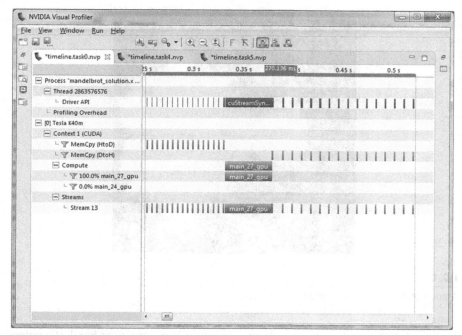

FIG. 5

NVIDIA Visual Profiler timeline of initial Mandelbrot generator.

The initial PCIe copy can be trivially eliminated by adding a *copyout* data clause, but then we run into a problem with the current code structure. As the code is currently written the copying of the image back to CPU memory can't occur until the completion of the main_20_gpu kernel. In order the enable the overlapping of computation and PCIe copies it is necessary to use a technique commonly referred to as *blocking* to break the problem into smaller chunks that can operate independently.

BLOCKING COMPUTATION

Blocking, or tiling, a computation is a technique of breaking a single large operation into smaller, independent pieces. When blocking is applied correctly, the final result should require the same amount of work and produce the correct results. Fig. 6 shows the same Mandelbrot set image that was generated previously and illustrates the image can be broken into multiple parts, in this case 4, that are generated separately because each pixel is generated independently. For this exercise we only block the image generation along rows, as shown, but the code can also be blocked by columns or by rows and columns. The decision to block by row ensures that the data for each block is contiguous in memory, thus simplifying the transfer of the data to and from the accelerator.

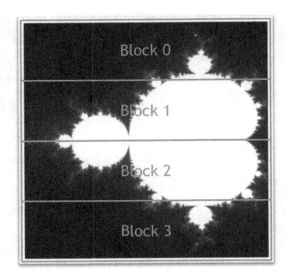

FIG. 6

Mandelbrot image broken into four blocks.

In order to operate in blocks along columns, it is necessary to break the outer, "y" loop into smaller parts by inserting a new outer loop that operates across blocks. The "y" loop now starts at the first row of each chunk and only iterates until the last row of the block. For simplicity we assume that the number of blocks always evenly divides into the height of the image so that the block sizes are always equal. Fig. 7 shows the code for this step, using 16 blocks rather than 4 shown in Fig. 6.

```
22    num_blocks = 16;
23   #pragma acc data copyout(image[:WIDTH*HEIGHT])
24     for(int block = 0; block < num_blocks; block++ ) {
25       int start = block * (HEIGHT/num_blocks),
26           end   = start + (HEIGHT/num_blocks);
27   #pragma acc parallel loop
28       for(int y=start;y<end;y++) {
29         for(int x=0;x<WIDTH;x++) {
30           image[y*WIDTH+x]=mandelbrot(x,y);
31         }
32       }
33     }
```

FIG. 7

Blocked Mandelbrot code.

At this point only the computation is blocked, but not the data movement. This is to ensure that if mistakes are made in figuring out the starting and ending values for the "*y*" loop then the mistakes are found and corrected early. Line 22 specifies the number of blocks to use in the "*y*" dimension. Line 23 adds a data region to ensure that the image array is only copied back to the host after all parallel loops finish executing on the accelerator. Lines 25 and 26 calculate the starting and ending value for the "*y*" loop respectively. Finally, line 28 is the modified loop, which iterates only over the rows in each block. Note that building and running the code at this step should still produce the correct image and should run in roughly the same amount of time as the previous step.

BLOCKING DATA COPIES

The next step in building the Mandelbrot pipeline is to block the data transfers in the same way as the computation. First add an *update* directive after the "*y*" loop, but before the end of the blocking loop. This directive copies only the part of the image array operated on by the current block. The starting value and count (or starting and ending value in Fortran) can be tricky, since they need to account for the width of each row, not just the number of rows. Line 34 in Fig. 8 shows the correct update directive. Lastly the `data` clause on line 24 must be changed from a `copyout` to a `create`, since the data transfers are now handled by the update directive. Fig. 8 shows the complete code for this step.

```
22    num_blocks = 16;
23    block_size = (HEIGHT/num_blocks)*WIDTH;
24 #pragma acc data create(image[WIDTH*HEIGHT])
25    for(int block = 0; block < num_blocks; block++ ) {
26      int start = block * (HEIGHT/num_blocks),
27          end   = start + (HEIGHT/num_blocks);
28 #pragma acc parallel loop
29      for(int y=start;y<end;y++) {
30        for(int x=0;x<WIDTH;x++) {
31          image[y*WIDTH+x]=mandelbrot(x,y);
32        }
33      }
34 #pragma acc update self(image[block*block_size:block_size])
35    }
```

FIG. 8

Mandelbrot code with blocked data transfers.

Once again, it is important to rebuild and rerun the code to ensure that the code still produces correct results. The runtime of the code at this step should be roughly comparable to the original runtime, since we have not yet introduced overlapping.

ASYNCHRONOUS EXECUTION

Now that both the computation and data transfers have been blocked they can be made asynchronous, freeing the host CPU to issue each block to the accelerator without waiting for the previous block to complete. This is done by using the *async* clause and *wait* directive. The *async* clause can be added to nearly any OpenACC directive to make it operate asynchronously with the CPU. When a directive includes the *async* clause the operation of that directive is placed in a work queue and execution immediately returns to the host CPU. Since all of the accelerator directives are now operating asynchronously with the host CPU, the CPU eventually reaches a point at which it needs the results. It is necessary to use the OpenACC wait directive to suspend host execution until the previously issued asynchronous operations complete. In the example code the right place to wait is between the end of the blocking loop and the end of the data region, since we need to ensure that all of the blocks are copied back to the host before the device arrays are destroyed at the end of the data region. Once all asynchronous operations are complete, the host CPU execution can use the results. Fig. 9 shows the resulting code.

```
19    num_blocks = 16;
20    block_size = (HEIGHT/num_blocks)*WIDTH;
21 #pragma acc data create(image[WIDTH*HEIGHT])
22    {
23      for(int block = 0; block < num_blocks; block++ ) {
24        int start = block * (HEIGHT/num_blocks),
25            end   = start + (HEIGHT/num_blocks);
26 #pragma acc parallel loop async
27        for(int y=start;y<end;y++) {
28          for(int x=0;x<WIDTH;x++) {
29            image[y*WIDTH+x]=mandelbrot(x,y);
30          }
31        }
32 #pragma acc update self(image[block*block_size:block_size]) async
33      }
34 #pragma acc wait
35    }
```

FIG. 9

Mandelbrot code with asynchronous blocks.

The final step in building the pipeline is to exploit the fact that each block is independent of each other block by putting blocks into different asynchronous queues. The async clause accepts a number representing the number of the queue in which to add the work. In theory each block could be given its own queue, but the creation of work queues can be an expensive operation on some architectures. Instead we use just two queues: one queue for computing and one queue for copying data back from the accelerator. The parallel loop and the update for each block must occur in order, so those should occur in the same queue, but different blocks are independent, so they may be placed in different queues. A convenient way to represent the queue number is to use the block number modulo the number of work queues. Fig. 10 shows the resulting code. The `wait` directive also accepts a queue number, but in this case we do not specify a queue number so the directive waits on all work queues to complete.

```
22    num_blocks = 16;
23    block_size = (HEIGHT/num_blocks)*WIDTH;
24  #pragma acc data create(image[WIDTH*HEIGHT])
25    {
26      for(int block = 0; block < num_blocks; block++ ) {
27        int start = block * (HEIGHT/num_blocks),
28            end   = start + (HEIGHT/num_blocks);
29  #pragma acc parallel loop async(block%2)
30        for(int y=start;y<end;y++) {
31          for(int x=0;x<WIDTH;x++) {
32            image[y*WIDTH+x]=mandelbrot(x,y);
33          }
34        }
35  #pragma acc update self(image[block*block_size:block_size]) async(block%2)
36      }
37    }
38  #pragma acc wait
```

FIG. 10

Mandelbrot code with alternating asynchronous queues.

At this point the execution time should be at least slightly improved from the original execution time, since the data copies and computation are now overlapped. The execution can be further improved by varying the number of blocks, which in turn varies the size of each block. Since it is necessary to find a balance between the added overhead of a large number of blocks and the benefit of overlapping small, evenly sized blocks, one should experiment to find the optimal number of blocks for a given system. The best number of blocks differs from system to system due to differences in the accelerator, host CPU, and data transfer speeds. Fig. 11 shows the Visual Profiler timeline with 16 blocks on an NVIDIA Tesla K40 GPU.

PIPELINING ACROSS MULTIPLE DEVICES

Since the image generation is now divided into independent blocks, it is not only possible to pipeline the blocks on a single accelerator, but the blocks could actually be executed across multiple devices. OpenACC provides an API for selecting which device the runtime should use based on a device type and number. Up to this point the example has used the default device, which is selected automatically by the runtime. It is possible to change which device the runtime uses by calling the `acc_set_device_num` function.

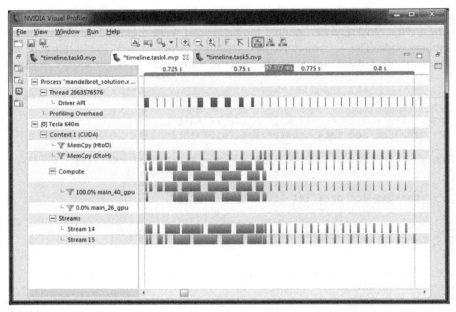

FIG. 11

NVIDIA Visual Profiler timeline for pipelined Mandelbrot code.

Multiple devices can be managed in a variety of different ways, including using the same CPU thread to manage all devices, using different processes per GPU, or using different threads. In this example the technique that requires the least code changes is to use OpenMP threads on the CPU to divide the blocks and assign each OpenMP thread to one of the available devices. Since the image array is small enough to fit in the memory of a single GPU, we simply replicate the entire image array on each device. When the data is too large to fit in a single accelerator's memory additional changes are required to only allocate enough space per accelerator to hold its part of the operation.

The PGI compiler used in this example allows using OpenACC and OpenMP in the same program, as long as they are not used on the same loop. In this example, OpenMP is used strictly on the blocking loop to workshare blocks to OpenMP threads and OpenACC is used for data management and for the "x" and "y" loops within each block. OpenMP must be enabled at compile-time using the *–mp* command line option. Fig. 12 shows how to use an OpenMP parallel construct to generate one thread per available device (line 22), using the *acc_get_num_devices* function (line 19) to query how many devices are available, and assign each thread a unique device (line 35). Each device still uses two asynchronous queues to enable overlapping of data transfers and computation.

```
19    int num_gpus = acc_get_num_devices(acc_device_nvidia);
20  // This parallel section eats the cost of initializing the
devices to
21  // prevent the initialization time from skewing the results.
22  #pragma omp parallel num_threads(num_gpus)
23  {
24    acc_init(acc_device_nvidia);
25    acc_set_device_num(omp_get_thread_num(),acc_device_nvidia);
26  }
27    printf("Found %d NVIDIA GPUs.\n", num_gpus);
28
29    double st = omp_get_wtime();
30  #pragma omp parallel num_threads(num_gpus)
31  {
33    int my_gpu = omp_get_thread_num();
34    acc_set_device_num(my_gpu,acc_device_nvidia);
35    printf("Thread %d is using GPU %d\n", my_gpu, acc_get_
device_num(acc_device_nvidia));
36  #pragma acc data create(image[WIDTH*HEIGHT])
37  {
38    #pragma omp for
39    for(int block = 0; block < num_blocks; block++ ) {
40      int start = block * (HEIGHT/num_blocks),
41          end   = start + (HEIGHT/num_blocks);
42  #pragma acc parallel loop async(block%2)
43      for(int y=start;y<end;y++) {
44        for(int x=0;x<WIDTH;x++) {
45          image[y*WIDTH+x]=mandelbrot(x,y);
46        }
47      }
48  #pragma acc update self(image[block*block_size:block_size])
async(block%2)
50      }
51  #pragma acc wait
52  }
53  } // OMP Parallel
54
55    double et = omp_get_wtime();
```

FIG. 12

Multi-device pipelining of Mandelbrot code.

Inspecting the GPU timeline using Visual Profiler (Fig. 13) reveals something peculiar. When run on 6 devices, devices 0 and 5 execute very quickly, while devices 1, 2, 3, and 4 execute relatively slowly. This phenomenon is due to an inherent load imbalance in the Mandelbrot generation. Looking at Fig. 2 notice that the middle part of the image is mostly white, while the outside of the image is mostly black. The white area in the Mandelbrot image indicates more iterations of the loop inside the *mandelbrot* function, meaning that the inner area takes longer to generate than the outer. In order to see the benefit of the multiple devices it is necessary to better balance the work between the devices. Most applications do not have such a load imbalance, so this next optimization is specific to this example code.

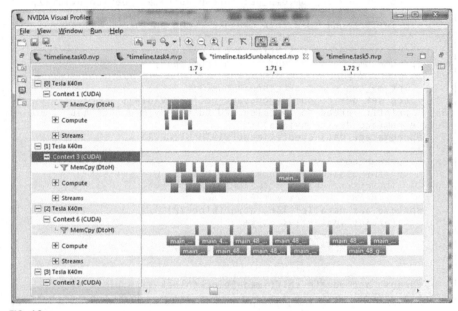

FIG. 13

Visual Profiler timeline for unbalanced multi-GPU work.

In order to load balance the four accelerators better, we change the way the blocks are assigned to each device. Since we are using OpenMP to assign the iterations of the block loops to different threads, and thus different devices, the simplest way to reassign the blocks is to change the schedule of the OpenMP loop. Using a static schedule with a *chunksize* of 1 assigns the loop iterations in a round robin manner to the devices rather than assigning contiguous chunks. One side effect of this change is that even and odd numbered threads only receive even and odd numbered blocks respectively. This change makes our logic to assign asynchronous queues insufficient to observe overlapping. Fortunately, this is easily fixed by introducing an additional variable to maintain the queue number within each thread. Fig. 14 shows the resulting code. Fig. 15 shows the final Visual Profiler timeline.

```
19    int num_gpus = acc_get_num_devices(acc_device_nvidia);
20  // This parallel section eats the cost of initializing the
devices to
21  // prevent the initialization time from skewing the results.
22  #pragma omp parallel num_threads(num_gpus)
23  {
24    acc_init(acc_device_nvidia);
25    acc_set_device_num(omp_get_thread_num(),acc_device_nvidia);
26  }
27    printf("Found %d NVIDIA GPUs.\n", num_gpus);
28
29    double st = omp_get_wtime();
30  #pragma omp parallel num_threads(num_gpus)
31  {
32    int queue = 1;
33    int my_gpu = omp_get_thread_num();
34    acc_set_device_num(my_gpu,acc_device_nvidia);
35    printf("Thread %d is using GPU %d\n", my_gpu,
acc_get_device_num(acc_device_nvidia));
36  #pragma acc data create(image[WIDTH*HEIGHT])
37  {
38    #pragma omp for schedule(static,1)
39    for(int block = 0; block < num_blocks; block++ ) {
40      int start = block * (HEIGHT/num_blocks),
41          end   = start + (HEIGHT/num_blocks);
42  #pragma acc parallel loop async(queue)
43      for(int y=start;y<end;y++) {
44        for(int x=0;x<WIDTH;x++) {
45          image[y*WIDTH+x]=mandelbrot(x,y);
46        }
47      }
48  #pragma acc update self(image[block*block_size:block_size])
async(queue)
49      queue = (queue + 1) % 2;
50    }
51  #pragma acc wait
52  }
53  } // OMP Parallel
54
55    double et = omp_get_wtime();
```

FIG. 14

Load balanced multi-device Mandelbrot code.

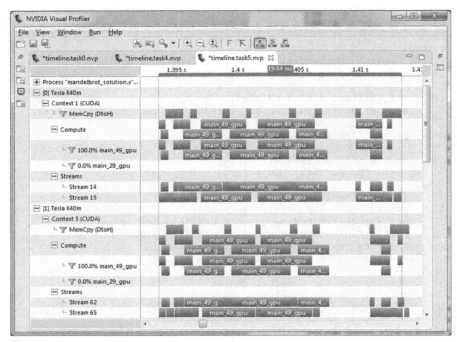

FIG. 15

Visual Profiler timeline for multi-GPU Mandelbrot code.

CONCLUSIONS

Pipelining is a powerful technique to take advantage of OpenACC's asynchronous capabilities to overlap computation and data transfer to speed up a code. On the reference system adding pipelining to the code results in a 2.9× speed-up and extending the pipeline across six devices increases this speed-up to 7.8× over the original. Pipelining is just one way to write asynchronous code, however. For stencil types of codes, such as finite difference and spectral element methods, asynchronous behavior may be used to overlap the exchange of boundary conditions with calculations on interior elements. When working on very large datasets, it may be possible to use asynchronous coding to divide the work between the host CPU and accelerator or to perform out-of-core calculations to stream the data through the accelerator in smaller chunks. Writing asynchronous code requires a lot of forethought and careful coding, but the end result is often better utilization of all available system resources and improved time to solution.

Advanced data management 5

Mathew Colgrove

The Portland Group (PGI), Beaverton, OR, United States

The purpose of this chapter is to teach the reader how to manage aggregate data structures, utilize global variables, and create device only data.

At the end of this chapter the reader will have a basic understanding of:

- Unstructured data regions
- Working with aggregate types with dynamic data members
- C++ class data management
- Using global static and Fortran module variables in device routines
- How to create device only data
- Sharing device memory between Message Passing Interface (MPI) processes

Previous chapters introduced data regions where data movement between the host and device is managed at the same point as where the computation is offloaded. However, as programs grow and data structures become more complex, it becomes better to take a top-down, whole program view of the device data along with a bottom-up approach to offloading computation. With this approach, the device data creation and deletion occur at a high level with data synchronization handled through an update directive. A first approach to achieving this is often to put the update directive before and after each compute region, and as more and more sections of the code are offloaded, the update directives can then be removed one by one. This enables incremental checking of the correctness of the program, and isolation of areas where data synchronization requires further investigation. If the program begins to exhibit incorrect answers, you can investigate if either data synchronization is necessary, or if the computation that is updating the data on the host could be offloaded onto the device to remove the data synchronization.

This chapter introduces unstructured data regions where the device data's lifetime is no longer defined by a lexical unit's beginning and ending, but rather the execution flow of the program. Unstructured data regions can be used to more easily create aggregate data structures which include dynamic data members by coupling device data creation at the same time as the data creation on the host. Unstructured data regions can also be used in C++ constructor and destructors allowing the lifetime of class

Parallel Programming with OpenACC. http://dx.doi.org/10.1016/B978-0-12-410397-9.00005-6

members on the host to match their lifetime on the device, as well as allowing for the encapsulation of data management within the class (Fig. 1).

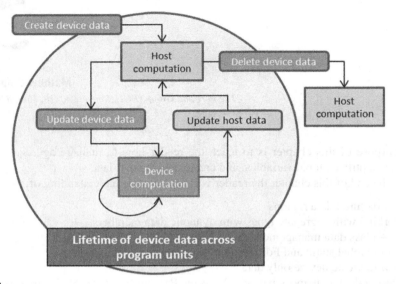

FIG. 1

Lifetime of device data across program units.

Other topics in this chapter include managing global static and Fortran module data using a declare directive as well as using device data without an associated host copy. The declare directive allows for global and module data to be accessed from within OpenACC device routines. Device only data is useful for interoperability with native device languages such as CUDA and OpenCL, creating memory pools, and sharing device data between different MPI ranks using the same device.

UNSTRUCTURED DATA REGIONS

One of the major additions to the OpenACC 2.0 standard was unstructured data regions. Prior to this, data regions had to have a lexically defined beginning and end. With unstructured data, the lifetime of the device data varies with the execution of the program and has the same scope as the associated host variable. While unstructured data regions can be used with static data, the intent is that they would match the lifetime and scope of dynamically allocated host data. The enter data create directive is used to define a variable on the device, and can be used just after allocating a dynamic variable via new, malloc, or allocate to match the creation of the host variable and the device variable. Likewise, the exit data delete directive just before the data is freed, deleted, or deallocated on the host then the lifetimes of the host and device variables will match (Box 1).

BOX 1 ENTER/EXIT DATA REGION SYNTAX

```
C/C++ syntax:
#pragma acc enter data [create | copyin] [ if, wait, async ]
#pragma acc exit data [delete | copyout ] [if, wait, async, finalize]

Fortran syntax:
!$acc enter data [ create | copyin ] [if, wait, async ]
!$acc exit data [delete | copyout ] [if, wait, async, finalize]
```

The enter data clause should only be used after the associated host variable has been created, likewise, the exit data clause should be used before the host variables is destroyed. The enter and exit data clauses are similar to structured data regions except that the enter directive can only create or copyin data and the exit directive can only copyout or delete data. Upon entering the data region, if the data is already present on the device, the device data will not be created again but rather its reference count is incremented. When an exit directive is encountered, the device data's reference count is decremented and only when no references remain, is the data deleted from the device. Adding a finalize clause to an exit data region will set the reference count to zero and delete the device data. Both directives support conditional execution using the if clause as well as asynchronous execution using the async and wait clauses (Boxes 2 and 3).

BOX 2 USING UNSTRUCTURED DATA REGIONS IN C

```
double * allocData(size_t size) {
    double * tmp;
    tmp = (double *) malloc(size*sizeof(double));
/* Create the array on device.
   The host copy must be allocated before creating the device copy   */
    #pragma acc enter data create(tmp[0:size])
    return tmp;
}

int deleteData(double * A) {
/* Delete the host copy.
   The device copy should be deleted before the host copy is freed.
*/
    #pragma acc exit data delete(A)
    free(A);
}
```

BOX 3 USING UNSTRUCTURED DATA REGIONS IN FORTRAN

```
module unstruct
    real, dimension(:,:), allocatable :: A, B

contains

    subroutine allocateData (N1,M1)
        integer(8) :: N1,M1
        allocate(A(N1,M1),B(N1,M1))
        ! Allocate device arrays after allocating on the host
        !$acc enter data create(A,B)
    end subroutine allocateData

    subroutine deallocateData()
        ! Deallocate device arrays before deallocating on the host
        !$acc exit data delete(A,B)
        deallocate(A,B)
    end subroutine deallocateData

end module unstruct
```

AGGREGATE TYPES WITH DYNAMIC DATA MEMBERS

Aggregate data types such as C++ Classes, C structs, and Fortran user-defined derived types can also be managed with data directives. If the aggregate type's size and shape is known at compile time, the compiler is able to manage the data movement allowing for fixed-sized types to be used in data clauses and update directives. However, if the aggregate type contains a dynamic data member, such as a C pointer or Fortran allocable object, the size and shape of the type's members is deferred to the runtime.

In Fortran where descriptors contain rank and bounds information about the allocable array, it may be possible for the runtime to determine how to create and update the aggregate type on the device. However, this is not part of the current OpenACC specification because for other cases such as a C++ pointer to an object where the runtime has little to no information about the data type, it is not possible to perform the data operations automatically. Further versions of the OpenACC standard may contain a shape directive giving users a method to describe the shape of the dynamic data members and a policy directive which allows for different shapes to be used in different situations.

The next few sections walk through examples on how to manually create and update device data structures. These methods manually implement the same steps a compiler runtime would do automatically if the shape directive was available.

BUILDING DATA STRUCTURES FROM THE TOP-DOWN

To begin, let's start with a simple C array of pointers, pointers to pointer, or multidimensional array. For the most common case where the dimensions are rectangular, the arrays can be used directly within data clauses (Box 4).

BOX 4 MULTIDIMENSIONAL C ARRAYS

```
#pragma acc enter data create(A[0:size1][0:size2])
#pragma acc update self(A[0:size1][0:size2])
```

However, if the array has a nonuniform space, for instance where each vector array is a different size, it is up to the programmer to manually create and update the data. The following example uses a top-down approach where we create an array of pointers on the device and then within the loop creates each vector. The vector array is "attached," i.e., where the vector's device pointer is assigned to the correct element of the device pointer array.

BOX 5 CREATING A JAGGED ARRAY

```
double ** allocData(size_t size1, int * sizes) {
    double ** tmp;
    int i;
    tmp = (double **) malloc(size1*sizeof(double*));
/* Create an array of pointers */
    #pragma acc enter data create(tmp[0:size1][0:1])
    for (i=0; i < size1; ++i) {
        tmp[i] = (double *) malloc(sizes[i]*sizeof(double));
/* Create the vector array and attach it to the pointer array */
        #pragma acc enter data create(tmp[i:1][0:sizes[i]])
    }
    return tmp;
}

int deleteData(double ** A, size_t size1) {
    int i;
    for (i=0; i < size1; ++i) {
        #pragma acc exit data delete(A[i:1])
        free(A[i]);
    }
    #pragma acc exit data delete(A)
    free(A);
}
```

Note that in the example from Box 5, each vector array needs to be individually created. When the data becomes available on the host, each vector array needs to be individually updated. If the pointer array itself were updated, then the code would be copying device or host memory addresses. This will cause runtime errors when dereferencing the pointers. *Be sure to only update fundamental, fixed size aggregate types, or arrays of those types!*

Let's now expand on this idea and in Box 6 create an array of "vector" structs each of which contains a size variable and an array of doubles (Box 7).

BOX 6 UPDATING JAGGED ARRAY VECTORS

```
/* Copy back the results for each vector */
    for (j=0; j < size1; ++j) {
      int nele = sizes[j];
      #pragma acc update self (A[j:1][0:sizes[j]])
    }
```

BOX 7 CREATING A STRUCT WITH A DYNAMIC DATA MEMBER

```
typedef struct {
   int size;
   double * data;
} vector;

vector * allocData(size_t size1) {
    vector * tmp;
    int i;
    tmp = (vector*) malloc(size1*sizeof(vector));

/* Create an array of vector structs */
    #pragma acc enter data create(tmp[0:size1])
    for (i=0; i < size1; ++i) {
        tmp[i].size = i+10;
        tmp[i].data = (double *) malloc(tmp[i].size*sizeof(double));

/* Create the data array and attach it to the data pointer */
        #pragma acc enter data create(tmp[i].data[0:tmp[i].size])

/* Update the size of the data so it can be used on the device */
        #pragma acc update device(tmp[i].size)
    }
    return tmp;
}

int deleteData(vector * A, size_t size1) {
    int i;
    for (i=0; i < size1; ++i) {
/* delete each vector's data array */
        #pragma acc exit data delete(A[i].data)
        free(A[i].data);
    }
/* delete the array of vectors */
    #pragma acc exit data delete(A)
    free(A);
}
```

When using these data structures within a compute region, it is important to use a present clause. Variables in a present clause indicate to the compiler that the data is already present on the device. If the variable is not in a present clause, the

compiler may attempt to put them into a copy clause which will cause problems given
that the shape isn't known (Box 8).

BOX 8 USING THE PRESENT CLAUSE ON COMPUTE REGIONS

```
#pragma acc parallel loop gang present(A,B)
    for (j=0; j < size1; ++j) {
        int size2 = A[j].size;
#pragma acc loop vector
        for (i=0; i < size2; ++i) {
            A[j].data[i]= B[j].data[i] + (double) ((j*size2)+i);
        }
    }
```

C++ CLASS DATA MANAGEMENT

In the previous section we created an array of a simple C "vector" struct. Let's now
expand on this by making the vector struct a C++ list Class. The data creation and
deletion can be moved into the class' constructors and destructors thus becoming
implicit when an object of the class is created or destroyed. We can also use tem-
plates allowing the same class definition be used for different fundamental data types
(Box 9).

BOX 9 EXAMPLE C++ CLASS CONSTRUCTOR AND DESTRUCTOR

```
template<typename T>
class myList {

    private:
        T* _A{nullptr};
        size_t _size{0};

    public:

    explicit myList(size_t size) {
        _size = size;
        _A = new T[_size];
        #pragma acc enter data copyin(this)
        #pragma acc enter data create(_A[0:_size])
    }

    ~myList() {
        #pragma acc exit data delete(_A[0:_size])
        #pragma acc exit data delete(this)
        delete [] _A;
        _A=NULL;
        _size=0;
    }
```

Note that the class' this pointer is also added to an enter data create directive. The this pointer is the actual instance of a particular object's data members. Although typically hidden from the programmer, all accesses to the object's data members are performed through the this pointer. So while the program may set a member using "_size=0," the program actually is accessing "this->_size = 0." When the this pointer is created on the device, space is created for each of the object's data members. If a this pointer is used in a copyin clause, then a shallow copy of the data members is performed. If any of the data members are pointers, then the associated host pointer is copied to the device (Fig. 2).

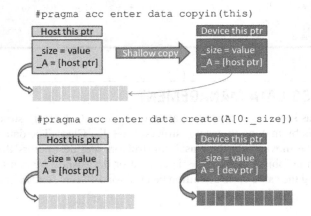

FIG. 2

Creating device data in a C++ constructor.

Next, the dynamic data members are allocated on the device and attached to the this pointer. Attaching will fill in the value of the data member's pointer to the address of the device data. Order matters. If the dynamic data member is created before the this pointer, there is nothing to attach to and the attach will be skipped. In the destructor, the reverse order is used where the dynamic data member is deleted from the device, then the this pointer is deleted.

Since the data is private, the class must provide methods to perform data synchronization between the host and device (Box 10).

BOX 10 ADDING CLASS UPDATE METHODS

```
void accUpdateSelf() {
    #pragma acc update self(A[0:_size])
}
void accUpdateDevice() {
    #pragma acc update device(A[0:_size])
}
```

Box 11 shows a simple program that uses the myList class. Other than deciding when to synchronize data, the programmer does not need to manage the creation, deletion, or updating of the underlying data.

BOX 11 USING THE CLASS

```cpp
#include "myList.h"

int main() {

    myList<double> A(N), B(N);
    for (int i=0; i < B.size(); ++i) {
        B[i]=2.5;
    }
    B.accUpdateDevice();
    #pragma acc parallel loop present(A,B)
    for (int i=0; i < A.size(); ++i) {
        A[i]=B[i]+i;
    }
    A.accUpdateSelf();
    for(int i=0; i<N; ++i) {
        cout << "A[" << i << "]: " << A[i] << endl;
    }
}
```

CREATING A GENERIC LIST CONTAINER CLASS

To make the container class more generic, it needs to be updated to allow for use with objects which themselves contain dynamic data. Since the generic container class will not have information about the object's data members, the contained object will need to manage its own device data. However, the container class must maintain the list of objects to ensure that the list is contiguous in device memory.

In this example, the container class, accList, contains a list of soaFloat3 struct which are composed of a size and three float pointers. In accList's constructor, an empty list of soaFloat3 is created on the device. Next for each list element, a new soaFloat3 is created. The soaFloat3 constructor creates the device arrays each of size M. Since the contained class manages its own data, the soaFloat3 copy constructor performs the copy into the list when inserted (Fig. 3).

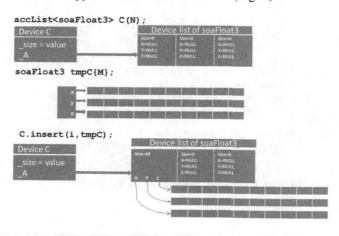

FIG. 3

Inserting a soaFloat3 into accList.

The accList constructor first creates its own this pointer on the device and then calls an initialization routine. There it creates a new empty list of objects and checks if the elements are already present on the device by calling the acc_is_present OpenACC Application Programming Interface (API) routine. If the element was allowed to create its own memory on the device, the objects may be scattered in device memory. This will cause errors when sequentially accessing the list elements on the device using the [] operator. To prevent this, the code will abort if the elements are present rather than crashing at runtime (Boxes 12 and 13).

BOX 12 accList CLASS CONSTRUCTORS

```
template<typename T>
class accList {
 public:
  explicit accList() {}
  explicit accList(size_t size) {
// Create the accList object on the device
    #pragma acc enter data copyin(this)
    allocate(size);
  }

  ~accList() {
    release();
// Delete the accList object from the device
    #pragma acc exit data delete(this)
  }
...
private:
  void release() {
    if (_size > 0) {
// Delete the _A list from the device
      #pragma acc exit data delete(_A[0:_size])
      delete[] _A;
      _A = nullptr;
      _size = 0;
    }
  }
  void allocate(size_t size) {
    if (_size != size) {
      release();
      _size = size;
// Update the device with the size of the _A list
      #pragma acc update device(_size)
      if (_size > 0) {
        _A = new T[_size];
#ifdef _OPENACC
// Make sure that the _A elements don't already exist on the device
        assert(!acc_is_present(&_A[0],sizeof(T)));
#endif
// Create the _A list on the device
        #pragma acc enter data create(_A[0:_size])
      }
    }
  }
```

BOX 13 METHOD TO INSERT AN OBJECT IN THE accList

```
void insert(size_t idx, const T& val) { _A[idx] = val; }
```

Next, add an insert method where objects can be added to the list. The actual update of the device data occurs in the copy constructor of the object since the list has no knowledge of the underlying data structure. In Box 14 is soaFloat3's copy constructor which makes a full copy of the data structures on both the host and device.

BOX 14 soaFloat3 COPY CONSTRUCTOR

```
  soaFloat3& operator=(const soaFloat3 &B) {
    size_t Bsize{B.size()};
    if (Bsize != _size)
      allocate(Bsize);
    size_t bytes = _size * sizeof *x;
    memcpy(x, B.x, bytes);
    memcpy(y, B.y, bytes);
    memcpy(z, B.z, bytes);
#if defined(USE_ACC_MEMCPY) && defined(_OPENACC)
    acc_memcpy_device(acc_deviceptr(x), acc_deviceptr(B.x), bytes);
    acc_memcpy_device(acc_deviceptr(y), acc_deviceptr(B.y), bytes);
    acc_memcpy_device(acc_deviceptr(z), acc_deviceptr(B.z), bytes);
#else
    accUpdateDevice();
#endif
    return *this;
  }
```

Instead of using accUpdateDevice method to update the device data, we could instead use the acc_memcpy_device API call to perform a device to device memory transfer. acc_memcpy_device takes two device pointers, the destination and source, and the size in bytes of the memory to copy. To obtain the device pointers associated with each array, make a call to acc_deviceptr. Either method works correctly with acc_memcpy_device being slightly faster than update at the cost being less portable given that an API call needs to be guarded by an _OPENACC macro while a directive is seen as a comment when OpenACC is not enabled.

accList UPDATE METHODS

Now that the accList and soaFloat3 classes manage the creation of device data, the accList class needs to call the update methods for each soaFloat3 elements in the list. This could be accomplished by adding a for loop in the accList update methods to traverse the list calling each elements' update method. However, this would cause issues if the contained object were a fundamental or fixed size aggregate type that didn't have an update method. Instead, the code needs to test at compile time if the contained class supports the accUpdateSelf and accUpdateDevice methods. To accomplish this, the code takes advantage of the "Substitution Failure Is Not An Error" (SFINAE) rules where a specialized method will be used if available and fall back to a more general method when it is not.

Here the decltype specifier returns the type of the object's accUpdate-Self method. If the method does exist, then the specialized accUpdateSelfT method is used. Otherwise the general case version which updates the list directly is used (Box 15).

BOX 15 TEST IF THE OBJECT SUPPORTS accUPDATE METHODS

```
void accUpdateSelf() { accUpdateSelfT(_A, 0); }
void accUpdateDevice() { accUpdateDeviceT(_A, 0); }

template<typename U>
void accUpdateSelfT(U *p, long) {
  #pragma acc update self(p[0:_size])
}

template<typename U>
auto accUpdateSelfT(U *p, int) -> decltype(p->accUpdateSelf()) {
  for (size_t j = 0; j < _size; ++j) {
    p[j].accUpdateSelf();
  }
}
```

Note that the full source listing for the example accList.h and soaFloat3.h header files are given at the end of the chapter.

USING GLOBAL AND MODULE VARIABLES IN ROUTINES

A host program's executable binary file is divided up into segments. One segment holds the instructions the program will run, another holds space for the stack, while a third contains the program's static (fixed size) data. Program data such as fixed size global arrays, C/C++ static variables, Fortran local variables with the save attribute, module variables, etc. are placed in this data segment. During compilation, the compiler doesn't know where in the data segment the static data will be placed. Instead it creates place holder references which the linker then resolves as an offset into the data segment.

While users can put static data into OpenACC data regions, the static data would need to be passed into any device routine that used it. To access the static data directly in a routine, the device would need to reference an offset into a data segment that doesn't exist in device memory. To solve this issue, OpenACC provides a declare directive which can be used in a nonexecutable, declaration section of a program (Box 16).

BOX 16 DECLARE DIRECTIVE

C/C++ syntax:

```
#pragma acc declare [ copy | copyin | copyout | present | deviceptr | link | device_resident ]
```

Fortran syntax:

```
!$acc declare [ copy | copyin | copyout | present | deviceptr | link | device_resident ]
```

The `declare` directive can be used at the start of routines, within modules, or globally as a way to define an implicit data region having the same scope and lifetime as the programing unit where it is defined. For static data, the compiler creates a device reference to the data which has a lifetime equal to the life of the program.

Box 17 shows an example of an OpenACC `routine vector` which uses a C static global array. The fixed size array is declared as an `extern` in a header file and then referenced in the vector routine.

BOX 17 USING A GLOBAL ARRAY IN A DEVICE ROUTINE

```
extern double A[N][M];
#pragma acc declare create (A)
...
#pragma acc routine vector
void setVal(int i, double val) {
    int j;
#pragma acc loop vector
    for(j=0;j<M;++j) {
        A[i][j] = val + (j*M)+i;
    }}
```

Note that `declare create` does not initialize the static data and an `update` directive should be used to synchronize the data between the host and device (Box 18).

BOX 18 UPDATING A GLOBAL DEVICE ARRAY

```
int main() {
    int i;
#pragma acc parallel loop gang
    for(i=0;i<N;++i) {
        setVal(i,2.5);
    }
#pragma acc update self(A[0:N][0:M])
...
```

Fortran module data must use a `declare` directive in order for it to be used in a OpenACC device routine. This includes scalars, fixed size arrays, and allocable arrays. When allocable arrays included in a `declare` directive are allocated or deallocated, the device copy is implicitly allocated and deallocated as well. The example from Box 19 declares two allocable arrays in one module and uses these arrays in a second module's device routine.

BOX 19 USING FORTRAN MODULE DATA IN AN OpenACC ROUTINE

```
module declare_data
    real, dimension(:,:), allocatable :: A, B
!$acc declare create(A,B)

    contains

    subroutine allocateData(n,m)
        integer n,m
! Data is implicitly allocated on the device
        allocate(A(n,m),B(n,m))
    end subroutine allocateData

    subroutine deallocateData
! Data is implicitly deallocated on the device
        deallocate(A,B)
    end subroutine deallocateData

end module declare_data

module use_data
    use declare_data
contains

    subroutine fillData (j,val)
!$acc routine vector
        integer(8), value :: j
        real(kind=dp), value :: val
        integer(8) :: i
!$acc loop vector
        do i=1,M
! the device copy of the declare_data arrays are used here
            A(j,i) = B(j,i) + ((j-1)*M)+(i-1)
        end do

    end subroutine fillData
end module use_data
```

USING DEVICE ONLY DATA

In general, it is recommended to use data regions to manage device data. However, in some cases the program may need to work with data that is only available on the device. For example, device only data would be used when interoperating with native device languages, CUDA or OpenCL, or when managing a memory pool on the device. OpenACC provides runtime API routines to dynamically allocate and free device memory (Box 20).

BOX 20 acc_malloc AND acc_free

C/C++ syntax:

```
d_void * acc_malloc( size_t number_of_bytes);
void acc_free( d_void *);
```

The acc_malloc and acc_free routines are used in the same way as the host's malloc and free except they create data only on the device. When using device only data within an OpenACC compute, data, or host_data region, the data should be declared in a deviceptr clause. Failure to use deviceptr may result in a runtime error. Also, device only data cannot be used in an update directive or other data clauses since there is no associated host copy.

BOX 21 CALLING A CUDA ROUTINE USING acc_malloc CREATED DEVICE DATA

```
int main() {
    double *A, *B;
    size_t size, i;
    size = N;
    A= (double*) malloc(size*sizeof(double));
    B= (double*) acc_malloc(size*sizeof(double));

    /* Call a CUDA routine to set the device data */
    cudaSet(B,size,2.5);

    /* Use the deviceptr clause on the compute region */
    #pragma acc parallel loop copyout(A[0:size]) deviceptr(B)
    for (i=0; i < size; ++i) {
        A[i] = B[i] + (double) i;
    }
    printData(A, size);
    free(A);  acc_free(B);
}
```

The following example in Box 21 creates device only data using acc_malloc and then uses this data in a CUDA kernel.

Where the cudaSet routine calls a CUDA kernel that uses the device array (Box 22).

```
BOX 22  setVal CUDA KERNEL
#include <cuda.h>

__global__ void setVal(double * B, size_t size, double val)
{
    int tid = threadIdx.x + blockDim.x * blockIdx.x;
    int stride = blockDim.x * gridDim.x;
    for(; tid < size; tid += stride)
        B[tid] = val;
}

extern "C"
{
void cudaSet(double * B, size_t size, double val) {
    setVal<<<1,128>>>(B,size,val);
  }
}
```

MAPPING DEVICE DATA

In some cases, the amount of data used by the program is too large for the device's memory. To accommodate, the program would need to be blocked, i.e., rewritten so that smaller portions of the data are divided into blocks and then the blocks are computed on the device one after the other. Instead of creating and destroying the device data for each block, a pool of device data could be created once and then each host block is mapped and unmapped to this pool.

```
BOX 23  acc_map_data AND acc_unmap_data
C/C++ syntax:

void acc_map_data(void *host_ptr, void * device_ptr, size_t number_of_bytes);
void acc_unmap_data(void * host_ptr );
```

The `acc_map_data` method associates a host address to a device address for a certain number of bytes. The device address does not need to be the base address of the device memory as returned by `acc_malloc`. Rather it could be the base address plus an offset allowing for different host variables to map to different sections of the device data (Box 23).

Box 24 shows a simple blocking algorithm where the same device memory pool is reused for each block of host data.

BOX 24 REUSING DEVICE DATA WITH acc_map_data

```
int main() {

    double **A, *tmpA;
    char * devMem;
    int i, j, nbytes;
    nbytes = N*sizeof(double);

    A= (double**) malloc(BLOCKS*sizeof(double*));
    for (i=0; i < BLOCKS; ++i) {
       A[i] = (double*) malloc(nbytes);
    }
    /* Create the device memory */
    devMem= (char*) acc_malloc(nbytes);

    for (i=0; i < BLOCKS; ++i) {
        /* use a tmp pointer to get the block's starting address */
        tmpA = A[i];

        /* map the host block to the device memory */
        acc_map_data(tmpA,devMem,nbytes);
        #pragma acc parallel loop present(tmpA)
        for (j=0; j < N; ++j) {
            tmpA[j] = 2.5 + (double) ((j*N)+i);
        }
        /* Copy the data back to the block */
        #pragma acc update host(tmpA[0:N])

        /* unmap the block */
        acc_unmap_data(A[i]);
    }

    printData(A,BLOCKS,N);
    for (i=0; i < BLOCKS; ++i) {
        free(A[i]);
    }
    free(A);
    acc_free(devMem);
}
```

SHARING DEVICE MEMORY BETWEEN MPI PROCESSES

Using OpenACC's data mapping routines and CUDA Inter Process Communication (IPC), MPI programs can share device data. Sharing device memory can help performance by eliminating or minimizing the need to copy device data back to the host, perform an MPI_send and MPI_recv, and finally copy the data back the device.

However, sharing device data is currently limited to MPI processes using the same NVIDIA Graphics Processing Unit (GPU) device. For target devices other than NVIDIA, the IPC would need to be replaced with the equivalent for the target device.

BOX 25 EXAMPLE SHARING DEVICE MEMORY BETWEEN MPI PROCESSES

```
#include <openacc.h>
// CUDA runtime includes
#include <cuda_runtime_api.h>
...
    /* Declare or host and device shared memory arrays */
    double * devSharedMemory;
    double * sharedMemory;

    /* IPC Handle variable */
    cudaIpcMemHandle_t mem_handle;
...
    /* All Ranks create a local host array */
    sharedMemory = (double*) malloc(N*sizeof(double));
    devSharedMemory = NULL;
```

First the example in Box 25 includes the `cuda_runtime_api.h` header file for the CUDA IPC function prototypes and type definitions. Next, it declares a host and device pointer for the shared memory array as well as a CUDA IPC memory handle. The example has all MPI ranks creating their own host array which will be associated with the shared device memory. However, if the data is never used on the host, this may be unnecessary and the techniques shown earlier on using device only data can be applied (Box 26).

BOX 26 CREATING A CUDA IPC MEMORY HANDLE

```
if ( rank == 0 ) {
/* Rank 0 creates and gets an IPC handle to the device memory */
    #pragma acc enter data create(sharedMemory[0:N])
    cudaIpcGetMemHandle(&mem_handle,acc_deviceptr(sharedMemory));
}
```

Rank 0 first creates the device memory by either using an unstructured data region or a call to `acc_malloc` if using device only data. Then it will request a CUDA IPC memory handle for this device data (Box 27).

BOX 27 OPENING A CUDA IPC MEMORY HANDLE

```
if ( rank == 0 ) {
  /* Rank 0 sends the IPC Handle to the Rank 1 */
  MPI_Send(&mem_handle,CUDA_IPC_HANDLE_SIZE,MPI_BYTE,
            1,1,MPI_COMM_WORLD);
} else {
  /* Rank 1 gets the IPC Handle from the Rank 0 */
  MPI_Recv(&mem_handle,CUDA_IPC_HANDLE_SIZE,MPI_BYTE,
            0,1,MPI_COMM_WORLD,&status);

  /* Open the IPC Handle and associate the memory
     to a local device pointer */
  cudaIpcOpenMemHandle(&devSharedMemory, mem_handle,
                       cudaIpcMemLazyEnablePeerAccess);

  /* Map the Rank 1's shareMemory host array to the
     shared device memory. */
  acc_map_data(sharedMemory,devSharedMemory,N*sizeof(double));
}
```

Rank 0 then sends the CUDA IPC memory handle to Rank 1. Rank 1 opens the CUDA IPC memory handle associating it with its local device pointer to the shared memory. Note that cudaIpcMemLazyEnablePeerAccess automatically enables peer-to-peer access between the processes. Rank 1 then uses acc_map_data to associate the host shared memory array with the device array.

Now Rank 1 can write to the device array with Rank 0 reading the memory (Box 28).

BOX 28 USING CUDA IPC SHARED MEMORY

```
if ( rank == 1 ) {
  /* The Rank 1 sets the shared device memory values. */
  #pragma acc parallel loop present(sharedMemory)
  for (size_t i=0; i < N; ++i) {
     sharedMemory[i] = (double) i / (double) N;
  }
}
MPI_Barrier(MPI_COMM_WORLD);
if ( rank == 0 ) {
  /* The Rank 0 updates the host array and prints out the
     values set by the Rank 1. */
  #pragma acc update self(sharedMemory[0:N])
  for (size_t i=0; i < N; ++i) {
     printf("sharedMemory[%d] = %f \n",i,sharedMemory[i]);
  }
}
MPI_Barrier(MPI_COMM_WORLD);
```

Finally, Rank 0 deletes the device memory and rank 1 unmaps the data and closes the CUDA IPC handle (Box 29).

BOX 29 CLOSING A CUDA IPC MEMORY HANDLE

```
if ( rank == 0 ) {
   /* Rank 0 deletes the device array */
   #pragma acc exit data delete(sharedMemory)
} else {
   /* Rank 1 unmaps the data and closes the IPC Handle */
   acc_unmap_data(sharedMemory);
   cudaIpcCloseMemHandle(devSharedMemory);
}
```

CODE EXAMPLES

Below are the full example source code listings for the accList container class (Boxes 30–32), soaFloat3 struct (Boxes 33–35), and example of their use (Boxes 36 and 37).

BOX 30 SOURCE FOR accList CLASS (accList.h)

```
 1
 2 #ifndef ACC_LIST_H
 3 #define ACC_LIST_H
 4
 5 #include <cstdlib>
 6 #include <cassert>
 7 #ifdef _OPENACC
 8 #include <openacc.h>
 9 #endif
10
11 template<typename T>
12 class accList {
13  public:
14    explicit accList() {}
15    explicit accList(size_t size) {
16       #pragma acc enter data copyin(this)
17       allocate(size);
18    }
19
20    ~accList() {
21       release();
22       #pragma acc exit data delete(this)
23    }
24
25    #pragma acc routine seq
26    T& operator[](size_t idx) { return _A[idx]; }
27
```

BOX 31 SOURCE FOR accList CLASS (CONTINUED)

```
28    #pragma acc routine seq
29    const T& operator[](size_t idx) const { return _A[idx]; }
30
31    size_t size() const { return _size; }
32
33    accList& operator=(const accList& B) {
34      allocate(B.size());
35      for (size_t j = 0; j < _size; ++j) {
36        _A[j] = B[j];
37      }
38      accUpdateDevice();
39      return *this;
40    }
41
42    void insert(size_t idx, const T& val) { _A[idx] = val; }
43    void insert(size_t idx, const T* val) { _A[idx] = *val; }
44
45    void accUpdateSelf() { accUpdateSelfT(_A, 0); }
46    void accUpdateDevice() { accUpdateDeviceT(_A, 0); }
47
48  private:
49    void release() {
50      if (_size > 0) {
51        #pragma acc exit data delete(_A[0:_size])
52        delete[] _A;
53        _A = nullptr;
54        _size = 0;
55      }
56    }
57
58    void allocate(size_t size) {
59      if (_size != size) {
60        release();
61        _size = size;
62        #pragma acc update device(_size)
63        if (_size > 0) {
64          _A = new T[_size];
65  #ifdef _OPENACC
66          assert(!acc_is_present(&_A[0],sizeof(T)));
67  #endif
68          #pragma acc enter data create(_A[0:_size])
69        }
70      }
71    }
72
73    // These template functions use the SFINAE pattern so as to call
74    // the element type's accUpdateSelf/Device() member functions, if
75    // they exist, on all of the elements, or otherwise use the
76    // "acc update self/device" directive on the raw data.
77    // This works because the versions of the template functions below
78    // that call those member functions look more specialized so
79    // are favored by C++'s function overload resolution rules
80    // over the more general versions that apply the directives.
81
```

BOX 32 SOURCE FOR accList CLASS (CONCLUSION)

```
82   template<typename U>
83   void accUpdateSelfT(U *p, long) {
84     #pragma acc update self(p[0:_size])
85   }
86
87   template<typename U>
88   auto accUpdateSelfT(U *p, int) -> decltype(p->accUpdateSelf()) {
89     for (size_t j = 0; j < _size; ++j) {
90       p[j].accUpdateSelf();
91     }
92   }
```

BOX 33 soaFloat3 CLASS SOURCE (soaFloat3.h)

```
 1
 2  #ifndef FLOATS3_H
 3  #define FLOATS3_H
 4
 5  #include <cstring>
 6  #ifdef _OPENACC
 7  #include <openacc.h>
 8  #endif
 9
10  using namespace std;
11
12  struct soaFloat3 {
13
14    float *x{nullptr}, *y{nullptr}, *z{nullptr};
15
16    soaFloat3() {
17      // Don't "acc enter data copyin(this)" for the default
18      // constructor, so that an instantiation as part of
19      // an array, as in accList, retains address contiguity
20      // in both host and device address spaces.
21    }
22
23    explicit soaFloat3(size_t n) : _created{true} {
24      #pragma acc enter data copyin(this)
25      allocate(n);
26    }
27
28    ~soaFloat3() {
29      release();
30      if (_created) {
31        #pragma acc exit data delete(this)
32      }
33    }
```

BOX 34 soaFloat3 CLASS SOURCE (CONTINUED)

```
34
35    soaFloat3& operator=(const soaFloat3 &B) {
36      size_t Bsize{B.size()};
37      if (Bsize != _size)
38        allocate(Bsize);
39      size_t bytes = _size * sizeof *x;
40      memcpy(x, B.x, bytes);
41      memcpy(y, B.y, bytes);
42      memcpy(z, B.z, bytes);
43 #if defined(USE_ACC_MEMCPY) && defined(_OPENACC)
44      acc_memcpy_device(acc_deviceptr(x), acc_deviceptr(B.x), bytes);
45      acc_memcpy_device(acc_deviceptr(y), acc_deviceptr(B.y), bytes);
46      acc_memcpy_device(acc_deviceptr(z), acc_deviceptr(B.z), bytes);
47 #else
48      accUpdateDevice();
49 #endif
50      return *this;
51    }
52
53 #pragma acc routine vector
54    void add(const soaFloat3& B) {
55      #pragma acc loop vector
56      for (size_t j = 0; j < _size; ++j) {
57        x[j] += B.x[j];
58        y[j] += B.y[j];
59        z[j] += B.z[j];
60      }
61    }
62
63 #pragma acc routine seq
64    void setValue(float xval, float yval, float zval) {
65 #pragma acc loop seq
66      for (size_t j = 0; j < _size; ++j) {
67        x[j] = xval;
68        y[j] = yval;
69        z[j] = zval;
70      }
71    }
72
73    size_t size() const { return _size; }
74
75    void accUpdateSelf() {
76      #pragma acc update self(x[0:_size])
77      #pragma acc update self(y[0:_size])
78      #pragma acc update self(z[0:_size])
79    }
80
81    void accUpdateDevice() {
82      #pragma acc update device(x[0:_size])
83      #pragma acc update device(y[0:_size])
84      #pragma acc update device(z[0:_size])
85    }
86
```

BOX 35 soaFloat3 CLASS SOURCE (CONCLUSION)

```
87   private:
88     void release() {
89       if (_size > 0) {
90         #pragma acc exit data delete(x[0:_size])
91         #pragma acc exit data delete(y[0:_size])
92         #pragma acc exit data delete(z[0:_size])
93         delete[] x;
94         delete[] y;
95         delete[] z;
96         _size = 0;
97         x = y = z = nullptr;
98       }
99     }
100
101    void allocate(size_t n) {
102      if (_size != n) {
103        release();
104        _size = n;
105        #pragma acc update device(_size)
106        if (_size > 0) {
107          x = new float[_size];
108          y = new float[_size];
109          z = new float[_size];
110          #pragma acc enter data create(x[0:_size])
111          #pragma acc enter data create(y[0:_size])
112          #pragma acc enter data create(z[0:_size])
113        }
114      }
115    }
116
117    size_t _size{0};
118  // Whether to "acc exit data delete(this)" in d'tor
119    const bool _created{false};
120  };
121  #endif
```

BOX 36 accList.soaFloat3.cpp EXAMPLE

```
1
2 #include <iostream>
3 #include "soaFloat3.h"
4 #include "accList.h"
5 #ifndef N
6 #define N 6
7 #define M 1024
8 #endif
9
10 int main() {
11
12   accList<soaFloat3> C{N};
13   for (size_t j = 0; j < C.size(); ++j) {
14     soaFloat3 tmpC{M};
15     C.insert(j, tmpC);
16   }
17
18   accList<soaFloat3> A{N}, B{N};
19   for (size_t j = 0; j < A.size(); ++j) {
20     soaFloat3 tmpA{M};
21     soaFloat3 tmpB{M};
22     A.insert(j, tmpA);
23     B.insert(j, tmpB);
24     B[j].setValue(2.5, 3.5, 4.5);
25   }
26   A.accUpdateDevice();
27   B.accUpdateDevice();
28 #pragma acc parallel loop present(A,B)
29   for (size_t j = 0; j < N; ++j) {
30     A[j].setValue(2.5, 3.5, 4.5);
31     A[j].add(B[j]);
32   }
33   A.accUpdateSelf();
34   for (size_t j = 0; j < 5; ++j) {
35     cout << "A[" << j << "]: " << A[j].x[1] << ","
36          << A[j].y[1] << "," << A[j].z[1] << endl;
37   }
38   cout << "......" << endl;
39   for (size_t j = N-5; j < N; ++j) {
40     cout << "A[" << j << "]: " << A[j].x[1] << ","
41          << A[j].y[1] << "," << A[j].z[1] << endl;
42   }
43 }
```

BOX 37 USING accList WITH A FUNDAMENTAL TYPE

```
1
2  #include <iostream>
3  #include <cstdlib>
4  #include <cstdint>
5  #include "accList.h"
6  using namespace std;
7  #ifndef N
8  #define N 1024
9  #endif
10
11 int main() {
12
13     accList<double> A(N), B(N);
14     for (int i=0; i < B.size(); ++i) {
15         B[i]=2.5;
16     }
17     B.accUpdateDevice();
18     #pragma acc parallel loop gang vector present(A,B)
19     for (int i=0; i < A.size(); ++i) {
20             A[i]=B[i]+i;
21     }
22     A.accUpdateSelf();
23
24     for(int i=0; i<10; ++i) {
25         cout << "A[" << i << "]: " << A[i] << endl;
26     }
27     cout << "......" << endl;
28     for(int i=N-10; i<N; ++i) {
29         cout << "A[" << i << "]: " << A[i] << endl;
30     }
31 }
```

RUNTIME RESULTS

The following example in Box 38 shows how to build and run the example accList using a soaFloat3 data type (Box 39).

BOX 38 BUILDING AND RUNNING accList EXAMPLE CODE

```
% pgc++  --c++11 -w -I. -fast  -acc  -Minfo=accel -o accList.soaFloat3.out
accList.soaFloat3.cpp
main:
     31, Generating present(A,B)
     31, Accelerator kernel generated
         Generating Tesla code
         33, #pragma acc loop gang /* blockIdx.x */
soaFloat3::soaFloat3(unsigned long):
      7, include "soaFloat3.h"
         27, Generating enter data copyin(this[:1])
soaFloat3::~soaFloat3():
      7, include "soaFloat3.h"
         34, Generating exit data delete(this[:1])
soaFloat3::add(const soaFloat3&):
      7, include "soaFloat3.h"
         56, Generating Tesla code
             58, #pragma acc loop vector /* threadIdx.x */
         56, Generating acc routine vector
         58, Loop is parallelizable
soaFloat3::setValue(float, float, float):
      7, include "soaFloat3.h"
         66, Generating acc routine seq
             68, #pragma acc for seq
soaFloat3::accUpdateSelf():
      7, include "soaFloat3.h"
         81, Generating update self(x[:_size],y[:_size],z[:_size])
soaFloat3::accUpdateDevice():
      7, include "soaFloat3.h"
         87, Generating update device(x[:_size],y[:_size],z[:_size])
soaFloat3::release():
      7, include "soaFloat3.h"
         95, Generating exit data delete(x[:_size],y[:_size],z[:_size])
soaFloat3::allocate(unsigned long):
      7, include "soaFloat3.h"
         108, Generating update device(_size)
         115, Generating enter data create(x[:_size],y[:_size],z[:_size])
accList<soaFloat3>::accList(unsigned long):
      8, include "accList.h"
         20, Generating enter data copyin(this[:1])
accList<soaFloat3>::~accList():
      8, include "accList.h"
         26, Generating exit data delete(this[:1])
accList<soaFloat3>::operator [](unsigned long):
      8, include "accList.h"
         29, Generating acc routine seq
accList<soaFloat3>::release():
      8, include "accList.h"
         55, Generating exit data delete(_A[:_size])
```

```
BOX 39  BUILDING AND RUNNING accList EXAMPLE (CONTINUED)
accList<soaFloat3>::allocate(unsigned long):
     8, include "accList.h"
        66, Generating update device(_size)
        72, Generating enter data create(_A[:_size])
decltype(((param#1->accUpdateSelf)()))
accList<soaFloat3>::accUpdateSelfT<soaFloat3>(T1 *, int):
     8, include "accList.h"
decltype(((param#1->accUpdateDevice)()))
accList<soaFloat3>::accUpdateDeviceT<soaFloat3>(T1 *, int):
     8, include "accList.h"
std::basic_ostream<T1, T2> & std::endl<char,
std::char_traits<char>>(std::basic_ostream<T1, T2> &):
     8, include "accList.h"

% ./accList.soaFloat3.out
A[0]: 5,7,9
A[1]: 5,7,9
A[2]: 5,7,9
A[3]: 5,7,9
A[4]: 5,7,9
......
A[1]: 5,7,9
A[2]: 5,7,9
A[3]: 5,7,9
A[4]: 5,7,9
A[5]: 5,7,9
```

SUMMARY

Managing the creation and synchronization of data between the host and device can be a challenge when moving beyond simple programs to full applications. Users of OpenACC can simplify this challenge by taking a whole program, top-down approach to data management. Utilizing unstructured data regions to create device data at the same time as the host data is allocated allows for the lifetime of device data to match that of the host data. The program's computation can then be offloaded incrementally with synchronization between the host and device enabled by using OpenACC update directives.

Utilizing OpenACC enter and exit directives you can mirror host and device data structures, including aggregate data types with dynamic data, as well as how to encapsulate data management within C++ class structures. The declare directive allows you to use static global and Fortran module data in device callable routines. For cases where the host data is too large to be contained in device memory, you can create device memory pools using acc_malloc in which host data can be mapped using acc_map_data. Finally, you can use CUDA IPC memory with acc_map_data to share device data between multiple host MPI processes.

Tuning OpenACC loop execution

6

Saber Feki*, Malek Smaoui†

KAUST Supercomputing Laboratory, King Abdullah University of Science and Technology, Thuwal, Saudi Arabia* Computer, Electrical, Mathematical Sciences and Engineering Division, King Abdullah University of Science and Technology, Thuwal, Saudi Arabia†

The purpose of this chapter is to help OpenACC developer who is already familiar with the basic and essential directives to further improve his code performance by adding more descriptive clauses to OpenACC loop constructs.

At the end of this chapter the reader will:

- Have a better understanding of the purpose of the OpenACC loop construct and its associated clauses illustrated with use cases
- Use the acquired knowledge in practice to further improve the performance of OpenACC accelerated codes

Whether you strive for scientific discovery or for professional achievement or may be working towards a degree, you certainly want to make the most of your resources. For instance, as a code developer/writer/programmer, you want to get the best of the computation devices available to you, whether it is Central Processing Unit (CPU) or accelerator. However, it is also known that such objective requires investing time and effort, which themselves are valuable resources—in both learning and applying the necessary skills. OpenACC design is based on a compromise between productivity and performance. Being a directive based paradigm, it is easier to learn and use compared to other code acceleration paradigms like CUDA for instance. So, make your life easy: start with the highest-level Application Programming Interface (API) (like OpenACC), then, eventually, delve down into lower-level APIs to achieve higher performance or to use a specific functionality.

If you are reading this chapter, you should already know how to run compute-intensive/parallelizable portions of your code on an accelerator using OpenACC. In other words, you should be familiar with the OpenACC `kernels` and the OpenACC `parallel` constructs which allow you to define a parallel execution section. If done properly, i.e., you managed data movements wisely with the OpenACC data constructs, you should have already seen significant performance improvement over native CPU code. But, it also means that you are striving for even better performance. Fortunately, simple as it is, OpenACC allows you to further improve your code performance, in a short time, while still using a high-level API.

For that purpose, and as it is very likely that the code portions that will be running on the accelerator are loops, you can apply the OpenACC loop construct to the loop which immediately follows, in order to provide hints to the compiler with more details about the parallelization and distribution of iterations. This implies that the loop already has to be part of a code section that will be executing on the accelerator. However, although perfectly legitimate, a bare loop construct is probably not very much useful (even risky). It is only through the multitude of associated clauses that you get to describe what type of parallelism should be used for executing the loop, and define any necessary reduction operations.

THE LOOP CONSTRUCT

Referring to OpenACC standard version 2.5, the general syntax of the loop construct is (Figs. 1 and 2):

–   In C/C++

```
#pragma acc loop [clause-list]
for(...
```

FIG. 1

OpenACC loop directive syntax in C/C++.

–   In Fortran

```
!$acc loop [clause-list]
do ...
```

FIG. 2

OpenACC loop directive syntax in Fortran.

where [clause-list] is one or a combination of clauses and their arguments properly selected from the following list (Fig. 3).

Throughout the rest of this chapter, the significance of most of these clauses and corresponding arguments will be explained and their usage illustrated using both a simple code example.

```
collapse( n )

gang [( gang-arg-list )]

worker [( [num:]int-expr )]

vector [( [length:]int-expr )]

seq

auto

tile( size-expr-list )

device_type( device-type-list )

independent

private( var-list )

reduction( operator:var-list )
```

FIG. 3

List of clauses associated with OpenACC loop directive.

The first code is a naïve sequential implementation of the matrix-matrix multiplication operation, preceded by an initialization loop. You will find that, though pretty simple, it is a tangible example where the use of the loop construct is quite valuable (Fig. 4).

You may have noticed that the operands a and b are initialized with artificial values as this is just an illustrative example. In a more useful/purposeful code, these operands would be input to the program or would be result of previous calculations. It is why only the computation loops are considered for acceleration (and performance measurement).

Compiling this code using the Portland Group (PGI) compiler version 15.10 gives the following output while using the compiler flags "-acc -fast ta=nvidia -Minfo= accel":

A quick analysis of this output reveals that the compiler decided to parallelize the two outermost loops (counters i and j). It also detected a data-dependency carried by the innermost loop and decided to execute this loop sequentially (Fig. 5).

BASIC LOOP OPTIMIZATION CLAUSES
THE auto CLAUSE

With the auto clause, you can specify that the compiler is responsible for analyzing the loop and determining whether its iterations are data-independent and, consequently decide whether to apply parallelism to this loop or whether to run the loop sequentially. When the parent compute construct is a kernels construct, the compiler treats a loop construct with no independent or seq clause as if it has the auto clause.

```
1       #include <sys/time.h>
2       #include <stdio.h>
3
4       /* matrix-acc-base.c */
5       #define SIZE 4000
6
7       double a[SIZE][SIZE];
8       double b[SIZE][SIZE];
9       double c[SIZE][SIZE];
10      double d[SIZE][SIZE];
11
12      int main()
13      {
14        int i,j,k;
15        struct timeval tim;
16        double t1, t2;
17
18        // Initialize matrices.
19        for (i = 0; i < SIZE; ++i) {
20          for (j = 0; j < SIZE; ++j) {
21            a[i][j] = (double)(i + j);
22            b[i][j] = (double)(i - j);
23            c[i][j] = 0.0f;
24            d[i][j] = 0.0f;
25          }
26        }
27        gettimeofday(&tim, NULL);
28        t1=tim.tv_sec+(tim.tv_usec/1000000.0);
29
30        // Compute matrix multiplication.
31        #pragma acc data copyin(a,b) copy(c)
32        #pragma acc kernels
33        for (i = 0; i < SIZE; ++i) {
34          for (j = 0; j < SIZE; ++j) {
35            for (k = 0; k < SIZE; ++k) {
36              c[i][j] += a[i][k] * b[k][j];
37            }
38          }
39        }
40
41        gettimeofday(&tim, NULL);
42        t2=tim.tv_sec+(tim.tv_usec/1000000.0);
43        printf("%.6lf seconds with OpenACC \n", t2-t1);
44
45        // ****************
46        // double-check the OpenACC result
47        // ****************
48        // Perform the multiplication, OpenMP parallel
49        #pragma omp parallel for default(none) shared(a,b,d) private(i,j,k)
50        for (i = 0; i < SIZE; ++i)
51          for (j = 0; j < SIZE; ++j)
52            for (k = 0; k < SIZE; ++k)
53              d[i][j] += a[i][k] * b[k][j];
54
55        // check all the OpenACC matrices
56        for (i = 0; i < SIZE; ++i)
57          for (j = 0; j < SIZE; ++j)
58            if(c[i][j] != d[i][j]) {
59              printf("Error %d %d %f %f \n", i,j, c[i][j], d[i][j]);
60              exit(1);
61            }
62        printf("OpenACC matrix multiplication test was successful!\n");
63
64        return 0;
65      }
```

FIG. 4

A matrix-matrix multiplication OpenACC accelerated code example.

```
main:
    31, Generating copyin(a[:][:],b[:][:])
        Generating copy(c[:][:])
    33, Loop is parallelizable
    34, Loop is parallelizable
    35, Complex loop carried dependence of c prevents parallelization
        Loop carried dependence of c prevents parallelization
        Loop carried backward dependence of c prevents vectorization
        Inner sequential loop scheduled on accelerator
        Accelerator kernel generated
        Generating Tesla code
        33, #pragma acc loop gang /* blockIdx.y */
        34, #pragma acc loop gang, vector(128) /* blockIdx.x
threadIdx.x */
```

FIG. 5

Compilation report of the matrix-matrix multiplication code example.

```
31      #pragma acc data copyin(a,b) copy(c)
32      #pragma acc kernels
33      #pragma acc loop auto
34        for (i = 0; i < SIZE; ++i) {
35      #pragma acc loop auto
36          for (j = 0; j < SIZE; ++j) {
37      #pragma acc loop auto
38            for (k = 0; k < SIZE; ++k) {
39                  c[i][j] += a[i][k] * b[k][j];
40            }
41          }
42        }
```

FIG. 6

Example of use of the auto clause.

The above example could be simply annotated with a loop construct either bare or with the auto clause before each of the nested loops, as follows (Fig. 6):

Since the compiler is still sole decider of the parallelization strategy, the compilation output does not change from previously and evidently neither does the code performance.

The above description of the auto clause, along with the example, might lead you to think that this clause is useless. Well, this clause is probably more useful when the parent compute clause is parallel and the explanation can be found right in the next section as it requires understanding of the more influential clause: independent.

THE independent CLAUSE

The independent clause allows you to indicate that the iterations of the loop are data-independent with respect to each other. As a result, the compiler will generate code that computes these iterations using independent asynchronous threads.

If you examine the loops in our previous example code, you will see that the computation of a single element of the product matrix does not depend on values of other elements of the same matrix. So, the two outermost computation loops are independent, which confirms the compiler's previous analysis. However, for the innermost loop, each iteration requires the value of c[i][j] from the previous one: that is a data-dependency that excludes the use of the independent clause.

Note that you must exercise caution when considering this clause. First, if you happen to miss a data-dependency in a specific loop and annotate it with the independent clause, your program will most probably give you incorrect and inconsistent results. Then, there is also the case where the independent clause is implied on all loop constructs, unless explicitly overridden using the auto or the seq clauses, and that is when the parent compute construct is a parallel construct. And here rises the importance of the auto clause: using the loop construct with the auto clause is always safer than keeping it bare.

THE seq CLAUSE

If for some reason (most often a data-dependency), a loop has to execute sequentially, you need only annotate it with the loop construct along with the seq clause. This clause will override any automatic parallelization or vectorization that might be attempted by the compiler. Let's note that compilers tend to operate on the safe side when it comes to data-dependency detection: false-positives are much more frequent than false-negatives. In other words, the seq clause is absolutely needed in the very rare cases where the compiler parallelizes a loop containing a data dependency, which would produce erroneous numerical results.

For it is quite straight forward, the compiler has already found out which loops were independent and which required sequential execution in our matrix-matrix multiplication example. So, the following annotation is only for the sake of illustrating the use of the independent and seq clauses but does not have any further influence on the extent of parallelization (Fig. 7).

```
31      #pragma acc data copyin(a,b) copy(c)
32      #pragma acc kernels
33      #pragma acc loop independent
34        for (i = 0; i < SIZE; ++i) {
35      #pragma acc loop independent
36          for (j = 0; j < SIZE; ++j) {
37      #pragma acc loop seq
38            for (k = 0; k < SIZE; ++k) {
39                    c[i][j] += a[i][k] * b[k][j];
40            }
41          }
42        }
```

FIG. 7

Example of use of the independent and seq clauses.

THE reduction CLAUSE

Some data-dependencies can be overcome with reductions. If you are not already familiar with reductions, then the best way to proceed is via example and it happens that our matrix-matrix multiplication example is perfect for that purpose. The innermost computation loop consists in gradually accumulating the sum of the a[i] [k] times b[k][j] multiplications performed at each iteration. The multiplication operations are independent through the iterations and thus could be performed in parallel, whereas the sum operations are what prevents parallelization of the whole loop. So, if the result of the multiplications could be individually saved to temporary variables, then it becomes possible to parallelize them. The sums are then performed with those temporary variables as operands after their values become available. This sounds like quite a bit of code modification and also extra storage that needs to be allocated. Fortunately, the compiler can do that automatically when hinted about this reduction operation via the reduction clause.

More generally, the reduction clause requires specifying arguments: a reduction operator and one or more scalar variables. For each reduction variable, a private copy is created and initialized for that operator according to the table in Fig. 8. While executing, threads will store partial results in their corresponding private copies of the variable. When all the threads finish the loop execution, the partial results are combined using the specified reduction operator along with the original value of the variable. The global result becomes available at the end of the parallel or kernels region if the loop has gang parallelism, and at the end of the loop otherwise.

In our example, the reduction result supposedly should go in c[i][j]. However, the variable argument to the reduction clause is required to be scalar. Thus, a slight

C and C++		Fortran	
Operator	Initialization value	Operator	Initialization value
+	0	+	0
*	1	*	1
max	least	**max**	Least
min	largest	**min**	Largest
&	~0	**iand**	All bits on
		0	**ior**	0
%	0	**ieor**	0
&&	1	.and.	.true.
||	0	.or.	.false.
			.eqv.	.true.
			.neqv.	.false.

FIG. 8

Reduction operators.

code modification is entailed, where a temporary scalar variable tmp replaces c[i] [j] within the loop annotated with the reduction clause. Then, a simple assignment outside the loop stores the computation result in its final destination (Fig. 9).

```
31      #pragma acc data copyin(a,b) copy(c)
32      #pragma acc kernels
33      #pragma acc loop independent
34        for (i = 0; i < SIZE; ++i) {
35      #pragma acc loop independent
36          for (j = 0; j < SIZE; ++j) {
37            tmp=0.0f;
38      #pragma acc loop reduction(+:tmp)
39            for (k = 0; k < SIZE; ++k) {
40              tmp += a[i][k] * b[k][j];
41            }
42            c[i][j] = tmp;
43          }
44        }
```

FIG. 9

Example of use of the reduction clause.

The compilation output after the reduction is as follows (Fig. 10):

```
    31, Generating copyin(a[:][:],b[:][:])
        Generating copy(c[:][:])
    34, Loop is parallelizable
    36, Loop is parallelizable
        Accelerator kernel generated
        Generating Tesla code
        34, #pragma acc loop gang /* blockIdx.y */
        36, #pragma acc loop gang, vector(128) /* blockIdx.x
threadIdx.x */
        39, Loop is parallelizable
```

FIG. 10

Compilation report of the code example with the reduction clause: note the difference in the innermost loop parallelization.

You can note the difference with the previous compilation output regarding the innermost loop parallelization.

On a side note, the PGI compiler is capable of detecting the reduction without even referring to a loop directive with a reduction clause, as long as a scalar variable is used instead of the matrix element c[i][j].

THE collapse CLAUSE

So far, you've seen that the OpenACC loop construct is associated with the immediately following loop. One directive is required for each nested loop. This tends to be cumbersome especially if multiple nested loops are to be treated in the same way. The collapse clause comes in handy in such a case. The argument to the collapse clause is a constant positive integer, which specifies how many tightly nested loops are associated with the loop construct. Consequently, you can describe the scheduling of the iterations of these loops using a single loop construct according to the rest of its clauses (other than the collapse).

In our example, we replace the two first loop directives with a single one that comes with a collapse(2) clause (Fig. 11).

```
31      #pragma acc data copyin(a,b) copy(c)
32      #pragma acc kernels
33      #pragma acc loop collapse(2) independent
34        for (i = 0; i < SIZE; ++i) {
35          for (j = 0; j < SIZE; ++j) {
36            tmp=0.0f;
37      #pragma acc loop reduction(+:tmp)
38            for (k = 0; k < SIZE; ++k) {
39            tmp += a[i][k] * b[k][j];
40            }
41            c[i][j] = tmp;
42          }
43        }
```

FIG. 11

Example of use of the collapse clause.

The corresponding compilation output is as follows (Fig. 12):

```
31, Generating copyin(a[:][:],b[:][:])
        Generating copy(c[:][:])
    34, Loop is parallelizable
    35, Loop is parallelizable
        Accelerator kernel generated
        Generating Tesla code
        34, #pragma acc loop gang, vector(128) collapse(2) /*
blockIdx.x threadIdx.x */
        35,    /* blockIdx.x threadIdx.x collapsed */
    38, Loop is parallelizable
```

FIG. 12

Compiler report when using the collapse clause.

Another case where the collapse clause is of great benefit is when the loop count in any of some tightly nested loops is relatively small compared to the available number of threads in the device. By creating a single iteration space across all the nested loops, the iteration count tends to increase thus allowing the compiler to extract more parallelism. Our example, however, is not a good illustration of this case.

ADVANCED LOOP OPTIMIZATION CLAUSES
THE `gang`, `worker`, AND `vector` CLAUSES

A typical accelerator architecture exhibits multiple levels of parallelism. For example, NVIDIA GPUs consists of multiple streaming multiprocessors, each of which can schedule multiple blocks of warps, which are 32-wide Single Instruction Multiple Data (SIMD) threads. On the other hand, Intel Xeon Phi, has a large number of x86_64 cores, each of which can execute up to four threads of 512-bits-wide SIMD instructions.

In line with these common architectural considerations, OpenACC has been equipped with the `gang`, `worker`, and `vector` clauses to allow you to map the loop iterations to the target device using up to three levels of parallelism. Please note that these clauses can also be associated with the `parallel` or `kernels` constructs parent to a loop construct. This chapter does not discuss this specific case and rather focuses on their usage while accompanying a loop construct.

The first level of parallelism can be specified using the `gang` clause, which suggests that the iterations of the associated loop or loops are to be executed in parallel across multiple gangs. Furthermore, you can add an integer argument to state the number of gangs to be scheduled on the device.

The second level of parallelism can be described using a `worker` clause to indicate that the iterations of the associated loops are to be executed in parallel across the workers within a gang. You can optionally add an integer argument to specify how many workers per gang to use to execute the iterations of this loop.

The third level of parallelism can be expressed using the `vector` clause, which specifies that the iterations of the associated loop or loops are to be executed with vector or SIMD processing. Similarly, you can an optional integer argument to determine the vector length. Typical vector lengths for Graphic Processing Unit (GPU) targets are multiple of the warp size, i.e., 32 in the latest generations.

If you do not specify these clauses and/or their arguments, the compiler will use its heuristics to make the best mappings.

On NVIDIA GPUs, a possible mapping could be `gang` to thread blocks, `worker` to warps, and `vector` to threads. Alternatively, you can omit the `worker` clause and map `gang` to thread blocks and `vector` to threads within a block.

In our example, we further annotate the outer loop construct with the `gang` clause and the subsequent nested loop with the `vector` clause. Then, the optional integer argument for both clauses is tuned to achieve better performance with the best combination of number of thread blocks and number of threads per block. While our example is tuned manually, it is possible to obtain the best values using some available auto-tuning tools (Fig. 13).

```
31      #pragma acc data copyin(a,b) copy(c)
32      #pragma acc kernels
33      #pragma acc loop gang(32)
34        for (i = 0; i < SIZE; ++i) {
35      #pragma acc loop vector(16)
36          for (j = 0; j < SIZE; ++j) {
37            tmp=0.0f;
38      #pragma acc loop reduction(+:tmp)
39            for (k = 0; k < SIZE; ++k) {
40              tmp += a[i][k] * b[k][j];
41            }
42            c[i][j] = tmp;
43          }
44        }
```

FIG. 13

Example using gang and vector clauses.

The corresponding compilation output is as follows (Fig. 14):

```
31, Generating copyin(a[:][:],b[:][:])
        Generating copy(c[:][:])
    34, Loop is parallelizable
    36, Loop is parallelizable
        Accelerator kernel generated
        Generating Tesla code
        34, #pragma acc loop gang(32), vector(8) /* blockIdx.y
threadIdx.y */
        36, #pragma acc loop gang, vector(16) /* blockIdx.x
threadIdx.x */
    39, Loop is parallelizable
```

FIG. 14

Compiler report when using the gang and vector clauses.

You can clearly see that the compiler took into consideration the hint provided with the additional clauses and their corresponding arguments.

THE tile CLAUSE

The tile clause causes each loop in the loop nest to be split into two loops: an outer tile loop and an inner element loop. Then, the tile loops will be reordered to be outside all the element loops, and the element loops will all be inside the tile loops. For instance, if you have two nested loops as follows (Fig. 15):

```
for (int i = 0; i < sizeX; i++)
    for (int j = 0; j < sizeY; j++)
        // loop body
```

FIG. 15

Example loops for tiling.

Splitting these loops into tiles of size tileX by tileY results in the following code (for simplicity, we shall assume that sizeX and sizeY are respectively multiples of tileX and sizeY but even if it is not the case, tiling is still possible with few tiles not reaching tileX by tileY size) (Fig. 16):

```
for (int k = 0; k < sizeX/tileX; k++)
    for (int m = 0; m < sizeY/tileY; m++)
        for(int i = 0; i < tileX; i++)
            for(int j = 0; j < tileY; j++)
                // loop body with adjusted indexes
```

FIG. 16

Splitting the loops into tiles.

Generally, you would use the tile clause to take advantage of data locality which in many cases is an important factor contributing in the improvement of the code performance. Tiling is an operation that can be parameterized where the parameters are obviously the tile sizes. Consequently, the tile clause takes as argument a list of one or more constant positive integer tile sizes. If there are *n* tile sizes in the list, the loop construct must be immediately followed by *n* tightly nested loops. Alternatively, you can use an asterisk instead to let the compiler select an appropriate value.

The first two nested loops in our example are tiled using the tile clause with two integer arguments that have been tuned for better performance of the kernel. The third nested loop could not be tiled, as it is not tightly nested with the two other loops (Fig. 17).

```
31      #pragma acc data copyin(a,b) copy(c)
32      #pragma acc kernels
33      #pragma acc loop tile(32,32)
34          for (i = 0; i < SIZE; ++i) {
35              for (j = 0; j < SIZE; ++j) {
36                  tmp=0.0f;
37      #pragma acc loop reduction(+:tmp)
38                  for (k = 0; k < SIZE; ++k) {
39                  tmp += a[i][k] * b[k][j];
40                  }
41                  c[i][j] = tmp;
42              }
43          }
```

FIG. 17

Example using the tile clause.

The corresponding compilation output is as follows (Fig. 18):

```
31, Generating copyin(a[:][:],b[:][:])
      Generating copy(c[:][:])
 34, Loop is parallelizable
 35, Loop is parallelizable
     Accelerator kernel generated
     Generating Tesla code
      34, #pragma acc loop gang, vector tile(32,32) /* blockIdx.x
threadIdx.x */
       35,   /* blockIdx.x threadIdx.x tiled */
 38, Loop is parallelizable
```

FIG. 18

Compiler report when using the tile clause.

The compiler output clearly reflects the effect of the tile clause and its corresponding argument. When using two asterisks (*,*) instead of (32,32) arguments, the compiler chose tile arguments (32,4) instead and resulted in a longer execution time.

PERFORMANCE RESULTS

In Fig. 19, you will find the performance results obtained using OpenMP and OpenACC with the different loop clauses described in this chapter. Please note that some time and effort were invested to fine-tune the argument values where it applied. These results are provided to illustrate the performance benefit that you could get from tuning your code but may not be the best ever possible.

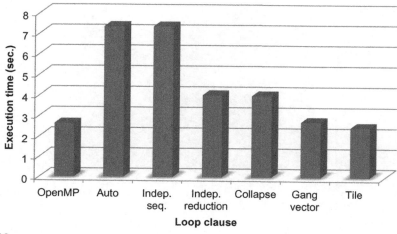

FIG. 19

Execution time (lower is better) of the matrix-matrix multiplication kernel using OpenMP on multicore and OpenACC with different loop clauses on GPU accelerator.

The test bed used for performance evaluation consists of a dual socket system hosting NVIDIA Kepler K20c GPU card. Each CPU socket contains an eight-core Sandy Bridge Intel(R) Xeon(R) CPU E5-2650, running at a clock speed of 2.00 GHz.

You can perceive a first good performance advantage when the third nested loop is parallelized using the `reduction` clause with the necessary code modification. A second significant performance gain is obtained by fine-tuning the execution of the loops using either the `gang` and `vector` clauses or the `tile` clause with careful choice of their corresponding optional parameters. The tuned OpenACC accelerated code running on the GPU was almost twice as fast as its OpenMP counterpart running on the multicore CPU.

CONCLUSION

The OpenACC standard allow for a multitude of options to annotate the `loop` construct in order to provide hints to the compiler about the type of parallelism that should be used for executing the loop and define any necessary reduction operations. Some of the clauses described in this chapter have special use cases; others are more common and applicable to the majority of codes. Further tuning of some integer arguments in some of the clauses is typically good to get better performance of the accelerated kernel on the target hardware. You can refer to some research work that has been conducted for auto-tuning these parameters. Even though this chapter focuses on explaining the different clauses that can be used with the `loop` construct, developer may use a combination of many of these in their kernels. Fig. 17 illustrates this aspect by using both `tile` and `reduction` clauses for example.

Multidevice programming with OpenACC

7

Jiri Kraus

NVIDIA GmbH, Würselen, DEU, Germany

The purpose of this chapter is to explain how to program multiple OpenACC devices to work cooperatively on a single problem.

At the end of this chapter the reader will have a basic understanding of:

- How to program multidevice systems or accelerated clusters with OpenACC using a single host thread, OpenMP, or MPI
- Coordinate the work of multiple devices using a domain decomposition strategy
- How to use the async clause to overlap computation and MPI communication
- How to use the NVIDIA® tools for MPI+OpenACC applications

INTRODUCTION

After accelerating your application using a single device, it is natural to consider extending your application to take advantage of multiple devices in a single node or in multiple nodes of an accelerated cluster. The two major reasons to use multiple devices are

- Compute faster—more devices equals faster time to solution
- Compute larger—more devices equals more memory for larger problems

Application acceleration often requires the use of multiple devices, because the problem does not fit into the memory of a single device or needs to be computed in a certain amount of time (e.g., numerical weather prediction).

In this chapter, you will learn how to program multidevice systems in accelerated clusters with OpenACC by example. To coordinate the work of multiple devices, domain decomposition is applied to a Jacobi solver for the 2D Poisson equation. The chapter covers OpenMP, Message Passing Interface (MPI), and single-threaded as different alternatives to program multiple devices with OpenACC. It focuses on accelerators with memory that is physically separate from host memory, for example, Graphics Processing Units (GPUs). For OpenACC targets where the memory of the host processors and the accelerator is the same, for example, the Portland Groups (PGI's) multicore target, doing a domain decomposition to utilize all processor cores within a shared memory node is not necessary. However, using MPI for multidevice programming with OpenACC applies for these targets and enables scaling across a cluster.

To simplify the understanding and focus on the aspects relevant for multidevice programming with OpenACC, the source code and code snippets accompanying this chapter make these simplifications:

- To simplify index arithmetic, the data arrays are defined as 2-dimensional global arrays.
- To simplify the logic necessary for the domain decomposition, the MPI version replicates the problem in each MPI rank.

It is not recommended to use these simplifications in production applications, as they are used solely for didactical reasons.

SCALABILITY METRICS FOR SUCCESS

Before we start, let us define some scalability metrics for success that we shall use throughout this chapter. The basic idea of these metrics is that if we double the number of resources to solve a given problem we expect to get a solution twice as fast. Therefore, we define the following (Hager & Wellein, 2010, pp. 122–123):

1. Serial time: T_s—how long it takes to run the problem with a single processor, for example, a GPU.
2. Parallel time: T_p—how long it takes to run the problem in parallel on multiple processors.
3. Number of processors: P—the number of processors operating in parallel.

With these we can define the following metrics to measure the success of our multidevice parallelization:

4. Speedup: $\dfrac{T_s}{T_p}$ —how much faster the parallel version is versus the serial version. The ideal speedup is P.
5. Parallel efficiency: $E = \dfrac{S}{P}$ —how efficiently the processors are being used. The ideal parallel efficiency is 1.

The source code provided for this chapter computes the same problem twice: once with a single devices and once with multiple devices. The runtimes of both executions are timed with host timers to compute the above metrics, and assess the implementation performance for multiple devices.

THREE WAYS TO PROGRAM MULTIPLE DEVICES WITH OpenACC

The three most common ways to program multiple devices with OpenACC are:

1. Controlling multiple devices from a single host thread
2. Controlling each device from its own dedicated host thread, for example, using OpenMP
3. Controlling each device from its own dedicated process, for example, using MPI

HANDLING DEVICE AFFINITY OR SELECTING A DEVICE

To program multiple devices, all alternatives need to express the device to target with a series of commands. In the case of a dedicated host thread or process controlling a single device, the assignment is often referred to as device affinity. In OpenACC selecting a device is done with the set directive and the device_num clause. An example of selecting the NVIDIA® GPU with the device ordinal 2 (assuming there are at least three NVIDIA® devices available) in a multiGPU system is shown in Fig. 1.

```
#pragma acc set device_num(2)
```

FIG. 1

How to change the OpenACC device to use.

After a set device_num, all subsequent OpenACC directives or Application Programming Interface (API) calls target the device selected with set device_num. The currently active device can be changed at any point in the program, even if an asynchronous operation is executing on a different device.

SINGLE-THREADED MULTIDEVICE PROGRAMMING

When controlling multiple devices from a single host thread, the basic idea is to launch operations asynchronously on one device and immediately switch to the next device to launch operations asynchronously. To perform asynchronous operations, we use the *async* clause. In this way, multiple devices can be utilized as shown in Fig. 2.

```
for ( int dn = 0; dn < num_devices; dn++ )
{
    #pragma acc set device_num(dn)
    #pragma acc kernels async
    for (int iy = iy_start[dn]; iy < iy_end[dn]; iy++)
    {
        ...
```

FIG. 2

How to launch work on multiple devices asynchronously.

As described below, the subfolder Jacobi_multi_device contains an example for this alternative to program multiple devices with OpenACC.

MULTITHREADED MULTIDEVICE PROGRAMMING

The basic idea when one host thread is dedicated to control each accelerator is to tie the OpenACC device number to the thread ID. An example of how to use OpenMP to create host threads to control multiple OpenACC devices is shown in Fig. 3.

The above snippet protects the calls to the OpenACC runtime API routines with preprocessor directives. The preprocessor symbol _OPENACC is defined to *yyyymm* by an OpenACC compiler when OpenACC is enabled, were *yyyy* is the year and *mm* is the month when the implemented OpenACC standard was released

```
int thread_num = 0;
int num_threads = 1;
#pragma omp parallel firstprivate(thread_num,num_threads)
{
#ifdef _OPENMP
    thread_num = omp_get_thread_num();
    num_threads = omp_get_num_threads();
#endif /*_OPENMP*/

#ifdef _OPENACC
    int num_devices=acc_get_num_devices(acc_device_nvidia);
    int device_num=thread_num%num_devices;
    acc_set_device_num(device_num,acc_device_nvidia);
    acc_init(acc_device_nvidia);
#endif /*_OPENACC*/
```

FIG. 3

Tie the ACC device number to an OpenMP host thread.

(OpenACC-Standard.org, 2016, p. 18). The same is done for the OpenMP API calls to keep the code working with non OpenMP or OpenACC compilers.

Multiple host threads can also be used to share a single device as device_num can be calculated from thread_num with a modulo operation using the number of available devices. The subfolder Jacobi_OpenMP_multi_device contains an example for this alternative to program multiple devices with OpenACC.

MULTIPROCESS MULTIDEVICE PROGRAMMING

Similar to multithreaded programming, the basic idea of multidevice programming is to setup the device once when the creating the process. After initialization, you can use the device throughout the program. An example of using MPI to create the host processes is shown in Fig. 4.

```
int rank = 0;
int size = 1;
MPI_Init(&argc, &argv);
MPI_Comm_rank(MPI_COMM_WORLD, &rank);
MPI_Comm_size(MPI_COMM_WORLD, &size);

#if _OPENACC
acc_device_t device_type = acc_get_device_type();
if ( acc_device_nvidia == device_type ) {
    int num_devices=acc_get_num_devices(acc_device_nvidia);
    int device_num=rank%num_devices;
    acc_set_device_num(device_num,acc_device_nvidia);
}
acc_init(device_type);
#endif /*_OPENACC*/
```

FIG. 4

Tie the ACC device number to a MPI host process.

The calls of the OpenACC API routines are protected by the preprocessor conditionals to maintain compatibility with nonOpenACC compilers. The query of the device type is added to skip the device selection for targets that do not require or support the selection of a device, for example, the multicore target of the PGI compiler. This allows the use MPI for internode communication, and OpenACC parallelization within a node on Central Processing Unit (CPU) clusters.

As described below, the subfolder `Jacobi_MPI_multi_device` contains an example for this alternative to program a multidevice with OpenACC.

EXAMPLE: JACOBI SOLVER FOR THE 2D POISSON EQUATION

The source code accompanying this chapter uses a Jacobi solver for the 2D Poisson equation

$$\Delta A(y,x) = e^{-10*(x^2+y^2)}$$

with periodic boundary conditions on the top/bottom and left/right boundaries (Jacobi Method, 2016; Poisson Equation, 2016). The solver essentially executes the following steps in a loop checking for convergence:

1. Execute a Jacobi step on all inner points of the domain by computing (Fig. 5).

$$A_{k+1}(iy,ix) = \frac{rhs(iy,ix) - \left(A_k(iy,ix-1) + A_k(iy,ix+1) + A_k(iy-1,ix) + A_k(iy+1,ix)\right)}{4}$$

```
error = 0.0;
#pragma acc kernels
for (int iy = 1; iy < NY-1; iy++) {
  for( int ix = 1; ix < NX-1; ix++ ) {
    Anew[iy][ix]=-0.25*(rhs[iy][ix]-(A[iy][ix+1]+A[iy][ix-1]
                                     +A[iy-1][ix]+A[iy+1][ix]));
    error = fmax( error, fabs(Anew[iy][ix]-A[iy][ix]));
  }
}
```

FIG. 5

Jacobi step on single OpenACC device.

2. Copy computed values from Anew to A to reuse A and Anew in the next iteration (Fig. 6).

```
#pragma acc kernels
for (int iy = 1; iy < NY-1; iy++) {
  for( int ix = 1; ix < NX-1; ix++ ) {
    A[iy][ix] = Anew[iy][ix];
  }
}
```

FIG. 6

Copy computed values from Anew to A.

3. Apply periodic boundary conditions. This is done by copying the first modified inner row to the bottom boundary, the last modified inner row to the top boundary, the first modified inner column to the right boundary and the last modified inner column to the left boundary (Figs. 7 and 8).

```
#pragma acc kernels
for( int ix = 1; ix < NX-1; ix++ ) {
  A[0][ix]     = A[(NY-2)][ix];
  A[(NY-1)][ix] = A[1][ix];
}

#pragma acc kernels
for (int iy = 1; iy < NY-1; iy++) {
  A[iy][0]     = A[iy][(NX-2)];
  A[iy][(NX-1)] = A[iy][1];
}
```

FIG. 7

Apply periodic boundary conditions.

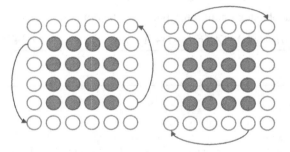

FIG. 8

Apply periodic boundary conditions.

See Jacobi_single_device for the complete source code.

DOMAIN DECOMPOSITION

To solve the 2D Poisson equation with the Jacobi method on multiple devices, it is necessary to distribute the work across all participating devices. To accomplish that domain decomposition is a common strategy (Hager & Wellein, 2010, pp. 117–119). The idea of domain decomposition is to divide the domain into a number of subdomains equal to the number of devices. These domains overlap with so called halo regions (highlighted in the lighter color in Fig. 9). The halo regions are the boundaries of each subdomain, and the boundary of one subdomain corresponds to an inner row or column of another subdomains. So in each iteration of the Jacobi solver, it is necessary to update the halo regions with new values computed in neighbor domains. To do one step of the Jacobi solver for each inner point of the domain we need the four nearest neighbors and a halo of 1. For a 2D problem like the given Jacobi solver, there are basically three options to do a domain decomposition summarized in Fig. 9.

Horizontal stripes	Vertical stripes	Tiles
• Minimizes number of neighbors • Optimal for latency bound communication • Contiguous halo exchanges when data layout is row major order (C)	• Minimizes number of neighbors • Optimal for latency bound communication • Contiguous halo exchange when data layout is column major order (Fortran)	• Minimizes surface area/volume ratio • Optimal for bandwidth bound communication • Requires non contiguous halo exchange

FIG. 9

Domain decomposition strategies.

Whether the domain decomposition strategy is the best depends on many factors such as the applied algorithm, the problem size, the number of devices used, and the available interdevice bandwidth. To avoid the complexities of noncontiguous halo exchange we apply a domain decomposition with horizontal stripes. For the Jacobi solver the following points need to be addressed for a multidevice parallelization:

1. Handle GPU affinity (see preceding text).
2. Apply the domain decomposition and compute which device should handle which subset of contiguous rows.
3. Compute the global error after applying the Jacobi step.
4. Halo exchange.

SINGLE-THREADED MULTIDEVICE PROGRAMMING

The start (iy_start) and end (iy_end) index for the loops running over the rows of the domain is computed for each device to apply the domain decomposition. For these two arrays (iy_start and iy_end) are created with one entry per device as shown in Fig. 10.

```
int chunk_size = ceil( (1.0*NY)/num_devices );
int iy_start[MAX_NUM_DEVICES];
int iy_end[MAX_NUM_DEVICES];
iy_start[0] = 1;
for ( int dn = 1; dn < num_devices; dn++ ) {
    iy_start[dn] = iy_start[(dn-1)] + chunk_size;
    iy_end[dn-1] = iy_start[dn];
}
iy_end[(num_devices-1)] = NY-1;
```

FIG. 10

Computing domain boundaries.

Knowing the subset of rows, the data region is created for each device as shown in Fig. 11.

```
for ( int dn = 0; dn < num_devices; dn++ ) {
#pragma acc set device_num(dn)
#pragma acc enter data
  copyin(A[(iy_start[dn]-1):(iy_end[dn]-iy_start[dn])+2][0:NX],
         rhs[iy_start[dn]:(iy_end[dn]-iy_start[dn])][0:NX])
  create(Anew[iy_start[dn]:(iy_end[dn]-iy_start[dn])][0:NX])
}
```

FIG. 11

Creating a data region for each domain.

The kernels in the main loop are dispatched asynchronously to the different devices on the computed subsets of rows. For example, applying the Jacobi step on the rows associated to each device is done with the code snippet shown in Fig. 12.

```
for ( int dn = 0; dn < num_devices; dn++ ) {
  #pragma acc set device_num(dn)
  #pragma acc kernels async
  for (int iy = iy_start[dn]; iy < iy_end[dn]; iy++) {
    for( int ix = ix_start; ix < ix_end; ix++ ) {
      Anew[iy][ix]=-0.25*(rhs[iy][ix]-(A[iy][ix+1]
                                      +A[iy][ix-1]
                                      +A[iy-1][ix]
                                      +A[iy+1][ix]));

    }
  }
}
```

FIG. 12

Executing Jacobi step for each domain on the assigned device.

The error is not computed for the single-threaded multidevice version. Computing the error would inhibit concurrent execution of the Jacobi step, because the OpenACC compiler needs to make sure that the result of the necessary reduction on the error variable is available after the kernels region (OpenACC-Standard.org, 2016, p. 24). If we did compute the error, we would wait for the current device to finish and error value to become available before work would be dispatched to the next device which essentially serializes the computation.

Since we are not computing the error in the single-threaded multidevice version, the step to compute the global error can be also omitted.

The halo exchange is done via the host copy of A by

1. Updating the host copy of the first (iy_start[dn]) and last processed row (iy_end[dn]-1) from each device (Fig. 13).

```
for ( int dn = 0; dn < num_devices; dn++ ) {
  #pragma acc set device_num(dn)
  #pragma acc update
  self(A[iy_start[dn]:1][0:NX],A[(iy_end[dn]-1):1][0:NX]) async
}
```

FIG. 13

Update halos on host.

2. Wait for all updates to complete (Fig. 14).

```
for ( int dn = 0; dn < num_devices; dn++ ) {
  #pragma acc set device_num(dn)
  #pragma acc wait
}
```

FIG. 14

Wait for host halo updates to complete.

3. Apply the top/bottom periodic boundary conditions to the host copy (Fig. 15).

```
for( int ix = 1; ix < NX-1; ix++ )
{
    A[0][ix]      = A[(NY-2)][ix];
    A[(NY-1)][ix] = A[1][ix];
}
```

FIG. 15

Apply periodic boundary conditions on the host.

4. Update the top boundary (iy_start[dn]-1) and the bottom boundary (iy_end[dn]) on each device from the just updated host copy (Fig. 16).

```
for ( int dn = 0; dn < num_devices; dn++ ) {
  #pragma acc set device_num(dn)
  #pragma acc update
  device(A[(iy_start[dn]-1):1][0:NX],
         A[iy_end[dn]:1][0:NX]) async
}
```

FIG. 16

Update halos on device.

Compiled with PGI 16.4 and running on the four GPUs of two NVIDIA® Tesla™ K80 doing 1000 iterations with a problem size of 4096×4096, a speedup of 2.78 and a parallel efficiency of 70% is achieved:

```
Num GPUs: 4.
4096x4096:
    1 GPU: 4.5793 s,
    4 GPUs: 1.6458 s, speedup: 2.78, efficiency: 69.56%
```

The reasons for the suboptimal parallel efficiency are

A. Parallel overhead: The serial version does not need to do the halo updates, and can do the top/bottom periodic boundary condition handling on the device.
B. The halo updates are executed serially, because the required update directives cannot fully run asynchronously. Depending on the target architecture and the used OpenACC implementation it might be required to pin host memory to get truly asynchronous data transfers, for example, on NVIDIA® hardware with the PGI® compiler it is necessary to use pinned host memory allocated on the heap. When adding the pinned sub option to the tesla target: -ta=tesla:pinned all heap memory is automatically pinned. As the host part of the update directive on A is a global variable it cannot be pinned with the pinned option and therefore the update directive does not run completely asynchronous (see the NVVP screenshot in Fig. 17).

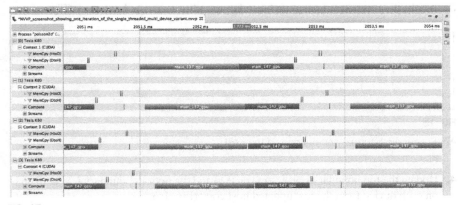

FIG. 17

NVVP screenshot showing one iteration of the single-threaded multidevice variant.

C. Due to the necessary serial dispatch of work to the different GPUs the kernels are not started all at the same time (see the NVVP screenshot in Fig. 17).
D. The data regions for the participating devices are created serially.

A production application would run for a longer time, so reason D would have a negligible impact on the application performance. Furthermore, it would be possible to improve the parallel efficiency by increasing the concurrent execution during the halo updates using heap memory and pinned memory.

MULTITHREADED MULTIDEVICE PROGRAMMING

Similar to the single-threaded multidevice version, domain decomposition is applied by computing the start (iy_start) and end (iy_end) index for the loops running over the rows of the domain for the device of the current thread as shown in Fig. 18.

```
// Ensure correctness if NY%num_threads != 0
int chunk_size = ceil( (1.0*NY)/num_threads );
int iy_start = thread_num * chunk_size;
int iy_end   = iy_start + chunk_size;
// Do not process boundaries
iy_start = max( iy_start, 1 );
iy_end = min( iy_end, NY - 1 );
```

FIG. 18

Computing domain boundaries.

The computed loop bounds are then used to create a data region with the part of the domain needed by the device associated with the current thread as shown in Fig. 19.

```
#pragma acc data
  copy(A[(iy_start-1):(iy_end-iy_start)+2][0:NX])
  copyin(rhs[iy_start:(iy_end-iy_start)][0:NX])
  create(Anew[iy_start:(iy_end-iy_start)][0:NX])
```

FIG. 19

Create a data region for each domain.

Launching all kernels only on the assigned subset of rows, for example, for the Jacobi step is shown in Fig. 20.
Computing the global error is done with an OpenMP critical section

1. Reset the global error to 0 (Fig. 21).
2. Compute the global error (Fig. 22).

Like in the single-threaded multidevice variant the halo updates are done via the host copy of A together with the top/bottom periodic boundary conditions as shown in Fig. 23.

```
#pragma acc kernels
for (int iy = iy_start; iy < iy_end; iy++) {
  for( int ix = ix_start; ix < ix_end; ix++ ) {
    Anew[iy][ix]=-0.25*(rhs[iy][ix]-(A[iy][ix+1]
                                    +A[iy][ix-1]
                                    +A[iy-1][ix]
                                    +A[iy+1][ix]));
    error=fmax(error,fabs(Anew[iy][ix]-A[iy][ix]));
  }
}
```

FIG. 20

Execute Jacobi step on the domain assigned to the executing OpenMP thread.

```
#pragma omp single
globalerror = 0.0;
#pragma omp barrier
```

FIG. 21

Reset global error.

```
#pragma omp critical
globalerror = fmax(globalerror,error);
#pragma omp barrier
error = globalerror;
```

FIG. 22

Compute the global error.

```
#pragma acc update
  self(A[iy_start:1][0:NX],A[(iy_end-1):1][0:NX])

#pragma omp barrier
if ( 0 == (iy_start-1) ) {
  for( int ix = 1; ix < NX-1; ix++ ) {
    A[0][ix]      = A[(NY-2)][ix];
  }
}
if ( NY-1 == iy_end ) {
  for( int ix = 1; ix < NX-1; ix++ ) {
    A[(NY-1)][ix] = A[1][ix];
  }
}

#pragma acc update
  device(A[(iy_start-1):1][0:NX],A[iy_end:1][0:NX])
```

FIG. 23

Apply periodic boundary conditions and do halo update.

In contrast to the single-threaded variant, the periodic boundary conditions on the top of the domain is handled by the thread computing the top most stripe. The periodic boundary condition on the bottom of the domain is handled by the thread computing the bottom most stripe. In addition a barrier after update self is required to avoid that a thread starts updating device halos before the neighboring thread finished writing these to the host copy.

Compiled with PGI 16.4 and running on the four GPUs of two NVIDIA® Tesla™ K80 doing 1000 iterations with a problem size of 4096×4096 a speedup of 3.35 and a parallel efficiency of 84% is achieved:

```
Num GPUs: 4.
4096x4096:
    1 GPU: 5.1182 s,
    4 GPUs: 1.5257 s, speedup: 3.35, efficiency: 83.87%
```

The reason for the suboptimal parallel efficiency for this variant is primarily the parallel overhead. The serial version does not need to do the halo updates, and can do the top/bottom periodic boundary condition handling on the device (see Fig. 24).

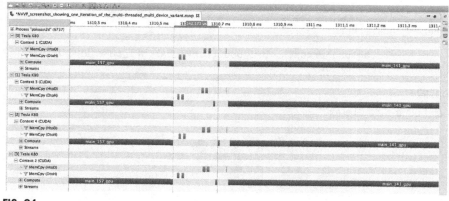

FIG. 24

NVVP screenshot showing one iteration of the multithreaded multidevice variant.

MULTIPROCESS MULTIDEVICE PROGRAMMING

The MPI variant is similar to the OpenMP variant. The domain decomposition is applied by computing the start (iy_start) and end (iy_end) index for the loops running over the rows of the domain for the device of the current MPI rank as shown in Fig. 25.

These loop bounds are used to launch all kernels only on the assigned subset of rows, for example, as it is shown for the Jacobi step in Fig. 26.

Computing the global error is done with an MPI_Allreduce as shown in Fig. 27.

Updating the halo regions and handling the top and bottom periodic boundary conditions is done in a single step with a ring exchange by taking rank size-1 as the top neighbor of rank 0 and rank 0 as the bottom neighbor of rank size-1. The periodic boundary conditions are implicitly handled via the rank 0-rank size-1 communication (Fig. 28).

```
// Ensure correctness if NY%size != 0
int chunk_size = ceil( (1.0*NY)/size );
int iy_start = rank * chunk_size;
int iy_end   = iy_start + chunk_size;
iy_start = max( iy_start, 1 );
iy_end = min( iy_end, NY - 1 );
```

FIG. 25

Computing domain boundaries.

```
#pragma acc kernels
for (int iy = iy_start; iy < iy_end; iy++) {
  for( int ix = ix_start; ix < ix_end; ix++ ) {
    Anew[iy][ix]=-0.25*(rhs[iy][ix]-(A[iy][ix+1]
                                    +A[iy][ix-1]
                                    +A[iy-1][ix]
                                    +A[iy+1][ix]));
    error=fmax(error,fabs(Anew[iy][ix]-A[iy][ix]));
  }
}
```

FIG. 26

Execute Jacobi step on the domain assigned to the executing MPI process.

```
real globalerror = 0.0;
MPI_Allreduce(
    &error,&globalerror,1, MPI_DOUBLE,MPI_MAX,MPI_COMM_WORLD);
error = globalerror;
```

FIG. 27

Compute the global error.

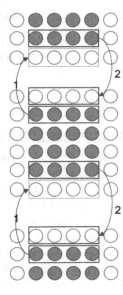

FIG. 28

Illustration of a halo exchange.

Two MPI_Sendrecv's are used to

1. Send the first modified row (iy_start) of a domain to the top neighbor and receive bottom boundary (iy_end) from the bottom neighbor (Fig. 29).

```
int top    = (rank == 0) ? (size-1) : rank-1;
int bottom = (rank == (size-1)) ? 0 : rank+1;
#pragma acc host_data use_device( A )
{
  MPI_Sendrecv(
    &A[iy_start][ix_start],(ix_end-ix_start),
    MPI_DOUBLE,top ,0,
    &A[iy_end][ix_start],(ix_end-ix_start),
    MPI_DOUBLE,bottom,0,
    MPI_COMM_WORLD, MPI_STATUS_IGNORE);
}
```

FIG. 29

Halo exchange step one.

2. Send the last modified row (iy_end-1) of a domain to the bottom neighbor while receiving the top boundary (iy_start-1) from the top neighbor (Fig. 30).

```
#pragma acc host_data use_device( A )
{
  MPI_Sendrecv(
    &A[(iy_end-1)][ix_start],(ix_end-ix_start),
    MPI_DOUBLE,bottom,0,
    &A[(iy_start-1)][ix_start],(ix_end-ix_start),
    MPI_DOUBLE,top ,0,
    MPI_COMM_WORLD, MPI_STATUS_IGNORE);
}
```

FIG. 30

Halo exchange step two.

By using the acc host_data use_device directive the device representation of A is passed directly to the MPI routine assuming the MPI can directly handle device memory, for example, a CUDA-aware MPI in case of NVIDIA® GPUs.

Compiled with PGI 16.4 using OpenMPI 1.10.2 and running on the four GPUs of two NVIDIA® Tesla™ K80 doing 1000 iterations with a problem size of 4096×4096, a speedup of 3.74 and a parallel efficiency of 93% is achieved:

```
Num GPUs: 4.
4096x4096:
    1 GPU: 5.2141 s,
    4 GPUs: 1.3949 s, speedup: 3.74, efficiency: 93.45%
```

The reason that we do not achieve optimal efficiency is parallel overhead because the halo exchange is not necessary in the serial version (Fig. 31).

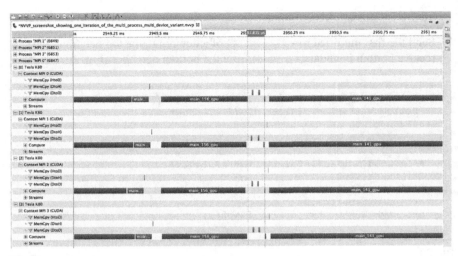

FIG. 31

NVVP screenshot showing one iteration of the multiprocess multidevice variant.

CUDA-aware MPI

A CUDA-aware MPI implementation allows you to exchange data directly to and from device memory buffers, avoiding the overhead of the host buffer staging in the user code. Without a CUDA-aware MPI it would have been necessary to stage data through host memory with update directives (see Fig. 32). If necessary, the host staging can be done far more efficiently when embedded in the internal pipelines of the MPI implementation. Furthermore a CUDA-aware MPI will transparently use acceleration technologies such as GPUDirect™ Peer-to-Peer (P2P) and Remote Direct Memory Access (RDMA) avoiding any host memory staging if possible (Kraus, 2016).

Remark: Direct GPU to GPU transfers (GPUDirect™ P2P) require using interprocess communication (IPC). CUDA-aware MPI implementations use CUDA IPC P2P mappings between GPUs controlled by different processes. Establishing the P2P mappings is often done lazily by the MPI implementation on the first communication, and has a significant overhead. In longer running applications the overhead is usually insignificant. To exclude it from the reported timing the MPI variant contains MPI warm up calls that isolate the costs of establishing the CUDA IPC connections. A similar technique was used to avoid the OpenACC initialization costs that slow down the first iterations of all discussed variants.

OVERLAPPING COMMUNICATION WITH COMPUTATION

The parallel efficiency of all presented variants suffers from the parallel overhead caused by the necessary halo exchange. Since the halo exchange only requires reading the first and last inner row of each domain, it is possible to hide these latencies behind the execution of the copy kernel (Hager & Wellein, 2010, pp. 216–220).

```
int top    = (rank == 0) ? (size-1) : rank-1;
int bottom = (rank == (size-1)) ? 0 : rank+1;

#pragma acc update
  self(A[iy_start:1][ix_start:(ix_end-ix_start)],
       A[(iy_end-1):1][ix_start:(ix_end-ix_start)])

MPI_Sendrecv(
  &A[iy_start][ix_start],(ix_end-ix_start),
  MPI_DOUBLE,top ,0,
  &A[iy_end][ix_start],(ix_end-ix_start),
  MPI_DOUBLE,bottom,0,
  MPI_COMM_WORLD, MPI_STATUS_IGNORE);
MPI_Sendrecv(
  &A[(iy_end-1)][ix_start],(ix_end-ix_start),
  MPI_DOUBLE,bottom,0,
  &A[(iy_start-1)][ix_start],(ix_end-ix_start),
  MPI_DOUBLE,top ,0,
  MPI_COMM_WORLD, MPI_STATUS_IGNORE);

#pragma acc update
  device(A[(iy_start-1):1][ix_start:(ix_end-ix_start)],
         A[iy_end:1][ix_start:(ix_end-ix_start)])
```

FIG. 32

Apply periodic boundary conditions and do halo update without CUDA-aware MPI.

Async queues are used for the halo exchange. An async queue is identified by a positive integer. Operations submitted to the same async queue are executed in the order they are submitted while operations submitted to different async queues are allowed to run concurrently. So, to achieve communication and computation overlap the copy kernel is first executed in async queue 1 on the rows that need to be sent to other processes (boundary), and the bulk of the async kernel is executed in async queue 2 as shown in Fig. 33.

This allows the communication times to be hidden for the necessary reduction of the error and the halo updates behind the execution of the copy kernel on the bulk of the data. For that the MPI_Allreduce call is moved after the two async kernel launches, and a wait for async queue 1 to finish before starting the halo exchange. After the halo updates are done, we need to wait for the kernel in async queue 2 to finish before we can start the next iteration (Fig. 34).

Compiled with PGI 16.4 using OpenMPI 1.10.2 and running on the four GPUs of two NVIDIA® Tesla™ K80 doing 1000 iterations with a problem size of 4096×4096, a speedup of 3.79 and a parallel efficiency of almost 95% is achieved (Fig. 35):

```
Num GPUs: 4.
4096x4096:
   1 GPU: 5.1756 s,
   4 GPUs: 1.3662 s, speedup: 3.79, efficiency: 94.71%
```

```
#pragma acc kernels async(1)
for(int ix=ix_start;ix<ix_end;ix++){
  A[iy_start][ix]=Anew[iy_start][ix];
  A[iy_end-1][ix]=Anew[iy_end-1][ix];
}

#pragma acc kernels async(2)
for (int iy=iy_start+1;iy<iy_end-1;iy++){
  for(int ix=ix_start;ix<ix_end;ix++){
    A[iy][ix]=Anew[iy][ix];
  }
}
real globalerror=0.0;
MPI_Allreduce(&error,&globalerror,1,
  MPI_DOUBLE,MPI_MAX,MPI_COMM_WORLD);
error=globalerror;

#pragma acc wait(1)

int top   =(rank==0)?(size-1):rank-1;
int bottom=(rank==(size-1))?0:rank+1;

#pragma acc host_data use_device(A)
{
  MPI_Sendrecv(
    &A[iy_start][ix_start],(ix_end-ix_start),MPI_DOUBLE,top,0,
    &A[iy_end][ix_start],(ix_end-ix_start),MPI_DOUBLE,bottom,0,
    MPI_COMM_WORLD,MPI_STATUS_IGNORE);
  MPI_Sendrecv(
    &A[(iy_end-1)][ix_start],(ix_end-ix_start),MPI_DOUBLE,bottom,0,
    &A[(iy_start-1)][ix_start],(ix_end-ix_start),MPI_DOUBLE,top,0,
    MPI_COMM_WORLD,MPI_STATUS_IGNORE);
}

#pragma acc wait(2)
```

FIG. 33

Using the async clause to execute MPI communication and OpenACC kernels concurrently.

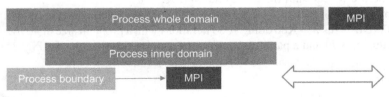

FIG. 34

Illustration of a communication time hiding.

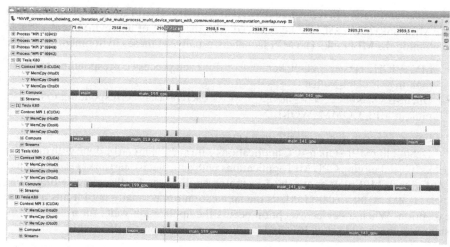

FIG. 35

NVVP screenshot showing one iteration of the multiprocess multidevice variant with communication and computation overlap.

Although this optimization was only demonstrated for the MPI variant, this optimization is also applicable to the single- and the multithreaded variant.

DEBUGGING AND PROFILING

For OpenACC targets building on the CUDA platform, it is possible to use the NVIDIA® debugging and profiling tools. This section summarizes tips and tricks on how to use the NVIDIA® debugging and profiling tools for an MPI+OpenACC application targeting NVIDIA® CUDA devices. Besides the discussed NVIDIA® tools other tools are also OpenACC aware, for example, pgprof, score-p, Vampir, and Tau for profiling or the DDT and TotalView debuggers.

DEBUGGING WITH cuda-memcheck AND cuda-gdb

To use cuda-memcheck on an MPI+OpenACC application it can be launched with the MPI launcher so that one cuda-memcheck instance is started for each MPI rank:

```
mpirun -np 2 cuda-memcheck ./myapp <args>
```

The main issue of this usage mode is that cuda-memcheck output is interleaved between different MPI ranks. This can be avoided by writing the output of cuda-memcheck to a file with using one of these cuda-memcheck command line options:

- --log-file name.%q{ENV_VAR}.log: to write the console output of cuda-memcheck to a text file.
- --save name.%q{ENV_VAR}.memcheck: to write a binary file that can be later read by cuda-memcheck with cuda-memcheck -read.

cuda-memcheck will replace %q{ENV_VAR} with the value of ENV_VAR. To get one file per MPI rank ENV_VAR should be replaced with the name of an environment variable containing the MPI rank. The MPI launchers usually set these environment variables.

- MVAPICH2 sets MV2_COMM_WORLD_RANK for each process corresponding to the rank in MPI_COMM_WORLD
- OpenMPI sets OMPI_COMM_WORLD_RANK for each process corresponding to the rank in MPI_COMM_WORLD

Other launcher might set different environment variables.

Debugging MPI+OpenACC applications with cuda-gdb can be done with the same tricks like debugging CPU MPI applications with gdb, that is, start an xterm with cuda-gdb for each MPI rank or attach to a running application. Furthermore setting CUDA_DEVICE_WAITS_ON_EXCEPTION let's the application run normally until it hits a device exception. When a device exception occurs the application waits for a cuda-gdb instance to attach and prints PID and hostname information similar to this:

```
<hostname>: The application encountered a device error and CUDA_
DEVICE_WAITS_ON_EXCEPTION is set. You can now attach a debugger
to the application (PID <pid>) for inspection.
```

Setting CUDA_ENABLE_COREDUMP_ON_EXCEPTION creates GPU or combined CPU/GPU core dumps on a device exception to allow offline inspection (NVIDIA, 2016).

PROFILING WITH nvprof AND THE NVIDIA® VISUAL PROFILER

Generating an nvprof profile for each MPI rank can be done by launching an nvprof instance for each MPI rank and writing the profile to a file:

```
mpirun -np 2 nvprof -o <filename>.%q{ENV_VAR}.nvprof ./myapp <args>
```

Like cuda-memcheck nvprof replaced %q{ENV_VAR} with the value of ENV_VAR. Using the environment variables provided by the MPI launcher, nvprof will produce one profile for each MPI rank (e.g., MVAPICH2: MV2_COMM_WORLD_RANK or OpenMPI: OMPI_COMM_WORLD_RANK). The produced profiles can be imported into the NVIDIA® Visual Profiler with the multiple processes import option. To ease mapping the different timelines to MPI ranks, it is possible to name the:

- process with the command line option: --process-name "MPI %q{ENV_VAR}"
- GPU context with the command line option: --context-name "MPI %q{ENV_VAR}"

Using the same environment variable names as for the output file.

CONCLUSION

In this chapter, you have learned three ways on how to compute faster or larger with multiple OpenACC devices. In summary, the presented alternatives to program multiple devices with OpenACC have the following advantages and disadvantages (Fig. 36).

	Advantages	Disadvantages
Single-threaded	• Does not add any further dependencies • Easy application startup	• Currently not possible to use direct device to device communication, e.g., GPUDirect™ P2P • Concurrency is limited in some cases, e.g., kernels with reductions and possibly data transfers from and to unpinned host memory
Multi-threaded	• Efficient shared memory coordination between controlling threads • Easy application startup	• Currently not possible to use direct device to device communication, e.g., GPUDirect™ P2P • Adds dependency to threading library, e.g., OpenMP
MPI	• Allows scaling beyond a node • Possible to used direct device to device communication on NVIDIA® Devices (GPUDirect™ P2P/RDMA) with a CUDA-aware MPI	• Adds dependency to MPI • Application startup requires to use a launcher, e.g., mpiexec

FIG. 36

Comparison of the alternatives to program multiple OpenACC devices.

Fig. 37 shows that running the MPI+OpenACC version using PGI® 16.4 and OpenMPI 1.10.2 nicely scales for the tesla and the multicore target of the PGI® compiler. The multicore target uses 16 threads per Socket/MPI rank.

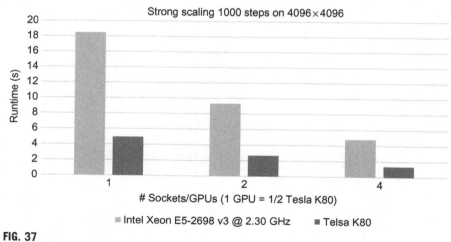

FIG. 37

Strong scaling on CPU and GPU.

REFERENCES

Hager, G., & Wellein, G. (2010). *Introduction to high performance computing for scientists and engineers.* Boca Ranton, FL: CRC Press.

Jacobi Method. (2016). *Encyclopedia of mathematics.* Retrieved from: http://www.encyclopediaofmath.org/index.php?title=Jacobi_method&oldid=34059.

Kraus, J. (2016). *An introduction to CUDA-aware MPI.* Retrieved from Parallel Forall: https://devblogs.nvidia.com/parallelforall/introduction-cuda-aware-mpi/.

NVIDIA. (2016). *CUDA-GDB.* Retrieved from CUDA Toolkit Documentation: http://docs.nvidia.com/cuda/cuda-gdb/#gpu-coredump.

OpenACC-Standard.org. (2016). *The OpenACC(R) application programming interface version 2.5.* June, Retrieved from OpenACC.org: http://www.openacc.org/sites/default/files/OpenACC_2pt5.pdf.

Poisson Equation. (2016). *Encyclopedia of mathematics.* Retrieved from: http://www.encyclopediaofmath.org/index.php?title=Poisson_equation&oldid=33144.

Using OpenACC for stencil and Feldkamp algorithms

8

Sunita Chandrasekaran*, Rengan Xu†, Barbara Chapman‡

Computer and Information Sciences, University of Delaware, Newark, DE, United States*
University of Houston, Houston, TX, United States† Stony Brook University, Stony Brook, NY,
United States‡

This chapter shows how a directive-based model can make it possible for application scientists to "keep" their codes, accelerate them with reduced programming effort, and achieve performance equal to or better than that obtained using hand-written code and low-level programming interfaces. Specifically, this chapter covers programmers' experiences porting two commonly used algorithms—Feldkamp and stencil—on single and multiple GPUs along with multicore platforms. These algorithms are representative of computational patterns used in a variety of domains including computational fluid dynamics, PDE solvers, MRI imaging, and image processing for computed tomography among several others. Additional discussion explains how OpenMP, another widely utilized directive-based programming model, can co-exist with OpenACC thus creating a hybrid programming strategy to target and distribute the workload across multiple GPUs.

At the end of this chapter the reader will have a basic understanding of:

- How to profile and gain a basic understanding of code characteristics for GPUs
- How to compile an OpenACC code using relevant compilation flags and analyze the compilation information
- How to incrementally improve an OpenACC code
- How to use OpenMP with OpenACC in the same code
- How to tune OpenACC code and provide relevant hints to achieve close to, or better performance than CUDA code

INTRODUCTION

Accelerators have gone mainstream in High Performance Computing (HPC), where they are being widely used in fields such as bioinformatics, molecular dynamics, computational finance, computational fluid dynamics, weather, and climate. Their power efficient, high compute capacity enables many applications to run faster and more efficiently than on general-purpose Central Processing Units (CPUs). As a

Parallel Programming with OpenACC. http://dx.doi.org/10.1016/B978-0-12-410397-9.00008-1

result, Graphics Processing Unit (GPU) accelerators are inherently appealing for scientific applications. However, in the past GPU programming has required the use of low-level languages such as OpenCL, CUDA, and other vendor-specific interfaces. These low-level programming models imply a steep learning curve and also demand excellent programming skills; moreover, they are time consuming to write and debug. OpenACC, a directive-based high-level model addresses these programming challenges for GPUs and simplifies the porting of scientific applications to GPUs whilst not unduly sacrificing performance.

In this chapter, we discuss experiences gained while porting two algorithms to single and multiple GPUs using OpenACC. We also demonstrate how OpenACC can be used to run on multicore platforms, thus maintaining a single code base. From our experimental analysis, we conclude that efficient implementations of high-level directive-based models plus user-guided optimizations can lead to performance close to that of hand-written CUDA code.

EXPERIMENTAL SETUP

The platform used for these experiments is a multicore server containing two NVIDIA Kepler80 GPUs (see Fig. 1 for configuration details). The most recent compiler versions are used for the experiments discussed in this chapter. PGI 16.4 with the compilation flag *-fast* is employed to translate the CPU and OpenACC versions of the programs. CUDA 7.5 is used to compile all CUDA programs. Wall-clock time is the basis for our evaluation: results of running CPU, OpenACC, and CUDA versions of the codes are collected and compared.

Item	Description
Architecture	Intel Xeon CPU E5-2660
CPU sockets	2
Core(s) per socket	10
CPU frequency	2.60 GHz
CPU memory	125 GB
GPU model	2 Kepler80
GPU DRAM	12 GB per GPU

FIG. 1

Experimental machine configuration.

FELDKAMP-DAVIS-KRESS ALGORITHM

Computerized Tomography (CT) is widely used in the medical sector to produce tomographic images of specific areas of the body. Succinctly, CT reconstructs an image of the original three-dimensional (3D) object from a large series of two-dimensional (2D) X-ray images. As a set of rays pass through an object around a single axis of rotation, the produced projection data is captured by an array of detectors, from which a filtered back-projection method based on the Fourier slice theorem is typically used to reconstruct the original object. Among various filtered back-projection algorithms, the Feldkamp-Davis-Kress (FDK) algorithm is mathematically straightforward and easy to implement. It is important that the image reconstructed from the acquired data be accurate. The goal of this work is to accelerate the reconstruction using directive-based programming models.

Fig. 2 shows pseudo-code for the FDK algorithm, which is comprised of three main steps:

1. Weighting—calculate the projected data.
2. Filtering—filter the weighted projection by multiplying their Fourier transforms.
3. Back-projection—back-project the filtered projection over the 3D reconstruction mesh.

```
Initialization;
foreach 2D image in detected images do
    foreach pixel in image do
        Pre-weight and ramp-filter the projection;
    end
end
foreach 2D image in detected images do
    foreach voxel in 3D reconstruct volume do
        calculate projected coordinate;
        sum the contribution to the object from all tilted fan
beams;
        end
    end
```

FIG. 2

Algorithm 1 pseudo-code of FDK algorithm.

The reconstruction algorithm is computationally intensive and it has biquadratic complexity ($O(N4)$), where N is the number of detector pixels in one dimension. The most time-consuming step of this algorithm is back-projection. As shown in Fig. 3, a profiled example of the application shows the back-projection routines in the application accounts for nearly all the runtime ($63.04\% + 20.85\% + 15.63\% = 99.52\%$ of the whole application). So the focus of our work is to parallelize the back-projection step.

```
Execution time of FDK: 159.57 seconds

======== CPU profiling result (bottom up):

Time(%)      Time   Name

 63.04%    100.7s   back_projection

 20.85%   33.3065s   __fsd_sincos_vex

 15.63%   24.9699s   floor

 15.63%   24.9699s   | back_projection

  0.18%   290.23ms   fourl

  0.11%   180.14ms   fread

  0.11%   180.14ms   | main

  0.05%   80.064ms   main
```

FIG. 3

Profiling result for CPU version of FDK (sin(), cos(), and floor() are called inside back_projection() function).

For implementation purposes we follow the steps given by Kak and Slaney (1988). As shown in Fig. 4A, the back-projection algorithm has four loops. The three outermost loops traverse each dimension of the output 3D object, and the innermost loop accesses each of the 2D detected image slices.

The code is first restructured so that the three outermost loops are tightly nested, and then the collapse clause from OpenACC is applied. This means that every thread sequentially executes the innermost loop. All detected images are transferred from the CPU to the GPU by using the copyin clause, and the output 3D object (i.e.,

```
void back_projection(…)

{

#pragma acc kernels copyin(fp_h[0:X_SIZE*Y_SIZE*Z_SIZE]) \

copyout(CT_numbers_h[0:RECONSIZE_Z*RECONSIZE*RECONSIZE])

{

    #pragma acc loop collapse(3) independent

  for(i=0;i<RECONSIZE_Z;i++)  {

      for(j=0;j<RECONSIZE;j++)  {

          for(k=0;k<RECONSIZE;k++){

              z=(Z_CENTER-zstart+i)*recon_step_z;

              y=(j-REC_XY_CENTER)*recon_step;

              x=(k-REC_XY_CENTER)*recon_step;


              reco = 0;

              for(l=view_start;l<view_end;l++)  {

                 ……

              }

          }

      }

  }

}

}
```

(A)

FIG. 4

(A) OpenACC code snippet of the back_projection kernel in FDK implementation and

Continued

```
__global__ void back_projection(…)
{
    idx = threadIdx.x + blockIdx.x*blockDim.x;
    size2 = RECONSIZE*RECONSIZE;
    i = (idx/size2)%RECONSIZE_Z;
    j = (idx/RECONSIZE)%RECONSIZE;
    k = idx%RECONSIZE;
    z=(Z_CENTER-zstart+i)*recon_step_z;
    y=(j-REC_XY_CENTER)*recon_step;
    x=(k-REC_XY_CENTER)*recon_step;
    reco = 0;
    for(l=view_start;l<view_end;l++) {
        ......
    }
}
int main()
{
    cudaMalloc((void**)&fp_d, X_SIZE*Y_SIZE*Z_SIZE*sizeof (float));
    cudaMemcpy(fp_d, fp_h, X_SIZE * Y_SIZE * Z_SIZE * sizeof (float),
cudaMemcpyHostToDevice);

    cudaMalloc((void**)&CT_numbers_d, RECONSIZE_Z * RECONSIZE * RECONSIZE *
sizeof (short int));
    cudaMemset((void*)CT_numbers_d, 0, RECONSIZE_Z * RECONSIZE * RECONSIZE *
sizeof (short int));
    dim3 dimBlock(THREADS, 1, 1);
    dim3 dimGrid((RECONSIZE_Z*RECONSIZE*RECONSIZE+THREADS-1)/THREADS,
1, 1);

    back_projection<<<dimGrid, dimBlock>>>(fp_d, CT_numbers_d,
view_start, view_end, X_SIZE, Y_SIZE, Z_SIZE);

    cudaMemcpy(CT_numbers_h, CT_numbers_d, RECONSIZE_Z * RECONSIZE *
RECONSIZE * sizeof (short int), cudaMemcpyDeviceToHost);
    }
```

(B)

FIG. 4, CONT'D

(B) CUDA code snippet of the back_projection kernel in FDK implementation.

many 2D image slices) is copied from GPU to CPU using the `copyout` clause. The implementations are evaluated using 3D Logan and Shepp (1975) head phantom data that has 300 detected images and the resolution of each image is 200×200. The algorithm produces a $200 \times 200 \times 200$ reconstructed cube. The input and output images are shown towards the end of this section.

Note that results for this application are sensitive to floating-point operation ordering and precision. Hence the floating-point values of the final output on a GPU can differ from the values computed on the CPU. One reason for this is the fused multiply add (FMA) operation Pullan (2009), where the computation `rn(X * Y + Z)` is carried out in a single step and is only rounded once. Without FMA, `rn(rn(X * Y) + Z)` is composed of two steps and rounded twice. Thus, using FMA will cause the results to differ slightly; but this does not mean that the FMA implementation is incorrect. The difference in results obtained with and without FMA, respectively, may matter for certain types of codes and not for others. In our case, the observed differences (with and without FMA) were minute. However, if a complex code, e.g., a weather modeling code is under consideration, even minute differences may not be tolerable.

To compile the C version of the FDK algorithm, the following command is used (Fig. 5):

```
$ pgcc -fast -acc -ta=tesla:cc35,nofma -Minfo=accel fdk.c -o acc_fdk
```

FIG. 5

Compilation command-line.

The flag "`-ta=tesla`" tells the compiler to generate code for the Tesla GPU. We use the option "`cc35`" to specify the compute capability of the targeted Tesla GPU since the Tesla GPU product family has evolved over time and now contains several generations of devices that differ with respect to their compute capabilities. The flag "`nofma`" tells the compiler to disable the FMA operation. The flag "`-Minfo=accel`" tells the compiler to output information when it translates the OpenACC code to GPU code, including information about loop scheduling, data movement, and data synchronization, and more.

In this way various implementation techniques can be explored even in the face of accuracy and precision differences.

The following is the information output by the PGI compiler (Fig. 6):

OpenACC is a model that targets different accelerator architectures. In order to use it for multicore architectures, the following command is required (Fig. 7):

```
back_projection:
    43, Generating copyin(fp_h[:Z_SIZE*(Y_SIZE*X_SIZE)])
        Generating copyout(CT_numbers_h[:8000000])
    47, Loop is parallelizable
    49, Loop is parallelizable
    51, Loop is parallelizable
        Accelerator kernel generated
        Generating Tesla code
        47, #pragma acc loop gang, vector(128) collapse(3)/* blockIdx.x threadIdx.x */
        49,    /* blockIdx.x threadIdx.x collapsed */
        51,    /* blockIdx.x threadIdx.x collapsed */
    58, Loop is parallelizable
```

FIG. 6

The output information by PGI compiler for FDK algorithm.

```
$ pgcc -fast -acc -ta=multicore -Minfo=accel fdk.c -o multicore_fdk
```

FIG. 7

Compiler command-line for multicore.

This command differs from the previous compiler command-line in the flags specified: -ta=multicore replaces -ta=tesla. On multicore platforms, a specification of the compute capability is not needed.

Our evaluation includes comparisons among sequential CPU versions, OpenACC versions targeting both multicore and GPUs as well as CUDA versions. The CUDA version was developed manually and the code snippet of back-projection kernel is shown in Fig. 4B.

In the OpenACC version, the three outer loops were collapsed. To keep the comparisons fair, a similar loop scheduling strategy is retained for the CUDA kernels. There are many loop schedules that can be applied by the compiler. The reader is directed to Tian et al. (2016) for more details on using different loop schedule options.

Fig. 8 shows the performance and speedup using different programming models/languages. Compared to the sequential version, the OpenACC multicore, OpenACC GPU, and CUDA versions achieved a speedup of 16.24×, 123.47×, and 98.93×, respectively. The performance of the OpenACC version is slightly better than that of the CUDA code. A probable reason for this is that the OpenACC compiler applied better optimizations while translating OpenACC kernels to CUDA than were implemented in the manually written CUDA kernel.

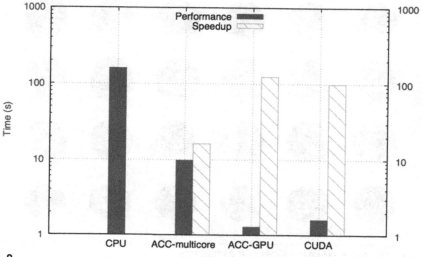

FIG. 8

The performance of FDK algorithm with different models.

```
resolution=200;

slice=180;

fid = fopen('output.img');

fseek(fid, resolution*resolution*slice, 'bof');

img = fread(fid, [resolution, resolution], 'short');

imtool(img, [-325, 1])
```

FIG. 9

Matlab script to visualize data.

Matlab can be used to view both the input and the output images. For instance, if the resolution of the output 3D image is 200×200, the following Matlab script can be used to view the 180th 2D image slice in the output image (Fig. 9).

The input and output data of the 2D images are shown in Figs. 10 and 11.

2D HEAT EQUATION

Our 2D heat equation application is a stencil-based algorithm with a high computation/communication ratio for which the workload can be distributed across several threads. The implementation uses the GPU's global memory and obtains good performance, but it could be further improved by using GPU shared memory.

The formula to represent 2D heat conduction is explained in Whitehead & Fit-Florea (2011) and is given in Fig. 12:

FIG. 10

The representative 2D image slices of the input image.

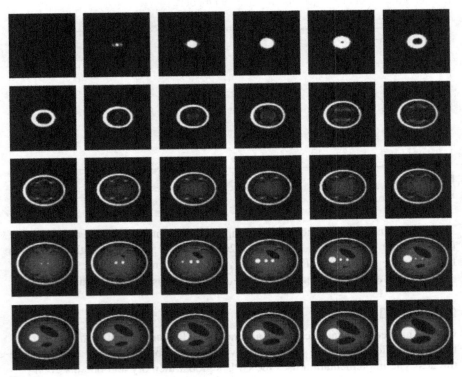

FIG. 11

The representative 2D image slices of the output image.

$$\frac{\partial T}{\partial t} = \alpha \left(\frac{\partial^2 T}{\partial x^2} + \frac{\partial^2 T}{\partial y^2} \right)$$

FIG. 12

2D heat conduction formula.

where T is temperature, t is time, α is the thermal diffusivity, and x and y are points in a grid. To solve this problem, one possible finite difference approximation is given in Fig. 13:

$$\frac{\Delta T}{\Delta t} = \alpha \left(\frac{T_{i+1,j} - 2T_{i,j} + T_{i-1,j}}{\Delta x^2} + \frac{T_{i,j+1} - 2T_{i,j} + T_{i,j-1}}{\Delta y^2} \right)$$

FIG. 13

One possible finite difference approximation.

where ΔT is the temperature change over time Δt and i, j are indices in a grid.

At program startup, a grid is set up that has boundary points with an initial temperature and inner points for which the temperature must be incrementally updated. Each inner point updates its temperature by using the previous temperature of its neighboring points and itself. The updating step diffuses the temperature from the boundary points through the grid, but it can only progress one grid point per iteration; this means that a large number of iterations can be required to reach a steady temperature state across all points in the grid.

A snippet from our code that implements the stencil-based temperature update is reproduced in Fig. 14. The number of iterations used in our experiments is 20,000, and the grid size is increased gradually from 256×256 to 4096×4096.

In order to parallelize the application, OpenACC directives are used: "#pragma acc kernels" is inserted at the top of the nested loop inside the temperature updating kernel, and "#pragma acc loop independent" is inserted right before each loop. The "independent" clause is used to tell the compiler that there is no loop-carried dependence in the annotated loop nest. In addition, the copyin and copyout data clauses are added to move the input to GPU and output data from GPU to CPU.

Results of profiling the basic implementation, shown in Fig. 15, indicate that the data is transferred back and forth in every main iteration step.

The cost of data transfer is so high that the parallelized code takes longer to execute than the original version on the host. To avoid transferring the data during each step, a data directive is added surrounding the main iterations; this ensures that the data is transferred only before and after the main loops. After all the iterations have completed, the data in temp1 instead of temp2 needs to be transferred from GPU to CPU since the pointers of temp1 and temp2 have been swapped earlier. In the kernel, the copyin and copyout clauses are replaced by the present clause which indicates that the data are already present on the GPU and thus there is no need to do any data movement.

Fig. 16A shows the OpenACC code snippet after applying data optimization and Fig. 17 shows the corresponding profile result. It is clear that the number of times the data is moved has been reduced from 40,000 to only 3. To enable a comparison, Fig. 16B shows a CUDA implementation of the same kernel.

```
void step_kernel(int ni, int nj, float fact, float* temp_in, float*
temp_out)
{
// loop over all points in domain (except boundary)
#pragma acc kernels copyin(temp_in[0:ni*nj]) copyout(temp_out[0:ni*nj])
{
#pragma acc loop independent
for (j=1; j < nj-1; j++) {
    #pragma acc loop independent
    for (i=1; i < ni-1; i++) {
/* find indices into linear memory for central point and neighbors */
            i00 = I2D(ni, i, j);   im10 = I2D(ni, i-1, j);
            ip10 = I2D(ni, i+1, j); i0m1 = I2D(ni, i, j-1);
            i0p1 = I2D(ni, i, j+1);
            // evaluate derivatives
            d2tdx2 = temp_in[im10]-2*temp_in[i00]+temp_in[ip10];
            d2tdy2 = temp_in[i0m1]-2*temp_in[i00]+temp_in[i0p1];
            // update temperatures
            temp_out[i00] = temp_in[i00]+tfac*(d2tdx2 + d2tdy2);
    }
  }
 }
}
int main(int argc, char* argv[]) {
for (istep=0; istep < nstep; istep++) {
        step_kernel(ni, nj, tfac, temp1_h, temp2_h);
        // swap the temperature pointers
        temp_tmp = temp1_h; temp1_h = temp2_h; temp2 _h= temp_tmp;
    }
}
```

FIG. 14

OpenACC implementation of 2D heat equation before data optimization.

```
Execution time of 2D Heat Equation: 6.65 s

==45380== Profiling application: ./unopt_heat_single_gpu 256 256 20000 out.dat

==45380== Profiling result:

Time(%)       Time     Calls      Avg        Min       Max   Name

 44.84%  1.41264s     20000  70.631us   70.111us  80.927us  [CUDA memcpy HtoD]

 44.72%  1.40874s     20000  70.437us   69.663us  84.031us  [CUDA memcpy DtoH]

 10.44%  328.74ms     20000  16.437us   16.064us  17.216us  step_kernel_cpu_27_gpu
```

FIG. 15

Profiling result for OpenACC version of 2D heat equation before data optimization.

```
void step_kernel(int ni, int nj, float fact, float* temp_in, float*
temp_out)
{
// loop over all points in domain (except boundary)
#pragma acc kernels present(temp_in[0:ni*nj], temp_out[0:ni*nj])
{
#pragma acc loop independent
for (j=1; j < nj-1; j++) {
    #pragma acc loop independent
    for (i=1; i < ni-1; i++) {
/* find indices into linear memory for central point and neighbors */
            i00 = I2D(ni, i, j);   im10 = I2D(ni, i-1, j);
            ip10 = I2D(ni, i+1, j); i0m1 = I2D(ni, i, j-1);
            i0p1 = I2D(ni, i, j+1);
            // evaluate derivatives
            d2tdx2 = temp_in[im10]-2*temp_in[i00]+temp_in[ip10];
            d2tdy2 = temp_in[i0m1]-2*temp_in[i00]+temp_in[i0p1];
            // update temperatures
            temp_out[i00] = temp_in[i00]+tfac*(d2tdx2 + d2tdy2);
    }
  }
 }
}
```

FIG. 16

(A) OpenACC implementation of 2D heat equation after data optimization and

Continued

```
int main(int argc, char* argv[]) {
#pragma acc data copy(temp1_h[0:(ni+2)*(nj+2)]) \
                            copyin(temp2_h[0:(ni+2)*(nj+2)])
{
    for (istep=0; istep < nstep; istep++) {
        step_kernel(ni, nj, tfac, temp1_h, temp2_h);
        // swap the temperature pointers
        temp_tmp = temp1_h; temp1_h = temp2_h; temp2 _h= temp_tmp;
    }
  }
}
```

(A)

```
__global__ void step_kernel(int ni, int nj, float fact, float* temp_in,
float* temp_out)
{
    j = blockIdx.y + 1;
    i = threadIdx.x + blockIdx.x*blockDim.x + 1;
    // loop over all points in domain (not boundary points)
    for (j=j; j < nj-1; j+=gridDim.y) {
        for (i=i; i < ni-1; i+=blockDim.x*gridDim.x) {
        // find indices into linear memory for central point and
neighbours
            i00 = I2D(ni, i, j);
            im10 = I2D(ni, i-1, j);
            ip10 = I2D(ni, i+1, j);
            i0m1 = I2D(ni, i, j-1);
            i0p1 = I2D(ni, i, j+1);
        // evaluate derivatives
            d2tdx2 = temp_in[im10] - 2*temp_in[i00] + temp_in[ip10];
            d2tdy2 = temp_in[i0m1] - 2*temp_in[i00] + temp_in[i0p1];
        // update temperatures
            temp_out[i00] = temp_in[i00] + tfac*(d2tdx2 + d2tdy2);
        }
    }
}
```

FIG. 16, CONT'D

```
int main(int argc, char* argv[]) {
    // allocate temperature arrays on device
    cudaMalloc((void **)&temp1_d, sizeof(double)*(ni+2)*(nj+2));
    cudaMalloc((void **)&temp2_d, sizeof(double)*(ni+2)*(nj+2));


    // transfer temperature array from host to device
    cudaMemcpy((void *)temp1_d, (void *)temp1_h,
sizeof(double)*(ni+2)*(nj+2), cudaMemcpyHostToDevice);

    cudaMemcpy((void *)temp2_d, (void *)temp1_h,
sizeof(double)*(ni+2)*(nj+2), cudaMemcpyHostToDevice);

    for (istep=0; istep < nstep; istep++) {
        step_kernel(ni, nj, tfac, temp1_h, temp2_h);
        // swap the temperature pointers
        temp_tmp = temp1_h; temp1_h = temp2_h; temp2 _h = temp_tmp;
    }

    cudaMemcpy((void *)temp1_h, (void *)temp1_d,
sizeof(double)*(ni+2)*(nj+2), cudaMemcpyDeviceToHost);
    }
```

(B)

FIG. 16, CONT'D

(B) CUDA implementation of 2D heat equation.

```
Execution time of 2D Heat Equation: 0.86 s

==46185== Profiling application: ./heat_single_gpu 256 256 20000 out.dat

==46185== Profiling result:

Time(%)      Time    Calls      Avg      Min      Max   Name

99.93%  327.37ms    20000  16.368us  15.999us  17.056us  step_kernel_cpu_27_gpu

 0.04%  142.94us        2  71.471us  71.359us  71.584us  [CUDA memcpy HtoD]

 0.02%  70.879us        1  70.879us  70.879us  70.879us  [CUDA memcpy DtoH]
```

FIG. 17

Profiling result for OpenACC version of 2D heat equation after data optimization.

HYBRID OpenMP/OpenACC

This section discusses the case where the application uses two GPUs. Fig. 18 reproduces the program details including comments. In this implementation, *ni* and *nj* are the X and Y dimensions of the grid (not including the boundary), respectively. As can be seen in Fig. 18, the grid is partitioned into two parts along the Y dimension, each of which will run on one GPU. The decomposed parts overlap at the boundaries and the overlapping regions are called halo regions. At the start of the computation, the initial temperature is stored in *temp1_h*; after updating the temperature, the new temperature is stored in *temp2_h*. Then the pointer is swapped so that in the next iteration the input of the kernel points to the current new temperature. Since each data point needs temperature values from its neighboring points in the previous iteration for the update, the two GPUs need to exchange halo data at every iteration. With today's technology, the data cannot be exchanged directly between different GPUs using high-level directives or runtime libraries. The only workaround is to first transfer the data from one device to the host and then from the host to the other device. This is illustrated in Fig. 19 for the 2D heat equation where different OpenACC devices exchange halo data through the CPU.

The profiling results in Fig. 20 also confirm that after every iteration, the pair of GPUs exchange data through the CPU. Because different GPUs use different parts of the data in the grid, separate memory for these partial data do not need to be allocated, instead only the private pointer needs to be used to point to the different positions of the shared variable `temp1_h` and `temp2_h`. If *tid* represents the id of a thread, then that thread's pointer points to the position $tid*rows*(ni+2)$ of the grid (because it needs to include the halo region) and it needs to transfer $(rows+2)*(ni+2)$ data to the device where *rows* is equal to *nj/NUM_THREADS*. The kernel that updates the temperature in the multiGPU implementation is exactly the same as the one in the single-GPU version.

Fig. 21 shows the results of profiling both OpenACC and CUDA multiGPU implementations. Note that their performance is similar. The kernel performance of the OpenACC implementation is slightly better than that of the CUDA implementation, which demonstrates that when translating OpenACC kernels, the OpenACC compiler may apply optimizations that are not available in the CUDA compiler.

Fig. 22 compares the performance obtained by different implementations. It is obvious that the execution time of the serial version of the code on a single CPU is always the slowest. The OpenACC multicore performance is slightly better than the GPU performance when the problem size is small, but poorer than GPU performance when the problem size is large. While comparing the performance of multiGPU with single GPU, we noticed that there is a trivial performance difference when the problem size is small. However, there is a significant increase in performance using multiple GPUs for larger grid sizes.

Fig. 23 shows the speedup in multicore and GPU compared to the CPU performance. For a grid size of 4096×4096, the speedup obtained using two GPUs is around twice that of the single GPU implementation. This is because as the grid size increases, the computation also increases significantly, while the halo-data exchange

```
        omp_set_num_threads(NUM_THREADS);
        rows = nj/NUM THREADS;
        LDA = ni + 2;


        // main iteration loop
        #pragma omp parallel private(istep)
        {
            float *temp1, *temp2, *temp tmp;
            int tid = omp get thread num();
            acc set device num(tid+1, acc device not host);
            temp1 = temp1 h + tid*rows*LDA;
            temp2 = temp2 h + tid*rows*LDA;
            #pragma acc data copyin(temp1[0:(rows+2)*LDA]) \
                                    copyin(temp2[0:(rows+2)*LDA])
            {
                for(istep=0; istep < nstep; istep++){
                    step_kernel(ni+2, rows+2, tfac, temp1, temp2);
/* all devices (except the last one) update the lower halo to the host */
                    if(tid != NUM_THREADS-1){
                        #pragma acc update host(temp2[rows*LDA:LDA])
                    }
/* all devices (except the first one) update the upper halo to the host */
                    if(tid != 0){
                        #pragma acc update host(temp2[LDA:LDA])
                    }
/* all host threads wait here to make sure halo data from all devices
                have been updated to the host */
                    #pragma omp barrier
/* update the upper halo to all devices (except the first one) */
                    if(tid != 0){
                        #pragma acc update device(temp2[0:LDA])
                    }
/* update the lower halo to all devices (except the last one) */
                    if(tid != NUM_THREADS-1){
                        #pragma acc update device(temp2[(rows+1)*LDA:LDA])
                    }
                    temp tmp = temp1; temp1 = temp2; temp2 = temp tmp;
                }
                /*update the final result to host*/
                #pragma acc update host(temp1[LDA:row*LDA])
            }
        }
```

FIG. 18

MultiGPU implementation of 2D heat equation with OpenMP/OpenACC.

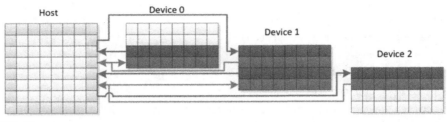

FIG. 19

The data movement in multiGPU implementation of 2D heat equation using OpenMP/
OpenACC hybrid model.

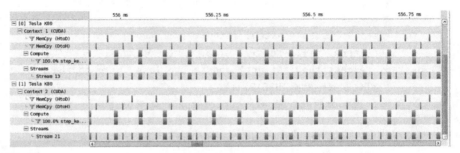

FIG. 20

Profiling result for multiGPU implementation of 2D heat equation.

```
==66180== Profiling application: ./cuda_multi _gpu 2 2048 2048 20000 cuda_multi_gpu.dat
==66180== Profiling result:
Time(%)        Time      Calls       Avg        Min        Max   Name
 97.67%    18.6972s      40000   467.43us   463.84us   471.61us   step_kernel
  1.21%    231.83ms      40004   5.7950us   5.2790us   2.7339ms   [CUDA memcpy HtoD]
  1.12%    214.22ms      40002   5.3550us   5.0240us   2.5506ms   [CUDA memcpy DtoH]


==66237== Profiling application: ./acc_multi_gpu 2 2048 2048 20000 acc_multi_gpu.dat
==66237== Profiling result:
Time(%)        Time      Calls       Avg        Min        Max   Name
 97.34%    16.4935s      40000   412.34us   407.49us   414.65us   step_kernel_cpu_42_gpu
  1.41%    239.50ms      40008   5.9860us   5.3110us   2.1293ms   [CUDA memcpy HtoD]
  1.24%    210.75ms      40004   5.2680us   4.9600us   2.5491ms   [CUDA memcpy DtoH]
```

FIG. 21

Comparison between OpenACC and CUDA implementation on multiGPU.

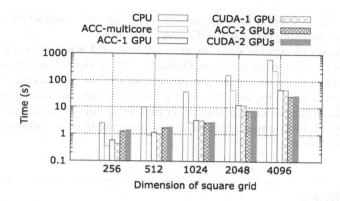

FIG. 22

The performance of 2D heat equation using different models.

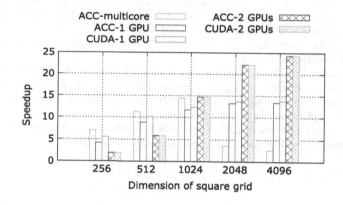

FIG. 23

The speedup of 2D heat equation compared to CPU.

remains small. Thus the computation/communication ratio increases; decomposing the computation to utilize multiple GPUs to can be quite advantageous. It is also apparent that the performance of the OpenMP/OpenACC implementation for multiple GPUs is comparable to the CUDA implementation.

SUMMARY

OpenACC, a directive-based programming model, can generate executables for more devices than just GPUs. This means that an application scientist can maintain a single code base whilst porting applications across a range of computing devices. This is critical since legacy codes usually contain several millions of lines of code, and it is impractical to rewrite them every time the device architecture changes.

Moreover it is expensive, time-consuming, and effectively impractical to rewrite them in low-level languages such as CUDA or OpenCL.

This chapter showcased some coding challenges and walks the reader through incremental code improvements using OpenACC. The reader will notice that the performance achieved depends primarily on the characteristics of the code, which can be discovered through the use of profiler tools. From our experimental results, we conclude that efficient implementations of high-level directive-based models, plus user-guided optimizations, are capable of producing the same performance as handwritten CUDA code.

REFERENCES

Kak, A. C., & Slaney, M. (1988). *Principles of computerized tomographic imaging*. IEEE Press.

Logan, B. F., & Shepp, L. A. (1975). Optimal reconstruction of a function from its projections. *Duke Mathematical Journal*, *42*(4), 645–659. http://dx.doi.org/10.1215/S0012-7094-75-04256-8. http://projecteuclid.org/euclid.dmj/1077311339.

Pullan, G. (2009). *Cambridge CUDA course*. 25–27 May http://www.many-core.group.cam.ac.uk/archive/CUDAcourse09.

Tian, X., Xu, R., Yan, Y., Chandrasekaran, S., Eachempati, D., & Chapman, B. (2016). Compiler transformation of nested loops for GPGPUs. *Journal of Concurrency and Computation: Practice and Experience*, *28*(2), 537–556. Special issue on programming models and applications for multicores and many cores.

Whitehead, N., & Fit-Florea, A. (2011). Precision and performance: Floating point and IEEE 754 compliance for NVIDIA GPUs. *rn* (*A*+*B*), *21*, 1–1874919424.

Accelerating 3D wave equations using OpenACC

9

Ty McKercher

NVIDIA Corporation, Houston, TX, United States

The purpose of this chapter is to learn how to express parallelism for a 3D finite difference code using OpenACC directives. It is common for scientific and engineering communities to use finite difference methods to solve partial differential equations.

After completing this chapter, you will have a basic understanding of:

- A finite difference code
- How to convert OpenMP code to OpenACC
- Practical techniques to profile and analyze performance behavior of finite difference codes
- How to use Unified Memory with OpenACC
- Testing portability targets including multicore systems

INTRODUCTION

In this chapter you will use a profile-driven approach to accelerate an application that solves the 3D scalar wave equation. This approach can be used across a variety of scientific domains on similar codes that simulate waves propagating through various medium. The code examples used in this chapter originated from "A Brief Introduction to OpenMP," from the Center for High Performance Computing at the Washington University School of Medicine in St. Louis, which contain both C and FORTRAN examples (Tobias, 2016).

First, you will use OpenMP tools to measure baseline host Central Processing Unit (CPU) scalability, then use enhanced OpenACC profiling capabilities to gain performance uplift for multicore host or Graphic Processing Unit (GPU) targets. To maximize your productivity, the OpenACC tools help you:

- Highlight parallel execution dependencies
- Identify critical optimization targets
- Measure code intensity regions (comparing memory bandwidth vs. floating point operations)

Parallel Programming with OpenACC. http://dx.doi.org/10.1016/B978-0-12-410397-9.00009-3

167

The profile-driven approach is an iterative method. With each iteration, you use enhanced dependency analysis to generate a timeline of functions on the critical path. Choosing which function to optimize is an important step. As shown in Fig. 1, the longest running kernel is not always the most critical optimization target (Harris, 2016).

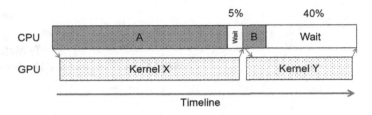

FIG. 1

Even though kernel X consumes more time than kernel Y, reducing kernel Y runtime will have the most performance impact since that will reduce overall wait time.

While you could use the command-line reports from the profiler, the visual-based Graphical User Interface (GUI) version makes it easier to identify these situations. Before illustrating how to use these tools, it is helpful to learn more details about the example code used in this chapter.

CODE EXAMPLE: SOLVING 3D SCALAR WAVE EQUATION

It is amazing how mathematical formulas can be used to express the behavior of natural phenomena, such as waves propagating through space and time. A complete understanding of the formulas derived in this section is not necessary. However, the details are provided here to help you gain insight about how the problem is solved, and how the code is structured. The example for this chapter uses standard Cartesian coordinates to express the 3D scalar wave equation in this form:

$$\frac{\partial^2 \phi}{\partial t^2} - \left(\frac{\partial^2 \phi}{\partial x^2} + \frac{\partial^2 \phi}{\partial y^2} + \frac{\partial^2 \phi}{\partial z^2} \right) = 0$$

where phi (ϕ) represents a scalar function that models wave displacement over time. For example, $\phi = \phi(x, y, z, t)$ could represent the propagation of sound waves in a fluid. In order to solve this second-order equation, two first-order equations are used:

$$f \equiv \phi, g \equiv \frac{\partial \phi}{\partial t}$$

where f represents a function $f(x, y, z)$ that assigns a scalar property value to each point in space, also known as a scalar wave field (Riffe, 2016). Here, g tells you how fast the scalar wave field is changing while traveling in a specific direction. Stated another way, g assigns a vector (magnitude + direction) to each point in space (also known as the linear time derivative of the field f). Using substitution leads to the following formulas:

$$\frac{\partial f}{\partial t} = g$$

$$\frac{\partial g}{\partial t} = \frac{\partial^2 f}{\partial t^2} = \left(\frac{\partial^2 f}{\partial x^2} + \frac{\partial^2 f}{\partial y^2} + \frac{\partial^2 f}{\partial z^2} \right)$$

Spatial (x, y, and z) data is arranged in the form of a uniform mesh, and a finite difference scheme is used to simulate how the scalar fields evolve over time. The structure of the example code used in this chapter can be summarized by pseudo code shown in Fig. 2.

```
 1 initialize x, y, and z arrays
 2 initialize f, and g arrays
 3 allocate fp and gp arrays
 4 set grid spacing dx, dy, dz, and time step interval dt
 5
 6 for n time steps:
 7     calculate predictor fp
 8     calculate boundary conditions gp
 9     use finite difference method to update gp from predictor fp
10     use average of g and gp to update fp
11     update f and g
12 end for
```

FIG. 2

Pseudo code for code example solving 3D scalar wave equation.

An important note about numerical stability using this algorithm: since a finite difference method is used to solve the wave equation, it is necessary for the variable dt (which represents the time step) to be much smaller than dx (which represents the mesh size) in order for the solution to converge. If you increase the time step and keep the mesh size fixed, or increase the mesh size and keep the time step fixed, the method may become unstable. A verification program is included in the source code for this chapter so you can check results after each optimization step. It does not matter how fast an application runs if you generate incorrect results.

The time domain finite difference method is commonly used to solve a set of partial differential equations due to efficiency of regular data access patterns. A sample code segment taken from the C program is shown in Fig. 3 that illustrates how the current array element is updated by contributions from neighboring elements using previous, current, and next values, commonly referred to as stencil operations. For this chapter, the original code was converted from double precision to single precision in order to target a broad range of GPUs. The core ideas covered in this chapter are applicable regardless of precision.

Perhaps Fig. 4 will help you understand this code fragment further by illustrating how two different wave field arrays g, and fp, are used to update the gp wave field array. The fp wave field uses a stencil pattern to add contributions from neighboring data elements at each time step.

```
...
for (i=1; i<NX-1; i++) {
    for (j=1; j<NY-1; j++) {
        for (k=1; k<NZ-1; k++) {
            gp[i][j][k] = g[i][j][k] + dt * (
                    (fp[i+1][j][k]-2.0f*fp[i][j][k]+fp[i-1][j][k])/dx/dx +
                    (fp[i][j+1][k]-2.0f*fp[i][j][k]+fp[i][j-1][k])/dy/dy +
                    (fp[i][j][k+1]-2.0f*fp[i][j][k]+fp[i][j][k-1])/dz/dz);
        }
    }
}
...
```

FIG. 3

C source code illustrating finite difference calculation using contributions from neighboring arrays.

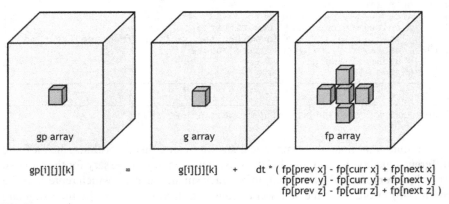

FIG. 4

A stencil pattern from array `fp` is used to add contributions from neighboring elements during the update of the `gp` wave field.

CONVERTING STACK TO HEAP

Now that you examined the pseudo code, you might be eager to dive-in and accelerate this code. Since the original C code for this chapter uses the program stack for arrays, you should first convert the code to use the heap (a larger free floating region of host memory) for allocation. This will allow you to experiment with larger problem sizes, which are typical in scientific applications.

During this transformation you will add code to accept input from the command-line that allows the user to specify dimensions of the problem size, and number of time steps for the simulation at runtime. This can be accomplished by parsing the command line arguments as shown in Fig. 5.

```
...
#define NX 256
#define NY 256
#define NZ 256
#define NSTEPS 500

int main(int argc, char *argv[]) {

    int i,j,k,n;

    int nx = NX;
    int ny = NY;
    int nz = NZ;
    int nsteps = NSTEPS;

    if( argc >= 4 ) {
        nx = atoi( argv[1] );
        ny = atoi( argv[2] );
        nz = atoi( argv[3] );
    }
    if( argc >=5 )
        nsteps = atoi( argv[4] );
...
```

FIG. 5

Define default values and allow user to specify problem dimensions by parsing command-line arguments.

Once the problem size has been defined, you next calculate the array size in bytes, and use the `malloc()` system call to allocate memory from the heap dynamically. Using the `restrict` keyword, as shown in Fig. 6, allows the compiler to be more aggressive during the analysis phase, because pointer alias concerns that might prevent automatic parallelization are eliminated.

```
...
    size_t nbytes = nx * ny * nz * sizeof(float);
    float *restrict x  = (float*)malloc( nbytes );
    float *restrict y  = (float*)malloc( nbytes );
    float *restrict z  = (float*)malloc( nbytes );
    float *restrict f  = (float*)malloc( nbytes );
    float *restrict g  = (float*)malloc( nbytes );
    float *restrict fp = (float*)malloc( nbytes );
    float *restrict gp = (float*)malloc( nbytes );
    if( 0==x || 0==y || 0==z || 0==f || 0==g || 0==fp || 0==gp ) {
        printf( "couldn't allocate fields on the host\n" );
        return (-1);
    }
...
```

FIG. 6

use `malloc()` to dynamically allocate memory from heap. The `restrict` keyword is helpful during the compiler analysis phase to indicate that pointer locations are not aliased.

Next is a very important part of the transformation from static memory allocation to dynamic heap allocation. You must define an OFFSET macro to calculate the proper 3D array index location, as shown in Fig. 7. If this step is not done correctly:

- The performance of your application will suffer due to inefficient data access patterns
- Your application may generate incorrect results

```
. . .
#define OFFSET(i,j,k,width,depth) ((k)+(width)*((j)+(i)*(depth)))

. . .

    for (i=0; i<nx; i++) {
        for (j=0; j<ny; j++) {
            for (k=0; k<nz; k++) {
                int offset = OFFSET(i, j, k, ny, nz);
                x[offset] = -1.0f + (i)*dx;
                y[offset] = -1.0f + (j)*dy;
                z[offset] = -1.0f + (k)*dz;
            }
        }
    }
. . .
```

FIG. 7

It is critical to properly define the OFFSET macro for efficient data access.

The final step in this transformation is to release the memory before exiting the program using the free() system call as shown in Fig. 8.

```
. . .
    free(x);
    free(y);
    free(z);
    free(f);
    free(g);
    free(fp);
    free(gp);
. . .
```

FIG. 8

For heap-based allocation, you need to free the memory before exiting the program.

MEASURING HOST BASELINE SCALABILITY

The original version of the example code contains OpenMP directives. This gives you the opportunity to measure scalability for host (CPU) systems, and determine baseline performance for comparison purposes. For each code example in this chapter, these timing routines are used (reference timer.h) to measure total runtime:

- For Windows-based systems: QueryPerformanceCounter()
- For Linux-based systems: gettimeofday()

CREATING THE OpenMP BUILD ENVIRONMENT

In order to gain the most insight from the profiling tools, you need to modify the Makefile to use an OpenMP compiler. This chapter will use the PGI (Portland Group Inc.) compiler, and corresponding PGProf profiler. As is shown in Fig. 9, the important compiler switches that you should use to assist with tuning are: -Minfo=all,ccff. Adding the ccff switch instructs the compiler to use the Common Compiler Feedback Format to store extra information in the executable about:

- Which code optimizations were implemented
- Which code optimizations could not be implemented (and why)
- How data is accessed
- Relationships between procedures

```
CC := pgcc
DEFINES := FP32
INCLUDES := -I.
OBJ := o
EXE := out
APP := 3Dwave_omp_dynamic

NX := 944
NY := 944
NZ := 944
NSTEPS := 500

UNAME := $(shell uname -a)
ifeq ($(findstring CYGWIN_NT, $(UNAME)), CYGWIN_NT)
    DEFINES := WIN32
    OBJ := obj
    EXE := exe
else
endif

CCFLAGS := -D$(DEFINES) -fast -Minline -Minfo=all,ccff -mp

all: build run verify

build: $(APP).c
        $(CC) $(INCLUDES) $(CCFLAGS) -o $(APP).$(EXE) $(APP).c

run: ./$(APP).$(EXE)
        export OMP_NUM_THREADS=8; ./$(APP).$(EXE) $(NX) $(NY) $(NZ) $(NSTEPS)
        export OMP_NUM_THREADS=4; ./$(APP).$(EXE) $(NX) $(NY) $(NZ) $(NSTEPS)
        export OMP_NUM_THREADS=1; ./$(APP).$(EXE) $(NX) $(NY) $(NZ) $(NSTEPS)

verify:       ../Verify/verify.$(EXE)
        ../Verify/verify.$(EXE) $(NX) $(NSTEPS) wave3d.xline.ref wave3d.xline

clean:
        @echo 'Cleaning up...'
        @rm -rf *.$(EXE) *.$(OBJ) *.dwf *.pdb prof
```

FIG. 9

Makefile for Linux or Windows systems, includes targets to build, run, and verify results for example, code in this chapter.

This information will help you increase performance, since the `pgprof` profiler uses `ccff` to present guided hints during code optimization. Also notice that the `-mp` flag is used to interpret the OpenMP directives. Finally, the Makefile includes a target to build a verification program to ensure proper values are being calculated.

COMPILING THE OpenMP CODE

The Portland Group (PGI) tool-chain includes a Command Shell Tool (PGI Bash) for command-line interaction with Windows or Linux environments. To compile the OpenMP version, type `make build` in the Command Shell to generate output similar to the information shown in Fig. 10. The `-fast` compile flag is used to generate optimal performance for the target platform. The `-Minline` flag allowed the compiler to substitute the body of `StartTimer` and `GetTimer` functions inline, and thus avoid function call overhead. Notice that the compiler reports that four parallel loops were activated using OpenMP static block schedule, and that three loops were not optimized using vector instructions due to data dependencies.

```
$ pgcc -I. -DFP32 -fast -Minline -Minfo=all,ccff -mp -o 3Dwave_omp_dynamic.out
3Dwave_omp_dynamic.c
main:
     59, Generated 2 alternate versions of the loop
     94, StartTimer inlined, size=2, file 3Dwave_omp_dynamic.c (32)
    104, Parallel region activated
    108, Parallel loop activated with static block schedule
    110, Generated 2 alternate versions of the loop
    118, Barrier
    119, Loop not vectorized: data dependency
    128, Loop not vectorized: data dependency
    137, Loop not vectorized: data dependency
    147, Parallel loop activated with static block schedule
    149, Generated 2 alternate versions of the loop
    169, Barrier
    170, Parallel loop activated with static block schedule
    172, Generated 2 alternate versions of the loop
    180, Barrier
    181, Parallel loop activated with static block schedule
    183, Generated vector sse code for the loop
    191, Barrier
    193, Parallel region terminated
    204, GetTimer inlined, size=10, file 3Dwave_omp_dynamic.c (51)
```

FIG. 10

Compiler output for OpenMP version using the PGI C-compiler on Linux-based system.

RUNNING THE OpenMP CODE

By typing `make run` in the Command Shell, you can measure the scalability improvements using 1, 4, and 8 OpenMP threads. Example run-times for the entire application, that were collected from a system with a single Intel Haswell-based CPU socket using a 3D grid-size that is $944 \times 944 \times 944$, and 500 time steps is reported in Table 1.

Table 1 Scalability Results Using OpenMP (on 8-Core, Intel CPU Socket, E5-2698 v3, 2.30 GHz)

Grid: 944×944×944 Time Steps: 500	Time (s)	Speedup	Efficiency (%)
OMP threads = 1	1835.32	1.00×	100.00
OMP threads = 4	671.23	2.73×	68.36
OMP threads = 8	436.37	4.21×	52.63

USING OpenACC TOOLS

Now that you measured the baseline host performance, you can use the OpenACC tools to target GPU-based accelerators. You will need access to a system that has an NVIDIA GPU, and PGI compilers installed. For this chapter example, a single NVIDIA™ Tesla® M40 24 GB GPU Accelerator (with 24 GB of GDDR5 GPU DRAM, and 3072 Maxwell GM200 CUDA® cores across 24 Multiprocessors) was added to the Haswell-based system. Since the original code was analyzed for parallel execution using OpenMP threads, you can confidently assert that the OpenACC directives are also parallel targets for corresponding loops.

ADDING OpenACC PARALLEL DIRECTIVES

There are two types of OpenACC parallel directives used at this stage:

- `#pragma acc kernels`
- `#pragma acc loop`

By inserting the `kernels` directive, you express your desire to parallelize any loops within the region, and place the burden of analysis on the compiler. In conjunction with the `kernels` directive, you add the `loop` directive before loops that you deem look interesting, and should be further analyzed by the compiler. Fig. 11 shows a portion of the C code using both the `kernels` and `loop` directives.

The additional clauses used in the `#pragma acc loop` directive are: `independent`, `collapse(N)`, `gang`, and `vector`. The `independent` clause informs the compiler that each iteration of the loop is independent (you have performed analysis on the code yourself, and are certain that there will be no race conditions or overwriting array locations). The `collapse(N)` clause will instruct the compiler to turn the next N loops into one flattened loop. This typically helps improve GPU occupancy. The `gang` and `vector` clauses allow you to provide hints to the compiler that specify how the parallel resources are scheduled. Multiple gangs work independently from each other, and are scheduled using a round-robin technique. This allows gangs to share resources such as multiprocessors, cache, etc. from a single GPU. Gangs have one or more workers, and each worker performs operations on a set of vector threads. Vector threads work in lock-step with same instruction operating on multiple data elements

```
...
        #pragma omp parallel private(i,j,k)
        #pragma acc kernels
        {
            // predictor
            #pragma omp for schedule(static)
            #pragma acc loop independent collapse(2) gang
            for (i=0; i<nx; i++) {
                for (j=0; j<ny; j++) {
                    #pragma acc loop independent vector
                    for (k=0; k<nz; k++) {
                        int offset = OFFSET(i, j, k, ny, nz);
                        fp[offset] = f[offset] + dt*g[offset];
                    }
                }
            }
            // static boundaries
            #pragma acc loop independent collapse(2)
            for (j=0; j<ny; j++) {
                for (k=0; k<nz; k++) {
                    int xbeg = OFFSET(0,    j, k, ny, nz);
                    int xend = OFFSET(nx-1, j, k, ny, nz);
                    gp[xbeg] = g[xbeg];
                    gp[xend] = g[xend];
                }
            }
...
```

FIG. 11

Adding OpenACC parallel directives.

at the same time. This is also known as single instruction multiple data (SIMD) or single instruction multiple threads (SIMT) style of computing.

COMPILING WITH OpenACC PARALLEL DIRECTIVES

To target an NVIDIA Tesla GPU, modify the Makefile by adding `-acc -ta=tesla` to the compile flags as shown in Fig. 12. You can also specify additional compile options for specific targets. For example, you can experiment with the fastmath

```
UNAME := $(shell uname -a)
ifeq ($(findstring CYGWIN_NT, $(UNAME)), CYGWIN_NT)
    CCFLAGS := -fast -Minline -Minfo=all -acc ta=tesla:fastmath
else
    CCFLAGS := -fast -Minline -Minfo=all -acc -ta=tesla:fastmath,managed
endif
```

FIG. 12

Add compiler flags to target Tesla GPUs.

compile option. This will generate code that takes advantage of hardware accelerated math routines, with emphasis on performance over accuracy, so take extra care to verify the results are correct while using this option.

UNDERSTANDING UNIFIED MEMORY

Wherever possible, you should take advantage of automation capabilities that improve programmer productivity. Such is the case with Unified Memory, which is one of the more dramatic programming model improvements for the Tesla platform. With Unified Memory, demand paging support was added so that memory allocated from a single managed pool can be automatically migrated between the host and GPU. The PGI tool-chain integrated Unified Memory support into the OpenACC environment. Under the right conditions, you can rely on the underlying system to ensure that the data is migrated to the right memory at the right time, without specifying any OpenACC data directives.

TAKING ADVANTAGE OF UNIFIED MEMORY

To take advantage of this convenient Unified Memory feature, you use a PGI-based compiler, and add the `managed` compiler option as shown in Fig. 12. This `managed` option exploits Unified Memory support with NVIDIA GPUs on Linux 64-bit systems, and requires that the program use data allocated from the heap. Since the heap is used after the first code transformation of this chapter, you can safely compile the code. The detailed report from the compiler, shown in Fig. 13, provides important

```
   . . .
  107, Generating copy(f[:])
       Generating copyout(fp[:])
       Generating copy(g[:])
       Generating copyout(gp[:])
  115, Accelerator kernel generated
       Generating Tesla code
   112, #pragma acc loop gang, vector(4) collapse(2)/*blockIdx.x threadIdx.y*/
   113,    /* blockIdx.x threadIdx.y collapsed */
   115, #pragma acc loop vector(32) /* threadIdx.x */
  124, Loop is parallelizable
  125, Loop is parallelizable
       Accelerator kernel generated
       Generating Tesla code
   124, #pragma acc loop gang, vector(128) collapse(2)/*blockIdx.x threadIdx.x*/
   125,    /* blockIdx.x threadIdx.x collapsed */

   . . .

  206, Generating update self(x[:nz*(ny*nx)])
```

FIG. 13

Compiler messages report that kernel has been automatically created.

information about how data is copied between the host and device. At this stage, there is no need for you to add OpenACC data clauses such as `copy` or `copyout` to migrate data, since the underlying system will perform this function automatically. Notice that the data clause `update self` is added automatically since the x array must be copied from device to host for results verification.

RUNNING WITH MANAGED MEMORY

The PGI-based managed memory feature is only supported on 64-bit Linux-based systems, and requires NVIDIA GPUs. The results shown in Table 2 were measured from a Haswell-based system that was augmented with a single Tesla M40 24 GB GPU Accelerator (with 24 GB GDDR5 memory, and 3072 Maxwell GM200 CUDA cores across 24 Multiprocessors), running the 64-bit version of CentOS v7.2.

Table 2 Performance Comparison, Adding OpenACC With Managed Memory on Tesla M40 GPU

Grid: 944 × 944 × 944 Time steps: 500	Time (s)	Speedup	Efficiency (%)
OMP threads = 1	1835.32	1.00×	100.00
OMP threads = 4	671.23	2.73×	68.36
OMP threads = 8	436.37	4.21×	52.63
OpenACC Tesla M40 managed memory	224.33	8.18× vs. HSW 1-core 1.94× vs. HSW 8-core	

PROFILING MANAGED MEMORY WITH VISUAL PROFILER

To help you visualize how the underlying system automatically migrates data, you can use the visual profiler by typing `pgprof` in the Command Shell. This will start the GUI-based profiler (assuming you have properly setup your remote display if accessing a remote system). Once the visual profiler has started, select the *New Session* menu item from the *File* menu. From the Executable Properties dialog box, shown in Fig. 14, make sure the following check boxes are selected:

- *Enable Unified Memory profiling*
- *Enable OpenACC profiling*

After you select the *Finish* button from Executable Properties dialog box, the visual profiler will collect application performance metrics, and generate a timeline display similar to that shown in Fig. 15.

From the timeline display, notice that the Unified Memory operations are performed in the following order:

1. Allocate memory on the host and GPU.
2. Transfer data from the device to host (DtoH row in Fig. 15).

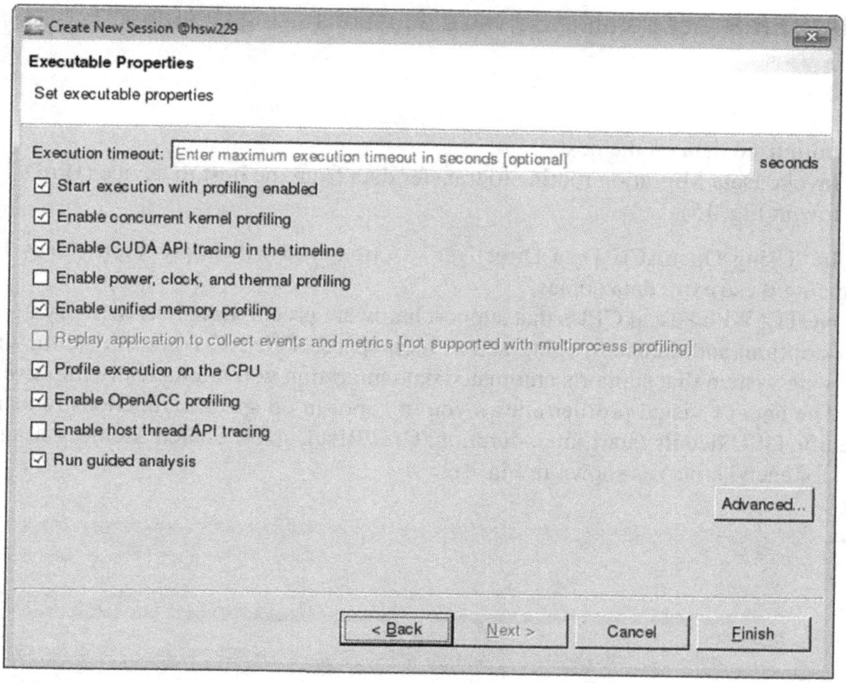

FIG. 14

Interactive session profiling allows you to display Unified Memory profiling information.

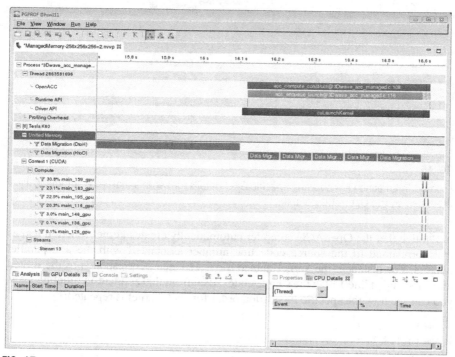

FIG. 15

Timeline view from the `pgprof` visual profiler showing Unified Memory data migration.

3. Initialized data on the host.
4. Invoke Data Migration routine to transfer data from the host to device (HtoD row in Fig. 15).

In "Using OpenACC Data Directives" section, you will improve efficiency by reducing these extra data copies.

NOTE: With Pascal GPUs that support hardware preemption, host memory over-subscription, and demand paging across high-speed NVLINK connections, the underlying system that supports automated data migration will dramatically improve.

The `pgprof` visual profiler allows you to zoom-in on specific functions to learn specific GPU details (start time, duration, Grid/Block sizes, Shared Memory usage, etc. for each kernel) as shown in Fig. 16.

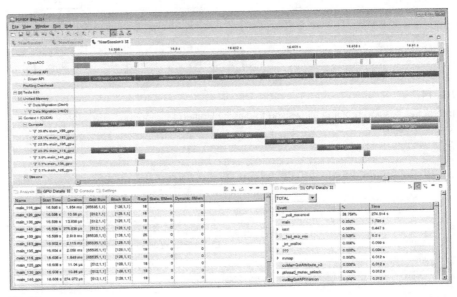

FIG. 16

Zoomed-in timeline view showing specific GPU details for kernels that were automatically generated by the OpenACC compiler.

Notice that the OpenACC compiler automatically creates kernel function names that correspond to the source code line number associated with the `acc parallel` pragma. For instance, the kernel named `main_159_gpu`, corresponds to the nested loops located at line 159 in the source code. Also, from this zoomed-in timeline view, you can see how the specific invocation order for each kernel is repeated:

1. `main_116_gpu`
2. `main_159_gpu`
3. `main_183_gpu`
4. `main_195_gpu`

It appears that enough time is spent in each kernel computing results for the inner data regions, that you could overlap boundary computation/communication using the OpenACC `async` directive. This will be left as an exercise for the reader.

USING OpenACC DATA DIRECTIVES

At this stage, you have

- Inserted OpenACC parallel pragmas adjacent to OpenMP directives
- Used Unified Memory *via* the PGI compiler `managed` option to automatically migrate data
- Used the `pgprof` visual profiler to identify redundant data copies

The next step is to use the detailed compiler reports that specify how data is copied with Unified Memory, to guide your precise insertion of OpenACC data directives. The data directives listed in Fig. 17 show you how to explicitly express data motion for this example code. The mesh data (x, y, and z arrays initialized on the host), and input field data (f, and g arrays initialized on the host) are annotated with

```
. . .

#pragma acc enter data copyin(x[0:nx*ny*nz], y[0:nx*ny*nz], z[0:nx*ny*nz])
#pragma acc enter data copyin(f[0:nx*ny*nz], g[0:nx*ny*nz])
#pragma acc enter data create(fp[0:nx*ny*nz], gp[0:nx*ny*nz])
{
    for (n=0; n<nsteps; n++) {

        step = step + dt;

        if (((n+1)%printevery)==0)
            printf("step = %9.6f \n",step);

        #pragma omp parallel private(i,j,k)
        #pragma acc kernels
        {

            // predictor
            #pragma omp for schedule(static)
            #pragma acc loop independent collapse(2) gang
            for (i=0; i<nx; i++) {
                for (j=0; j<ny; j++) {
                    #pragma acc loop independent vector
                    for (k=0; k<nz; k++) {
                        int offset = OFFSET(i, j, k, ny, nz);
                        fp[offset] = f[offset] + dt * g[offset];
                    }
                }
            }

. . .
```

FIG. 17

OpenACC data directives provide explicit control of data motion to avoid redundant copies.

the `copyin` data directive which will copy data once from host to the device before any kernels are invoked. The propagator fields (`fp`, and `gp`) are annotated with the `create` data directive which will avoid extra copies by creating and accessing the data on the device.

COMPILING USING OpenACC DATA DIRECTIVES

After you have inserted the OpenACC data directives, remember to remove the `managed` compiler option from the Makefile before building the executable. The key compiler options you should use for Tesla GPU target architectures are: `-ta=tesla:pinned,fastmath`. The `pinned` compiler option is used to allocate non-pageable host memory for maximum transfer performance between host and device. Fig. 18 shows a portion of the detailed report from the PGI compiler, specifying how data is migrated, and how kernels are generated.

```
 . . .

 98, Generating enter data copyin(f[:nz*(ny*nx)],g[:nz*(ny*nx)])
 98, Generating enter data copyin(x[:nz*(ny*nx)],y[:nz*(ny*nx)],z[:nz*(ny*nx)])
 99, Generating enter data create(fp[:nz*(ny*nx)],gp[:nz*(ny*nx)])
117, Accelerator restriction: size of the GPU copy of fp,g is unknown
     Generating copyin(f[:])
     Generating copyout(fp[:])
     Generating copyin(g[:])
     Accelerator kernel generated
     Generating Tesla code
 114, #pragma acc loop gang, vector(4) collapse(2) /*blockIdx.x threadIdx.y*/
 115,    /* blockIdx.x threadIdx.y collapsed */
 117, #pragma acc loop vector(32) /* threadIdx.x */
126, Loop is parallelizable
127, Accelerator restriction: size of the GPU copy of g,gp is unknown
     Generating copyin(g[:])
     Generating copyout(gp[:])
     Accelerator kernel generated
     Generating Tesla code
 126, #pragma acc loop gang, vector(128) collapse(2)/*blockIdx.x threadIdx.x*/
 127,    /* blockIdx.x threadIdx.x collapsed */

 . . .
```

FIG. 18

Detailed report from PGI compiler using OpenACC data directives.

PROFILING WITH OpenACC DATA DIRECTIVES

Now that you have inserted the OpenACC data directives, you can use the `pgprof` visual profiler to examine data migration patterns, as shown in Fig. 19. If you compare Fig. 19 against Fig. 15 (shown in "Profiling Managed Memory with Visual Profiler" section), you will notice that the redundant data migrations have been removed.

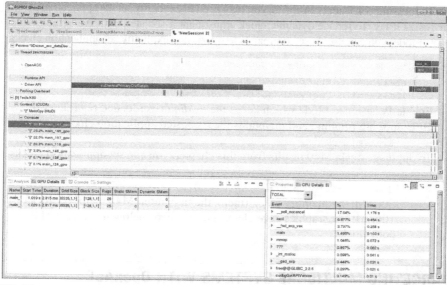

FIG. 19

Visual profiler timeline using OpenACC data directives.

RUNNING WITH OpenACC DATA DIRECTIVES

Once the GPU target is built using OpenACC data directives, you should be able to duplicate the performance results listed in Table 3 (collected from a Haswell-based system complemented by a Tesla M40 with 24 GBs of GPU memory). Notice that the best performance was measured using OpenACC data directives (greater than 2× speedup compared to single Haswell CPU socket with 8-cores). Also note that the performance using managed memory was on-par with data directives for this test case. This shows that under the right conditions, you might be able to measure good performance uplift by just inserting OpenACC parallel directives, and avoiding OpenACC data directives.

Table 3 Performance Comparison, Adding OpenACC Data Directives on Tesla M40 GPU

Grid: 944 × 944 × 944 Time Steps: 500	Time (s)	Speedup	Efficiency (%)
OMP threads = 1	1835.32	1.00×	100.00
OMP threads = 4	671.23	2.73×	68.36
OMP threads = 8	436.37	4.21×	52.63
OpenACC Tesla M40 managed memory	224.33	8.18× vs. HSW 1-core 1.94× vs. HSW 8-core	
OpenACC Tesla M40 data directives	214.92	8.54× vs. HSW 1-core 2.03× vs. HSW 8-core	

To measure consistent run-times, you may need to explicitly set the application clocks on Tesla GPUs. To reduce dynamic clock adjustment associated with the default Auto-boost mode, you can use these commands to query, and explicitly set application clocks:

- `nvidia-smi --help-query-supported-clocks`
  - `nvidia-smi --query-supported-clocks=mem --format=csv`
  - `nvidia-smi --query-supported-clocks=gr --format=csv`
- Enable Persistence Mode which keeps the *nvidia* driver loaded regardless if GPU apps are running, and maintains the requested application clocks
  - `nvidia-smi -pm 1`
- To duplicate Tesla M40 results from this chapter, you can set application clocks using:
  - `nvidia-smi -ac 3004,1063`
    - 3004 MHz = memory clock (mem, the maximum M40 memory clock)
    - 1063 MHz = graphics core clock (gr, two steps below maximum M40 core clock)

TARGETING MULTICORE SYSTEMS WITH OpenACC

By using a single set of OpenACC compiler directives, you can write clean, portable code, and have the compiler generate binaries that will work on multicore host systems, in addition to GPU accelerators. With OpenACC directives, you present the desire to parallelize regions to the compiler. The OpenACC compiler handles the details to automatically create kernels, migrate data, and make decisions about resource scheduling for the specific accelerator architecture.

COMPILING FOR OpenACC MULTICORE

To target multicore systems, you specify the `-ta=multicore -tp=haswell` compiler option for the PGI compiler, as shown in the Makefile listing in Fig. 20.

```
...
UNAME := $(shell uname -a)
ifeq ($(findstring CYGWIN_NT, $(UNAME)), CYGWIN_NT)
    CCFLAGS := -fast -Minline -Minfo=all -acc ta=multicore -tp=haswell
else
    CCFLAGS := -fast -Minline -Minfo=all -acc -ta=multicore -tp=haswell
Endif

...
```

FIG. 20

Use OpenACC directives and compiler to generate code for Intel Haswell multicore systems.

Fig. 21 shows output from compiler using multicore options using only a single set of OpenACC directives (no OpenMP directives).

```
. . .
     114, Loop is parallelizable
          Generating Multicore code
          114, #pragma acc loop gang
     115, Loop is parallelizable
     117, Accelerator restriction: size of the GPU copy of f,fp,g is unknown
          Generated 2 alternate versions of the loop
     126, Loop is parallelizable
          Generating Multicore code
          126, #pragma acc loop gang
     127, Accelerator restriction: size of the GPU copy of g,gp is unknown
     136, Loop is parallelizable
          Generating Multicore code
          136, #pragma acc loop gang
     137, Accelerator restriction: size of the GPU copy of g,gp is unknown
     146, Loop is parallelizable
          Generating Multicore code
          146, #pragma acc loop gang
     147, Accelerator restriction: size of the GPU copy of g,gp is unknown
     157, Loop is parallelizable
          Generating Multicore code
          157, #pragma acc loop gang
     158, Loop is parallelizable
     160, Accelerator restriction: size of the GPU copy of fp,g,gp is unknown
          Generated 2 alternate versions of the loop
     181, Loop is parallelizable
          Generating Multicore code
          181, #pragma acc loop gang
     182, Loop is parallelizable
     184, Accelerator restriction: size of the GPU copy of f,fp,g,gp is unknown
          Generated 2 alternate versions of the loop
     193, Loop is parallelizable
          Generating Multicore code
          193, #pragma acc loop gang
. . .
```

FIG. 21

Detailed compiler report using OpenACC directives, and compiler options to target multicore systems.

RUNNING WITH OpenACC ON MULTICORE SYSTEMS

The final performance comparison is shown in Table 4, where the OpenACC-based multicore binary was measured on an Intel Haswell system with dual CPU sockets. For a fair comparison to OpenMP, the number of CPU cores were restricted to eight cores, using the Linux-based `numactl` utility. You can use the `numactl --hardware` command to query the system and list available NUMA (nonuniform memory access) nodes.

```
numactl --hardware
```

To bind a process to specific cores from a specific NUMA node (e.g., NUMA node 0, and cores 0–7) you can use:

```
numactl --cpunodebind=0 --physbindcpu=0,1,2,3,4,5,6,7 <program>
<arguments>
```

Table 4 Performance Comparison, Adding OpenACC Data Directives, and Targeting Haswell Multicore System

Grid: 944 × 944 × 944 Time Steps: 500	Time (s)	Speedup	Efficiency (%)
OMP threads = 1	1835.32	1.00×	100.00
OMP threads = 4	671.23	2.73×	68.36
OMP threads = 8	436.37	4.21×	52.63
OpenACC Tesla M40 managed memory	224.33	8.18× vs. HSW 1-core 1.94× vs. HSW 8-core	
OpenACC Tesla M40 data directives	214.92	8.54× vs. HSW 1-core 2.03× vs. HSW 8-core	
OpenACC multicore using 8-core Haswell	371.74	4.93× vs. HSW 1-core	61.71

SUMMARY

In this chapter, you learned how to accelerate a 3D finite difference code by using a profile-driven approach. You converted directives from OpenMP to OpenACC, and with enhanced dependency analysis tools identified critical path optimization targets. A key transformation from stack-based allocation to heap-based allocation allowed you to take advantage of Unified Memory, and use the underlying system to automatically migrate data between host and GPU. You used detailed compiler reports to guide precise insertion of OpenACC data directives. This last transformation allowed you to take advantage of OpenACC portability by specifying GPU and multicore targets. A simple set of directives combined with powerful OpenACC tool-chain delivered a nice performance uplift for this example code.

REFERENCES

Harris, M. (2016). *CUDA 8 features revealed*. April, https://devblogs.nvidia.com/parallelforall/cuda-8-features-revealed/.

Riffe, M. (2016). *3D wave equation and plane waves/3D differential operators*. April, http://www.physics.usu.edu/riffe/3750/Lecture%2018.pdf.

Tobias, M. (2016). *A brief introduction to OpenMP*. April, https://www.mir.wustl.edu/Research/Research-Support-Facilities/Center-for-High-Performance-Computing-CHPC/For-Researchers/A-very-Brief-Introduction-to-OpenMP/.

The detailed development of an OpenACC application

10

Andy Herdman, Wayne Gaudin, Oliver Perks

AWE plc, Reading, United Kingdom

This chapter describes the step-by-step approach, along with the incremental performance gains and issues inhibiting performance, of applying the OpenACC directive model to the CloverLeaf mini-app, resulting in a fully resident, multiGPU version of the application. Although this chapter primarily discusses development using the Cray compiling environment and a Cray XK6 hardware platform, the authors believe the concepts and step-by-step approach can be applied to anyone wishing to utilize OpenACC as a mechanism to accelerate their current serial, MPI, OpenMP or hybrid MPI + OpenMP application.

At the end of the chapter, the reader will have a basic understanding of:

- A range of optimizations based on how each compute kernel is utilizing the GPU's threads
  - The creation of a robust, optimal fully resident OpenACC code
  - Extension of the code to use multiple GPUs by developing a hybrid MPI/OpenACC implementation
- Analyzing why the GPU code ran faster than a single CPU core, but showed detrimental performance compared to an entire CPU socket
- How to examine a code to eliminate inner loop dependencies, re-factor nested loops, and eliminate serial execution, unnecessary memory allocations, and hidden data transfers
- The use of asynchronous data transfers

INTRODUCING CloverLeaf
HYDRODYNAMICS SCHEME

CloverLeaf, co-authored by AWE and University of Warwick, is part of the R&D 100 award winning Mantevo test suite, is an explicit Eulerian hydro mini-app that solves the compressible Euler equations, a series of equations describing the conservation of energy, mass, and momentum in a system. The equations are solved

Parallel Programming with OpenACC. http://dx.doi.org/10.1016/B978-0-12-410397-9.00010-X

on a Cartesian grid in two dimensions. Each grid cell stores three quantities: energy, density and pressure, and each cell corner, or node, stores a velocity vector. CloverLeaf solves the equations with second-order accuracy, using an explicit finite-volume method.

Each cycle of the application consists of two steps: (i) a Lagrangian step advances the solution in time using a predictor-corrector scheme, distorting the cells as they move with the fluid flow; and (ii) an advection step is used to restore the cells to their original positions.

The advection routine calculates updates based on the direction of the "wind" (the material flow), and performs sweeps in the x and y directions to update quantities in a 1D temporary array, corresponding to one row/column of cells. Using a larger, temporary, 2D array allows all cells in the mesh to be updated in parallel.

The computational intensive sections of CloverLeaf are implemented via twelve individual kernels. In this instance, we use *kernel* to refer to a self-contained function which carries out one specific aspect of the overall hydrodynamics algorithm.

CloverLeaf is written with the purpose of assessing emerging hardware and programming models. The simple hydrodynamics scheme is written in such a way as to cause unnecessary dependencies in key computational sections. All scientific computation is carried out in small kernel functions, making long complex loops containing many subroutine calls unnecessary.

The initial implementation of CloverLeaf was in Fortran 90 and was used to develop an optimized and highly vectorizable, hybrid Message Passing Interface (MPI)/OpenMP code. This version was ported to an OpenACC implementation using Cray's Compiling Environment (CCE) compiler, on an NVIDIA™ accelerated Cray XK6. This initial OpenACC version was then used as the basis of an implementation that would compile and perform under the Portland Group, Inc. (PGI) and CAPS Enterprise OpenACC compilers. This ultimately led to the two OpenACC implementations presented here, the "parallel" and "kernel" versions.

CloverLeaf's C, MPI/OpenMP hybrid, OpenCL, CUDA, Intel's Heterogeneous Offload model and OpenMP 4.0 implementations are utilized, hardware permitting, to compare each of the OpenACC variants. Copies of all of CloverLeaf's implementations are available for download, and can be found under the download section of the Mantevo Suite.

TEST CASE

A simple yet representative asymmetric test problem is used throughout the study. The problem consists of two regions of idealized gas; one of high density and energy, adjacent to that of a lower density and energy region. As the simulation proceeds a shock wave forms and penetrates the low density region.

Initially a simulation time is created of 0.5 µs, on a problem size of 0.25 million (500^2 cells). This gave a relatively quick turnaround time, yet it was still long enough to see compute as the main work load. With refinements and improvements in the code, larger cell counts for the same simulation are used to maximize the size able to fit onto a Central Processing Unit (CPU) core and subsequently a node. These are detailed at the relevant points throughout the chapter.

DEVELOPMENT PLATFORM: Cray XK6

Chilean Pine is a Cray XK6 with 40 Advanced Micro Devices (AMD), 16-core Opteron 6272 Interlagos processors. Each compute node has one of these Opteron 6272 CPUs plus a companion NVIDIA™ X2090 Graphics Processing Unit (GPU). Each node has 32 GB of 1600 MHz Double Data Rate (DDR3) memory, supplying the CPUs. The XK6 utilizes the "Cray Gemini Network" (Gemini) as the interconnect. The Opteron 6272 CPU shares resources at the "Bulldozer module" level. That is the two cores that make up a "module" both have access to the shared Floating Point Unit (FPU). This FPU has two 128-pipelines which can be combined into one 265-bit pipeline housing a single 256 Advanced Vector Extension (AVX) instruction. This still only provides four double precision Floating-Point Operations Per Second (FLOPs)/clock cycle. However, AMD does have a 256-bit fused multiply add instruction that can theoretically double the floating point performance to 8 FLOPs/clock cycle. The Opteron in Chilean Pine has a 2.1 1 GHz clock frequency equating to a total CPU peak performance of 10.75 teraflop/s (TFLOPs). The default Fortran and C compilers are the CCE version 8.0.7 (although for this study, a beta release is used from Cray of CCE, 8.1.0.157) with the MPI of choice being MPICH2 via Cray's xt-mpich2 version 5.5.1.

DEVELOPMENT OF OpenACC CLOVERLEAF

This section describes the step-by-step approach, along with the incremental performance gains and issues inhibiting performance, of applying the OpenACC directive model to the CloverLeaf mini-app, resulting in a fully resident multiGPU version of the application.

CloverLeaf contains both C and Fortran implementations of the computationally intense code sections. The Fortran versions form the basis of this study and are targeted first; the C implementations are subsequently produced after the development of the fully optimal Fortran code. This is for two reasons: firstly the majority of applications developed within AWE are Fortran based, hence an insight as to the issues and process required to take Fortran source code and accelerate on a GPU architecture is of highest interest from an industry view point. Secondly, at the time of development Cray focused on the Fortran implementation of OpenACC in their CCE programming environment; hence, the Fortran offered a more mature toolset with greater support than their C implementation.

The implementation of the OpenACC directives is helped in that the CloverLeaf code has implemented an already developed OpenMP-based shared memory parallelization scheme. This immediately identified those areas requiring the application of OpenACC directives to achieve acceleration. However, as becomes apparent, this does not imply that simply adding or replacing OpenMP directives with OpenACC gives a suitably accelerated code. Ultimately, the number of accelerated kernels and applied OpenACC directives to produce an efficient accelerated version is summarized as follows:

- 14 Unique kernels
- 25 ACC data constructs
- 121 ACC parallel + loop regions
- 4 Reduction loops
- 12 ASYNC
- 4 Update host
- 4 Update device

The following sections detail the progressive approach applied to the code to produce the efficient accelerated OpenACC version. The first step is to identify those subroutines, or kernels, that are computationally intensive, or *hot spots.*

HOT SPOTS

Using a simple profiler, Table 1 shows a flat, single CPU core profile for CloverLeaf. These six computationally intense subroutines, or kernels, account for almost 95% of the codes execution time. On this basis, these kernels are targeted for initial acceleration.

Table 1 CloverLeaf CPU Profile

Subroutine	% Runtime
advec mom	41.79
advec cell	20.54
PdV	12.72
calc dt	9.06
Accelerate	5.32
Viscosity	5.24

ACCELERATION OF INDIVIDUAL KERNELS

The six kernels identified are taken individually and OpenACC directives were applied to each kernel. This is done by taking the existing OpenMP version of those kernels as a starting point. The advantage being that the OpenMP version necessitated the scoping of the kernels variables which is also required for OpenACC implementation.

As a first step the *acc data* and *acc parallel loop*, in-conjunction with the matching end directives, are required to accelerate a particular computation loop within each kernel.

Fig. 1 schematically shows this applied to representative pseudo code. However, this implicitly copies all of the data to the device for execution, and subsequently copies all the data back to the host on kernel completion. This can be rectified by adding clauses to the OpenACC directives which describe data dependencies between the CPU and GPU. With these clauses added, the code is executed with one kernel running in its accelerated mode at a time. This process is repeated for each of the six kernels.

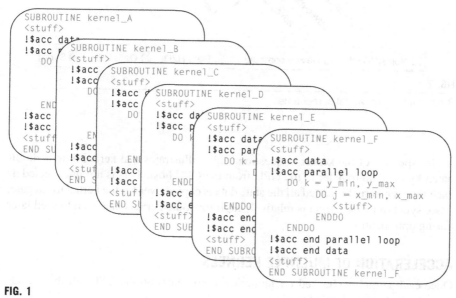

FIG. 1

Pseudo code: individual kernels accelerated.

Fig. 2 shows the breakdown of the individual kernels into "*Non-ACCed*" (code exclusively running on the CPU), "*Device Compute*" (pure execution time on the GPU), "*Data H2D*" (time taken to transfer data from the host to the device), "*Data D2H*" (data transfer time from device to host) and "*Sync*" (synchronization time on the device, that is time spent on the device not including compute, such as allocations and waiting).

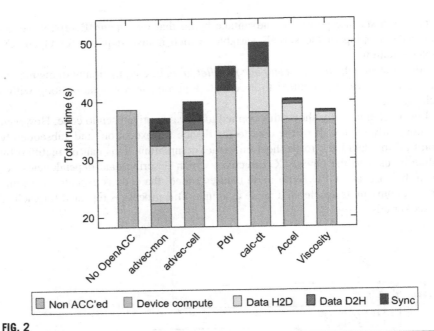

FIG. 2

Breakdown of individual kernel times.

Irrespective of the kernel in question, Fig. 2 illustrates that kernel time is dominated by the data transfer to the GPU from the CPU host. This is not unexpected as each time the kernel is called all the state data is copied over for the kernel to execute. Also, synchronization time is relatively high for some kernels and is addressed later during optimization.

ACCELERATION OF MULTIPLE KERNELS

Once each kernel is checked for numerical correctness on the GPU, all the kernels are executed in accelerated mode.

Fig. 3 shows the comparison between the original, nonaccelerated, version of the code and that with all six computationally "hot" kernels accelerated, broken down into the respective categories of *Non-ACCed, Device Compute, Data H2D, Data D2H*, and *Sync*.

Although now less than 5% of the code is executed on the CPU, the overall execution time is significantly greater than that of the nonaccelerated original. Even more apparent is the effect of the data transfers. On every time step each kernel is copying data (multiple times in the case of some kernels) to the device ready for computation. This data transfer can be reduced to a minimum by making the entire application resident on the GPU.

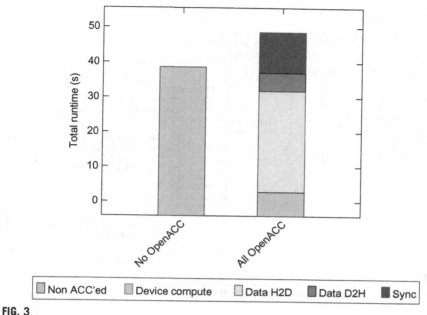

FIG. 3

Breakdown of multiple kernel times.

ACHIEVING FULL RESIDENCY ON THE GPU

The pseudo code in Fig. 4 shows how to use the OpenACC *copyin* and *copyout* data transfer directives in the *main* entry point of the CloverLeaf program to move data to and from the accelerator. Subsequent use of the OpenACC *present* clause on the *data* construct in each kernel indicates that data is already on the device and no copy is required before using the data on the device.

In addition to restricting the data transfer to an initial copy, in order to enable full code residency additional kernels to the original six kernels need to be placed on the GPU. These additional kernels are not computationally intensive kernels, but without placement on the GPU implicit data transfers occur to and from the host for each invocation of these sections of code.

With the exception of the initial set-up routine, a total of 14 unique kernels (including the previously identified six kernels) are required to be accelerated on the GPU. Fig. 5 shows the impact of accelerating these additional kernels and applying an additional one off data transfer.

With the all kernels now executing on the GPU there is virtually no computation remaining to be carried out by the CPU (compare against Fig. 2). This is observed in the visible increase in device compute. The most marked difference is that the data transfer overhead is dramatically reduced by implementation of the initial transfer. As this data is a "one off" event, it is reasonable to hypothesize that if the problem size was large enough, or computation long enough, the data transfer overhead would be a relatively small percentage of the overall execution time.

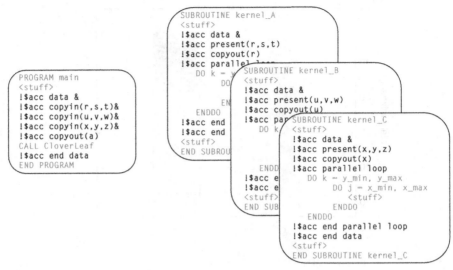

FIG. 4

Pseudo code: achieving residency with OpenACC.

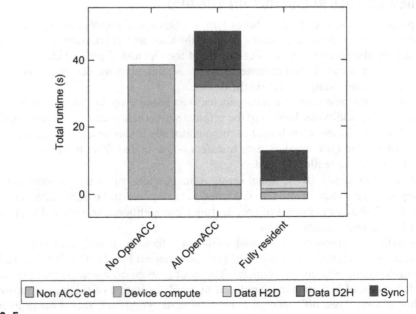

FIG. 5

Breakdown of resident kernel times.

INCREASING THE PROBLEM SIZE

The modest 500^2 problem size realizes a gain of 3.01 when executed on the GPU over the equivalent CPU. Fig. 6 shows this along with problems sizes of 960^2, 2040^2, and 4096^2 where the relative performance gains over the CPU are 4.91, 5.82, and 5.76, respectively. As expected, as the problem size increases the percentage of runtime is reduced for the data transfer. Indeed, for the 4096^2 problem the data transfer accounts for only 5.07%, compared to 18.24% for the 500^2.

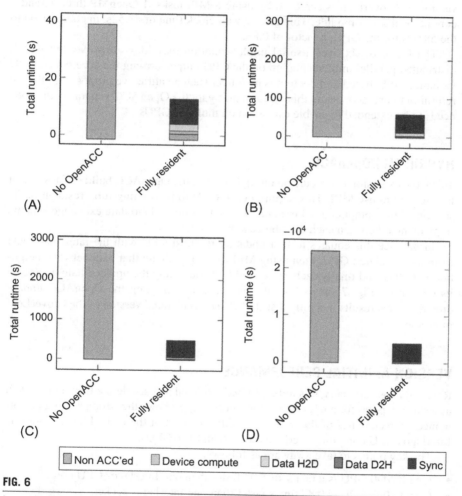

FIG. 6

Increase in problem size: (A) 500, (B) 960, (C) 2048, and (D) 4096.

For a sufficiently large enough problem, the GPU performance is approaching 6× of the performance of the nonaccelerated serial code on the Opteron CPU.

COMPARISON OF HYBRID MPI/OpenMP

At face value, a factor of six improvement in the accelerated code over the original nonaccelerated code sounds like a significant gain. However, this is comparing the performance of the entire X2090 GPU against that of a single Opteron core. A more realistic comparison is to compare against the performance achievable by using all the cores on the Opteron socket.

At the time of the study, the optimal performance using the hybrid MPI/OpenMP version of CloverLeaf is achieved by using 8 MPI tasks, 1 OpenMP threads, and 1 core per Bulldozer module. This gives a wall clock time of 43.52s, in comparison to the 58.03s for the GPU; a factor of 0.88.

The factor of six over a serial implementation may look attractive, but with a distributed parallel implementation on the CPU outperforming the accelerated GPU variant, a GPU-based architecture is no longer such an attractive proposition. Before returning to and addressing this performance gap, the OpenACC version of the code needs to be extended to enable execution on multiple GPUs.

HYBRID MPI/OpenACC

To enable extension to execute on multiple GPUs, the OpenACC build of CloverLeaf is extended to use MPI. This required each GPU to be running fully resident on its section of the computational domain, with a traditional halo data exchange scheme implemented between each distributed subdomain.

In practice this equates to first updating the host CPU with the latest halo data from its associated GPU, then using MPI to communicate that data between neighboring CPUs, and finally each associated GPU obtaining the updated halo data from its CPU host. Fig. 7 shows how this is implemented using the OpenACC *update* directive. This results in a fully distributed and accelerated version of the CloverLeaf mini-app.

VERSION A: INITIAL PERFORMANCE

Referred to as version A, this initial, fully distributed and accelerated version is taken as a starting point for analyzing performance. Fig. 8 shows the strong scaling performance characteristics of the initial multiGPU version of the code. Plots are for one Interlagos CPU core, one Interlagos socket, and 1–6 GPUs.

The key points to take away are as follows:

- One X2090 GPU is a factor of 5.97 faster than one Interlagos CPU core.
- One X2090 GPU is 0.88 times faster than one Interlagos socket.
- MultiGPU scaling turns over after utilizing 6 GPUs.

To see if these initial findings can be improved on, understanding these performance figures is crucial.

```
SUBROUTINE exchange
!$acc data &
!$acc present(snd_buffer)
!$acc parallel loop
   DO k = y_min_dpth, y_max_dpth
      DO j = 1, dpth
         <pack snd_buffer>
      ENDDO
   ENDDO
!$acc end parallel loop
!$acc update host (snd_buffer)
!$acc end data
CALL MPI_IRECV(rcv_buffer)
CALL MPI_ISEND(snd_buffer)
CALL MPI_WAITALL
!$acc data &
!$acc present(rcv_buffer)
!$acc update device(rcv_buffer)
!$acc parallel loop
   DO k = y_min_dpth, y_max_dpth
      DO j = 1, dpth
         <unpack rcv_buffer>
      ENDDO
   ENDDO
!$acc end parallel loop
!$acc end data
END SUBROUTINE exchange
```

FIG. 7

Pseudo code: hybrid MPI/OpenACC.

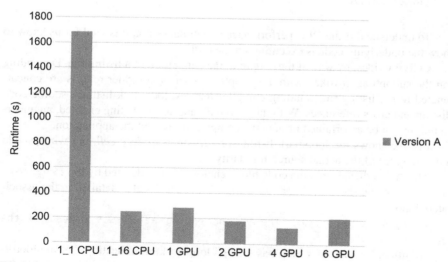

FIG. 8

Version A initial performance of multiCPU and GPU.

VERSION B: INNER LOOP DEPENDENCIES

On the XK6, Cray's analysis tool suite, Perftools measures GPU performance including that of a flat profile. Fig. 9 shows a flat profile for version A that indicates *advec cell* and *advec mom* are the two routines that dominated runtime. This is not entirely unexpected; indeed, running the code exclusively on the CPU results in a not dissimilar profile.

```
Time% |    Time |  Calls | Function

100.0% | 83.010479 | 415631.0 |Total
| --------------------------------------------------------------------
| 100.0% | 83.010473 | 415629.0 |USER
|| --------------------------------------------------------------------
|| 33.6% | 27.873962 |  2000.0 | advec_cell_kernelACC_SYNC_WAIT@li.238
|| 24.1% | 19.985739 |  4000.0 | advec_mom_kernel_.ACC_SYNC_WAIT@li.216
|| 15.5% | 12.873780 |  1000.0 | timestep.ACC_SYNC_WAIT@li.51
||  5.2% |  4.329525 |  4000.0 | advec_mom_kernel_.ACC_COPY@li.216
||  2.9% |  2.443764 |  1000.0 | accelerate_kernel_.ACC_SYNC_WAIT@li.101
||  2.6% |  2.166314 |  2000.0 | advec_cell_kernel_.ACC_COPY@li.238
||  2.4% |  1.970592 |  4000.0 | advec_mom_kernel_.ACC_COPY@li.68
||  1.5% |  1.278792 |  1000.0 | pdv_kernel_.ACC_SYNC_WAIT@li.133
||  1.2% |  1.034328 |  2000.0 | pdv_kernel_.ACC_SYNC_WAIT@li.137
||  1.2% |  0.987142 |  2000.0 | advec_cell_kernel_.ACC_COPY@li.58
||  1.2% |  0.976646 |  4000.0 | timestep_.ACC_COPY@li.51
```

FIG. 9

Flat profile version A.

To understand if the GPU performance is optimal or not, it is vital for us know to how the underlying code is executing on the GPU.

CCE provides, by way of the -r option, the generation of a listing file. Depending on the suboptions invoked with the -r option, a set of compiler reports are concatenated to the listing file detailing compiler listings, loopmark listings, source code listing and cross references. With the loopmark and source listing enabled, an understanding can be ascertained of how the compiler translated the application.

Fig. 10 shows the loopmark listing for version A's *advec cell*, but with pseudo code in place of the actual source for clarity.

The "G" indicates that the code block enclosed is accelerated by the !$acc parallel loop and the !$acc end parallel loop. This is also detailed in the associated dialog:

A region starting at line 93 and ending at 99 was placed on the accelerator

Additionally, the outer loop has the "g" loopmarking indicating that the loop is distributed across the thread blocks and subsequently the threads within those blocks. The associated dialog spells this out:

```
G-----<  !$acc parallel loop
G g---<   DO k = y_min, y_max
G g 3-<      DO j = x_min, x_max
G g 3-<         <stuff>
G g 3-<      ENDDO
G g---<   ENDDO
G-----<  !$acc end parallel loop
```

```
G - Accelerated  g - partitioned
```

Ftn-6405 ftn: ACCEL File=advec_cell.f90, Line=93
A region starting at line 93 and ending at line 99 was placed on
the accelerator

Ftn-6430 ftn:ACCEL File=advec_cell.f90, Line=94
A loop starting at line 94 was partitioned across the threadblocks
and the 128 threads within a threadblock

Ftn-6411 ftn: ACCEL File advec_cell.f90, Line=95
A loop starting at line 95 will be serially executed

FIG. 10

Compiler listing *advec cell* version A.

`A loop starting at line 94 was partitioned across the threadblocks and the 128 threads within a threadblock`

Both of these statements and loopmarkings are the desired result, indicating that each thread is working on its own instance of loop counter k.

However, on inspection of the inner loop the loopmarking specifies a numerical value (in this case "3"), along with the optimization message: "`A loop starting at line 95 will be serially executed.`" This indicates that j is split among the threads, and all the threads are iterating the same j at the same time—not the intended result. The dependencies need to be addressed, or at least the dependencies the compiler perceives, in the code.

In the case of *advec cell* for each iteration of the inner loop, a value is calculated for pre- and postmass, energy and volume. These updated values are then used in the same loop. This dependency is easily rectified by splitting the loop into two separate loops. One to calculate the values and a second to use these updated values.

Once implemented an updated listing file (Fig. 11) shows that the inner loop is now being correctly partitioned across the threads. The re-profile in Fig. 12 shows *advec cell* dropping from over-27s to under-12s.

This modified version of the code, version B, is compared to version A in Fig. 13.

```
G-----<  !$acc parallel loop
G g---<   DO k = y_min, y_max
G g g-<      DO j = x_min, x_max
G g g-<         <stuff>
G g g-<      ENDDO
G g---<   ENDDO
G-----<  !$acc end parallel loop
```

```
G - Accelerated  g - partitioned
```

Ftn-6405 ftn: ACCEL File=advec_cell.f90 , Line=93
A region starting at line 93 and ending at line 99 was placed on
the accelerator

Ftn-6430 ftn:ACCEL File=advec_cell.f90, Line=94
A loop starting at line 94 was partitioned across the threadblocks

Ftn-6430 ftn:ACCEL File=advec_cell.f90, Line=95
A loop starting at line 95 was partitioned across the 128 threads
within a threadblock

FIG. 11

Compiler listing *advec cell* version B.

```
Time% |   Time   | Calls  | Function
100.0% | 66.375613 | 415631.0 |Total
| -----------------------------------------------------------------
| 100.0% | 66.375607 | 415629.0 |USER
|| ----------------------------------------------------------------
|| 29.2% | 19.370430 |  4000.0 |advec_mom_kernel.ACC_SYNC_WAIT@li.216
|| 19.3% | 12.785822 |  1000.0 |timestep.ACC_SYNC_WAIT@li.51
|| 17.9% | 11.913056 |  2000.0 |advec_cell_kernel_.ACC_SYNC_WAIT@li.240
||  6.5% |  4.327830 |  4000.0 |advec_mom_kernel_.ACC_COPY@li.216
||  3.7% |  2.444010 |  1000.0 |accelerate_kernel.ACC_SYNC_WAIT@li.101
||  3.3% |  2.165092 |  2000.0 |advec_cell_kernel.ACC_COPY@li.240
||  3.0% |  1.970679 |  4000.0 |advec_mom_kernel_.ACC_COPY@li.68
||  1.9% |  1.278686 |  1000.0 |pdv_kernel_.ACC_SYNC_WAIT@li.133
||  1.6% |  1.033906 |  2000.0 |pdv_kernel_.ACC_SYNC_WAIT@li.137
||  1.5% |  1.019408 |  4000.0 |timestep_.ACC_COPY@li.51
||  1.5% |  0.986405 |  2000.0 |advec_cell_kernel_.ACC_COPY@li.58
```

FIG. 12

Flat profile version B.

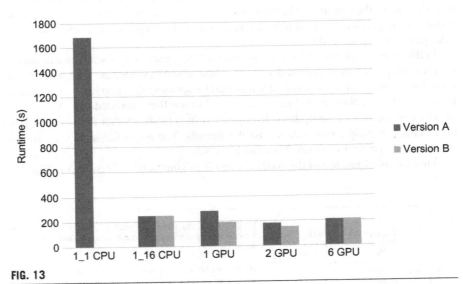

FIG. 13

Version B performance comparison.

VERSION C: NESTED LOOPS AND GLOBAL VARIABLES

Fig. 12 illustrates that *advec mom* is now dominating the runtime. Evaluating the loopmarking in the listing file shows that loops are not being accelerated containing multiple levels of nesting.

By splitting the nested loops, only one loop is not being partitioned as desired for acceleration. In the case of this nonpartitioned loop, it can be forced to be scheduled across all the threads by addition of the OpenACC vector clause to the `!$acc loop` construct.

Fig. 14 illustrates the original nested loop structure alongside its re-factored accelerated pseudo code. The re-factored code the *advec mom* kernel time drops from 19s to 8s as highlighted in Fig. 15's re-profile. Fig. 15 also shows that the *timestep* routine is now dominating the runtime. Consulting the associated listing file for *timestep* reveals that the kernel is only executing on a single GPU thread.

```
                                    !$acc parallel loop
                                    DO k = y_min, y_max
                                      DO j = x_min, x_max
                                        <flux stuff>
                                      ENDDO
                                    ENDDO
                                    !$acc end parallel loop
                                    !$acc parallel loop
                                    DO k = y_min, y_max
                                      DO j = x_min, x_max
                                        <mass stuff>
                                      ENDDO
                                    ENDDO
                                    !$acc end parallel loop
                                    !$acc parallel loop
                                    DO k = y_min, y_max
 !$acc parallel loop                !$acc loop vector
 DO k = y_min, y_max                  DO j = x_min, x_max
   DO j = x_min, x_max                  <vel stuff>
     <flux stuff>                     ENDDO
   ENDDO                            ENDDO
   DO j = x_min, x_max              !$acc end parallel loop
     <mass stuff>
   ENDDO
   DO j = x_min, x_max
     <vel stuff>
   ENDDO
 ENDDO
 !$acc end parallel loop

     (A)                               (B)
```

FIG. 14

Nested and re-factored pseudo code for *advec mom*: (A) version B and (B) version C.

The cause is traced to the use of global variables. As all threads have the potential to write to these global variables, the compiler is taking a conservative approach and only allowing the scheduling of the kernel on a single thread. The global variables in question are used in the *timestep* kernel to return the (i,j,k) coordinate of the sell which contains the minimum timestep values for the iteration. This functionally can be retained without the need of global variables by use of the Fortran intrinsic MINLOC.

Constituting version C, the flat profile (Fig. 16) shows the *timestep* kernel's execution time is reduced from 13s to less than 1s.

```
Time% |   Time  | Calls | Function
100.0% | 48.804249 | 447631.0 |Total
| ----------------------------------------------------------------
| 100.0% | 48.804243 | 447629.0 |USER
|| ----------------------------------------------------------------
|| 26.4% | 12.874175 |  1000.0 |timestep.ACC_SYNC_WAIT@li.51
|| 16.6% |  8.094541 |  4000.0 |advec_mom_kernel.ACC_SYNC_WAIT@li.247
||  9.8% |  4.794964 |  2000.0 |advec_cell_kernel_.ACC_SYNC_WAIT@li.236
||  8.9% |  4.328033 |  4000.0 |advec_mom_kernel_.ACC_COPY@li.247
||  5.0% |  2.442117 |  1000.0 |accelerate_kernel.ACC_SYNC_WAIT@li.101
||  4.4% |  2.164464 |  2000.0 |advec_cell_kernel_.ACC_COPY@li.236
||  4.0% |  1.969379 |  4000.0 |advec_mom_kernel$_.ACC_COPY@li.68
||  2.6% |  1.278651 |  1000.0 |pdv_kernel$_.ACC_SYNC_WAIT@li.133
||  2.1% |  1.034398 |  2000.0 |pdv_kernel$_.ACC_SYNC_WAIT@li.137
||  2.0% |  0.985912 |  2000.0 |advec_cell_kernel$_.ACC_COPY@li.58
||  2.0% |  0.972801    4000.0 |timestep$_.ACC_COPY@li.51
```

FIG. 15

Flat profile with re-factored *advec mom.*

```
Time% |   Time  | Calls | Function
100.0% | 48.804249 | 447631.0 |Total
| ----------------------------------------------------------------
| 100.0% | 48.804243 | 447629.0 |USER
|| ----------------------------------------------------------------
|| 26.4% | 12.874175 |  1000.0 |timestep.ACC_SYNC_WAIT@li.51
|| 16.6% |  8.094541 |  4000.0 |advec_mom_kernel.ACC_SYNC_WAIT@li.247
||  9.8% |  4.794964 |  2000.0 |advec_cell_kernel_.ACC_SYNC_WAIT@li.236
||  8.9% |  4.328033 |  4000.0 |advec_mom_kernel_.ACC_COPY@li.247
||  5.0% |  2.442117 |  1000.0 |accelerate_kernel.ACC_SYNC_WAIT@li.101
||  4.4% |  2.164464 |  2000.0 |advec_cell_kernel_.ACC_COPY@li.236
||  4.0% |  1.969379 |  4000.0 |advec_mom_kernel$_.ACC_COPY@li.68
||  2.6% |  1.278651 |  1000.0 |pdv_kernel$_.ACC_SYNC_WAIT@li.133
||  2.1% |  1.034398 |  2000.0 |pdv_kernel$_.ACC_SYNC_WAIT@li.137
||  2.0% |  0.985912 |  2000.0 |advec_cell_kernel$_.ACC_COPY@li.58
||  2.0% |  0.972801    4000.0 |timestep$_.ACC_COPY@li.51
```

FIG. 16

Flat profile version C.

Fig. 17 adds plots the calculation using version C of the code that includes the re-factored nested loops and the removal of the global variables. In comparison to version B significant gains are now observed on comparative executions using a single GPU. However, the performance gain is still turning over once 6 GPUs are being utilized.

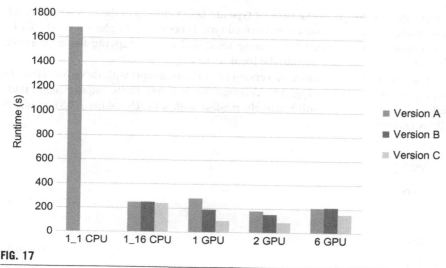

FIG. 17

Version C performance comparison.

VERSION D: MULTIGPUs, REDUCING HIDDEN TRANSFERS

To understand why the scaling on the accelerator is limited to a few GPUs, attention is needed on determining the bottlenecks of the multiGPU execution. The first area of interest is the data transfers between the host CPU and GPU. Depending on the variable in question, different depths of halo exchange cells are required for spatial domain decomposition. By default, the MPI distributed code sets the halo cell depth consistently for all variables. That default depth matches the maximum depth required for the worst case variable. As MPI communication overhead is a stepping function rather than a linear progression, the overhead in communication of one or two extra layers of data is negligible, if at all. However, any halo exchange data when running on distributed GPUs first needs to be transferred from the GPU to the host memory prior to CPU to CPU MPI communication, and the receiving CPU needs to transfer the new data from host memory to the GPU.

As previously detailed, PCIe data transfers to and from the GPU are a major bottleneck, so any reduction in data transfers should prove beneficial. With this in mind the code is modified to only exchange data genuinely required. Assisting in this was the CRAY ACC DEBUG environment variable documented from version 8.1.0.165 of CCE. The variable has three informational setting levels. Each level providing increasing amounts of information relating to what and how much data is transferred to and from the GPU.

Enabling the CRAY ACC DEBUG environment variable shows unexpected data transfers in the *accelerate* kernel not associated to the halo exchange data. Although a relatively small in size (2376 bytes), the output shows that a Fortran derived type is being transferred and allocated on the GPU. On further investigation, the scalar components of that particular derived type are being utilized in the *accelerate* kernel, and an implicit copy of the entire derived type is occurring to place it on the GPU. The implicit copy stopped by creating local scalars and copying the appropriate fields from the derived type into the local scalars.

The resultant performance of version D of the mini-app with these two changes implemented is shown in Fig. 18. Although this is a significant improvement, multiple GPU scalability is still relatively modest with 4 GPUs taking 63.57s while 6 GPUs take 67.01s.

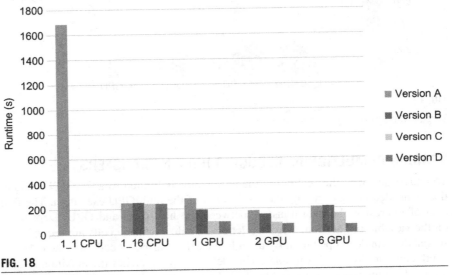

FIG. 18

Version D performance comparison.

VERSION E: "ACC SYNC WAITS"

A profile of version D is shown in Fig. 19. What is now dominating are a number of routines all with the overhead of ACC SYNC WAIT. On further investigation, what all of these routines have in common is that they allocate data on the GPU.

By preallocating temporary arrays at the same high level of the calling tree as described in the "Achieving Full Residency on the GPU" section and carrying out an initial data copy to the device, device memory is re-used multiple times by passing the relevant arrays through subroutine arguments. This removes the need to check if the data is present, and negates the need to create it on the device via an allocation.

Fig. 20 shows pseudo code for both the original allocation method and the preallocation implementation. A new code profile of version E (that with the preallocations implemented) is displayed in Fig. 21. This shows the implementation of the preallocation removed the ACC SYNC WAIT overhead.

```
Time% |   Time  | Calls | Function
100.0% | 37.151994 | 447631.0 |Total
|-------------------------------------------------
| 100.0% | 37.151988 |  447629.0 |USER
||------------------------------------------------
|| 21.8% | 8.103629 |  4000.0 |advec_mom_kernel_.ACC_SYNC_WAIT@li.247
|| 12.9% | 4.797456 |  2000.0 |advec_cell_kernel_.ACC_SYNC_WAIT@li.236
|| 11.6% | 4.322071 |  4000.0 |advec_mom_kernel_.ACC_COPY@li.247
||  6.6% | 2.447886 |  1000.0 |accelerate_kernel_.ACC_SYNC_WAIT@li.101
||  5.8% | 2.160784 |  2000.0 |advec_cell_kernel_.ACC_COPY@li.236
||  5.3% | 1.965759 |  4000.0 |advec_mom_kernel_.ACC_COPY@li.68
||  3.4% | 1.278799 |  1000.0 |pdv_kernel_.ACC_SYNC_WAIT@li.133
||  3.4% | 1.261867 |  1000.0 |timestep_.ACC_SYNC_WAIT@li.51
||  2.8% | 1.034047 |  2000.0 |pdv_kernel_.ACC_SYNC_WAIT@li.137
||  2.7% | 0.985090 |  2000.0 |advec_cell_kernel_.ACC_COPY@li.58
||  2.6% | 0.976743 |  4000.0 |timestep_.ACC_COPY@li.51
```

FIG. 19

Version D: ACC SYNC WAIT dominated profile.

```
SUBROUTINE advec_mom(a,b)
REAL ALLOCATABLE(:,:):: node_flux

ALLOCATE( node_flux(xmin:ymax))

!$acc data present_or_create(node_flux)
!$acc parallel loop
DO k = y_min, y_max
  DO j = x_min, x_max
     <flux stuff>
  ENDDO
ENDDO
!$acc end parallel loop
!$acc end data
DEALLOCATE( node_flux )
END SUBROUTINE
```

```
SUBROUTINE advec_mom(a,node_flux,b)
REAL DIMENSION(xmin,ymax)::node_flux

!$acc data present(node_flux)
!$acc parallel loop
DO k = y_min, y_max
  DO j = x_min, x_max
     <flux stuff>
  ENDDO
ENDDO
!$acc end parallel loop
!$acc end data
END SUBROUTINE
```

(A)   (B)

FIG. 20

Pseudo code for pre- and post-pre-allocations: (A) version D and (B) version E.

```
Time% |   Time  | Calls  | Function
100.0% | 26.698295 |  437621.0 |Total
|-------------------------------------------------
| 100.0% | 26.698290 |  437619.0 |USER
||------------------------------------------------
|| 17.8% | 4.749553 |  1000.0 |pdv_kernel_.ACC_SYNC_WAIT@li.132
||  8.6% | 2.297537 |  2001.0 |update_halo_kernel_.ACC_KERNEL@li.451
||  4.7% | 1.258818 |  1000.0 |timestep_.ACC_SYNC_WAIT@li.51
||  4.6% | 1.234257 |  2001.0 |update_halo_kernel_.ACC_KERNEL@li.442
||  3.6% | 0.970250 |  4000.0 |timestep_.ACC_COPY@li.51
```

FIG. 21

Flat profile version E.

Adding version E runtimes to the plot of previous versions (Fig. 22) shows a significantly improved accelerated version of the code. Indeed, version E gives a 67% improvements in total turnaround time over that of the initial version A on a single GPU.

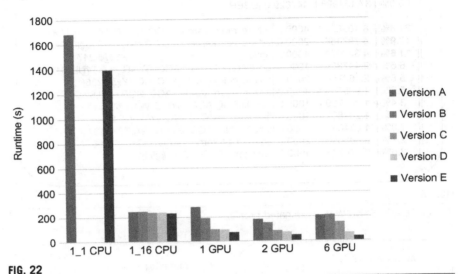

FIG. 22

Version E performance comparison.

Recall version A's initial performance:

- One X2090 GPU is a factor of 5.97 faster than one Interlagos CPU core
- One X2090 GPU is 0.88 times faster than one Interlagos socket
- MultiGPU scaling turns over once 6 GPU are utilized

These same metrics for version E are now:

- One X2090 GPU is a factor of 19.34 faster than one Interlagos CPU core
- One X2090 GPU is 4.91 times faster than one Interlagos socket
- MultiGPU scaling is still scaling with utilization of 6 GPUs

With a TDP of 115W for the Opteron and 225W for the X2090, this implies a performance increase of over 2.5 for the X2090 for the same power footprint.

IMPACT OF GPU OPTIMIZATIONS ON CPU

An interesting and relevant aside is to look at the relative performance of version A and version E when running exclusively on the CPU. Recall, all optimizations carried out between these two versions are aimed at improving/fixing issues detrimental to performance on the GPU. Yet, comparing single CPU performance version E gives over a 17% improvement over that of version A.

This is greater emphasized when the derived metrics for each version's performance are compared as in Fig. 23. Although version A is realizing a respectable 652 MFLOPs (Fig. 23A), version E (Fig. 23B) increases to over 1 GFLOP. This increase comes from an increase in L1 cache utilization (up a factor of 2.3) that is now averaging 4.164 uses per operand.

```
Total
-------------------------------------------------------------------------
Time%                                                 100.0%
Time                                               52.054641 secs
Imb. Time                                                 -- secs
Imb. Time%                                                --
Calcs                               107.656 /sec      5604.0 calls
PAPI_L1_DCM                         72.452M/sec   3771487818 misses
PAPI_TLB_DM                          63.664 /sec        3314 misses
PAPI_L1_DCA                       1043.884M/sec  54339011642 refs
PAPI_FP_OPS                        652.655M/sec  33973718491 ops
Average Time per Call                               0.009289 secs
CrayPat Overhead : Time               0.0%
User time (approx)                  52.055 secs  109315113219 cycles 100.0% Time
HW FP Ops / User time              652.655M/sec  33973718491 ops   3.9%peak(DP)
HW FP Ops / WCT                    652.655M/sec
Computational intensity               0.31 ops/cycle       0.63 ops/ref
MFLOPS (aggregate)                  652.65M/sec
TLB utilization                16396804.96 refs/miss     32025 avg uses
D1 cache hit,miss ratios             93.1% hits           6.9% misses
D1 cache utilization (misses)        14.41 refs/miss      1.801 avg hits
```

(A)

```
Total
-------------------------------------------------------------------------
Time%                                                 100.0%
Time                                               31.776925 secs
Imb. Time                                                 -- secs
Imb. Time%                                                --
Calcs                               220.725 /sec      7014.0 calls
PAPI_L1_DCM                         32.501M/sec   1032780862 misses
PAPI_TLB_DM                          73.386 /sec        2332 misses
PAPI_L1_DCA                       1082.638M/sec  34403038765 refs
PAPI_FP_OPS                       1032.789M/sec  32819004724 ops
Average Time per Call                               0.004530 secs
CrayPat Overhead : Time               0.1%
User time (approx)                  31.777 secs   66732042821 cycles 100.0% Time
HW FP Ops / User time             1032.789M/sec  32819004724 ops   6.1%peak(DP)
HW FP Ops / WCT                   1032.789M/sec
Computational intensity               0.49 ops/cycle       0.95 ops/ref
MFLOPS (aggregate)                 1032.79M/sec
TLB utilization                14752589.52 refs/miss     28814 avg uses
D1 cache hit,miss ratios             97.0% hits           3.0% misses
D1 cache utilization (misses)        33.31 refs/miss      4.164 avg hits
```

(B)

FIG. 23

Derived metrics: (A) version A and (B) version E.

MULTIGPU SCALABILITY

Increasing the problem size from 960^2 to 3840^2 enables a better case to consider strong scaling performance of the code.

Results for scaling this larger case on the GPU are presented in Fig. 24. Utilizing all 32 GPUs on Chilean Pine, parallel efficiency dips just under 50% with a speed up of 15.42 over 1 GPU.

Weak scaling figures, for micro-seconds per cell, are presented in Fig. 25.

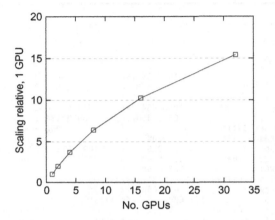

FIG. 24

0.5 μs, 3840^2, strong scaled.

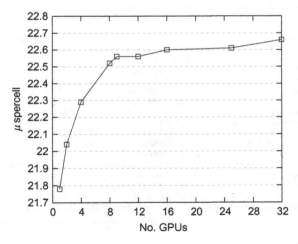

FIG. 25

0.5 μs, 3840^2, weak scaled.

After deploying 9 GPUs and instigating a communication in both dimensional planes, the cost per cell per timestep stays constant while increasing GPUs. At over 96% parallel efficiency, this shows good scaling on the whole of the machine.

CONCLUSION

OpenACC is a directive-based programming model to allow the code developer to identify areas of code to be accelerated on a hosted device. Adding directives to an existing code base is an attractive proposition when compared to re-writing in a new language and realizes some of the benefits from an open, nondisruptive approach. Vendors are developing backends that can still utilize their proposed methodology, yet have the OpenACC standard as a common interface. By investigating the OpenACC programming model, through the hydrodynamic mini-app CloverLeaf, an idea of the steps and understanding needed to accelerate an application has been gained. It has been shown that it is not just the case to "hot spot" an application and apply directives, but that the time has to be taken to understand what is happening on a hardware level in those targeted subroutines and kernels.

The re-factoring of compute kernels to be data parallel is key. As the number of processing elements on accelerated hardware can run into the thousands, it is essential to make sure all kernels are scheduled across all the device threads. In some cases this will be at the expense of additional memory usage to remove dependencies.

Data transfers destroy performance. It has been shown that this can even be true for the smallest most innocuous piece of data, which instigates a much larger implicit data transfer.

Optimizations required for a performant GPU implementation can give rise to significant benefits when applied to a CPU implementation. These optimizations forced the kernels to be data parallel, which not only meant they threaded well on the GPU, but also when running multithreaded via OpenMP on a CPU. Additionally, the re-factoring of the code also allowed the compiler to perform better scale and vector optimizations.

OpenACC ON THE CPU

Throughout the development of the OpenACC version of CloverLeaf the similarities with the OpenMP version have become obvious.

At a core level, both programming models provide a method to annotate the inherent parallelism within the algorithm, once it has been structured in such a way to exploit it.

Historically, CloverLeaf has maintained two codebases for the OpenMP and OpenACC variants, although no fundamental differences exist within the code, the directives used obviously differ.

This structure thus allowed us to have one code base to target the CPU and one to target the GPU.

However, with the more recent versions of the PGI compiler there is now the facility to target the CPU with OpenACC code.

Currently you must build the binaries with a separate target, specifying multicore for targeting the CPU threads. However, this can be done with the same source code as used for the GPU variant, from a maintainability perspective this is significantly beneficial.

OpenACC provides a perfect framework for such variance in targets due to the descriptive nature of the language. Within the OpenACC port of CloverLeaf we make use of the Kernels construct, then marking each loop as "Loop Independent;" this works especially well with nested loops.

The descriptive nature of OpenACC, allowing us to state this but without making any further restriction on how it should be executed is crucial.

We simply state that the loop iterations can be processed in parallel, without having to worry about placement. This means that the compiler is free to make decisions about how to generate threaded code based on this information.

By taking an OpenACC code we implicitly know that there is enough parallelism in the kernel, to make it worth processing on a GPU.

Currently this works on the CPU by taking the outermost independent loop as the parallel loop. In many scenarios this will be the desired behavior; however, without making use of nested parallelism this may not expose sufficient parallelism for the number of CPU threads the code is running on.

There is one inherent difference between the GPU and CPU environment is data movement.

With GPU programming, there are currently two distinct memory spaces, that of the CPU and that of the GPU. OpenACC as a language reflects that, supporting directives for the placement and movement of data.

With the CPU thread support, the code now executes in the same memory space as the host code, thus there is no need to be explicit about the data movement.

For the CloverLeaf mini-app, we were able to simply recompile the codebase with "−ta=multicore" rather than "−ta=tesla" or the desired GPU target.

This compilation took place without any fault and generated a binary which could be run on the CPU threads.

Using the PGI 15.7 compiler, with support for targeting multicore, we were able to compile and run CloverLeaf both as OpenMP and OpenACC builds. We are then able to perform a side by side analysis of the resulting performance.

We then strong scaled the binaries, running flat threads (no MPI) across the whole of a dual socket, 24 core, Intel Xeon (Haswell) node, for both data sets (Figs. 26 and 27).

From the results we can see that for both problem sizes there is negligible performance difference between the two parallelism options. This is very reassuring, as it facilitates the use of a single source codebase to target two very different hardware options, with no loss of performance.

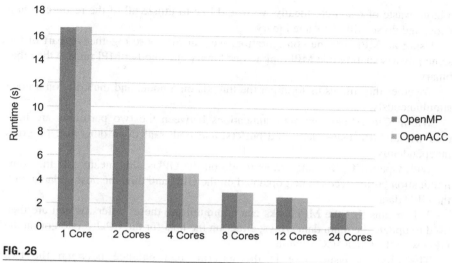

FIG. 26

CloverLeaf 960² OpenMP/OpenACC comparison.

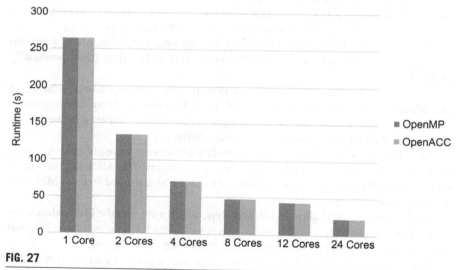

FIG. 27

CloverLeaf 3840² OpenMP/OpenACC comparison.

HETEROGENEOUS COMPUTING

One component that this new capability enables is the compilation of two binaries, from exactly the same source code, one targeting the GPU and one targeting the CPU.

When running OpenACC code on the GPU of a node the CPU is generally idle. As we look towards future fat nodes, such as the OpenPower system, this would be a large waste of resource. Ideally we would like to utilize all of the resources on a node, and do so with the same binary.

Using an MPI runtime configuration, we can run these together as part of the same job, associating one MPI rank to one binary and another MPI rank to the other binary.

Together this allows us to target the threads on a node, and the GPU on a node simultaneously.

Within CloverLeaf, the communications between the two partitions are handled within MPI, using dedicated buffers, and both ranks can otherwise progress independently.

With OpenACC, the data arrays reside on the GPUs, this means that the communication buffer needs to be populated on the GPU and then the host updated with the GPU data.

This means that the MPI ranks can communicate these buffers, which are then used to update the main data arrays, either on the host for the CPU version or on the GPU with the OpenACC version.

The obvious issue here is the natural load balance between the two architectures.

In testing, we have seen around a 4× performance difference between the dual-socket CPU and the GPU version. This would suggest that if we were to utilize all of the resource then we would be looking at around a 20% performance gain.

However, we still need to assign some CPU resource to the OpenACC rank—to drive the GPU. Thus our expected performance gain is less than this—potentially around 10%.

This is in an idealized scenario. Currently the decomposition scheme in CloverLeaf assigns equal work to each MPI rank. However, with our heterogeneous scheme we would actually want a much larger portion of the data set allocated to the GPU, proportional to the relative performance difference.

As a mini-app, CloverLeaf is sufficiently flexible that we were able to implement a new decomposition scheme, driven by input deck parameters. Allowing the user to simply state what fraction of the problem set should be allocated to each MPI rank of the problem.

Whilst unwieldy, this allows us to prototype a hardware specific load balance. As the load balance in CloverLeaf is static, this is sufficient for now; however, it would act as a precursor for a dynamic load balance for more complex codes.

Testing on a Nehalem X5650 (dual hex-core socket) with an attached NVIDIA K20, running the CloverLeaf 3840^2 problem (PGI 15.7, OpenMPI 1.8.1).

CPU time (2 MPI × 6 OpenMP)	64.9 s
GPU time (1 MPI)	19.6 s

Our best heterogeneous version is a configuration of 4 MPI ranks, 1 for GPU and 3 for CPU. Each of the CPU ranks has 3 OpenMP threads associated with it, thus totaling 1 GPU and 9 CPU cores. The best load balance configuration we have found is 82% of the problem assigned to the GPU and then each of the remaining 3 CPU ranks gets 6% of the problem domain.

1 GPU, 3 MPI×3 OpenMP—0.82 0.06 0.06 0.06	17.9 s

This gives an 8.5% speedup over the GPU version. Obviously this speedup is dependent on the performance ratio between the GPU and the CPU, but may be significant.

SUMMARY

Once identified, OpenACC was applied to each kernel on an individual basis, and the breakdown of compute and data transfer to and from the CPU can be assessed on a kernel by kernel basis.

Once all the main compute kernels were accelerated, they were then executed in unison. This then showed the overall performance being achieved form execution on the GPU. However, as each kernel was still transferring data to and from the host, it also highlighted the overhead of the data transfer.

To remove the impact of the data transfers, the code was made fully resident on the GPU device. This removed all but an initial copy to the GPU and a final copy back to the host CPU.

However, to make fully resident, and run exclusively on the GPU, not only did all of the data need to be identified for the initial transfer, but also those parts of the code that were not necessarily computationally intense also needed to be made to execute on the GPU.

Once the entire application was resident and running exclusively on the GPU, the performance was then investigated to determine bottlenecks. Firstly the impact of increasing the problem size was explored, and once a large enough case identified that suitably fed the GPU, the performance was compared against the best CPU performance possible from the most optimal variant of the code (MPI, OpenMP, MPI/OpenMP hybrid) available at the time of study. Based on these comparisons, a range of optimizations were applied by analyzing how each kernel is utilizing the GPU's threads.

Finally, attaining a robust, optimal fully resident OpenACC version of the code, the application was extended to use multiple GPUs by developing a hybrid MPI/OpenACC implementation. This resulted in a performance increase of 5.82× performance gain over a single Interlagos CPU core, but showed detrimental performance compared to an entire CPU socket.

A study was carried out which identified those areas inhibiting performance, as summarized in Table 2.

Once rectified, a single GPU now realizes a factor of 19.34 over a single Interlagos CPU core, and a factor of 4.91 over an entire socket.

Table 2 Summary of Performance Issues

Issue	Remedy
Inner loop dependencies	Split loops into
"Calculating and using"	"Calculating" and "use"
Nested loops not accelerating	Re-factor loops into own entity
Global variables, single thread execution	Remove
Hidden data transfers	Identified and removes/minimized
"ACC SYNC WAITS"	Temporary array allocation and reuse

Increasing the problem size, strong and weak scaling showed almost 50% parallel efficiency for the former, and over 96% for the latter when executed across the entirety of the Chilean Pine XK6 platform.

Additionally, by using the multicore target for the PGI compiler we have demonstrated how the same source can be run using OpenACC at two levels. As one of the main benefits of heterogeneous computing is to target different compute kernels at different hardware, depending on their level of parallelism, or data dependency; this becomes a viable option within a single source codebase.

FOR MORE INFORMATION

The UK-MAC web page (http://uk-mac.github.io) contains a selection of mini-apps, developed as part of collaborations with a number of UK-based institutions.

CloverLeaf (http://uk-mac.github.io/CloverLeaf) was the first of our mini-apps and is part of the larger Mantevo (https://mantevo.org) project which provides a suite of application performance proxies covering a wide range of algorithmic domains. Mantevo was the recipient of an R&D 100 Award (https://mantevo.org/mantevo-suite-1-0-chosen-for-rd-100-award) in 2013.

GPU-accelerated molecular dynamics clustering analysis with OpenACC

11

John E. Stone, Juan R. Perilla, C. Keith Cassidy, Klaus Schulten
University of Illinois at Urbana-Champaign, Urbana, IL, United States

This chapter explores the use of OpenACC directives to accelerate the calculation of a so-called dissimilarity matrix, the most costly computation required for clustering analysis of molecular dynamics simulations.

By the end of this chapter, the reader will have an understanding of:

- Key algorithmic analysis steps that help guide decision making involved in application acceleration and parallelization and help set realistic performance targets for a successful OpenACC implementation on GPUs and other accelerators
- Differences in development and maintenance of directive-based kernels and compiler autovectorization as compared with data-parallel languages such as CUDA and OpenCL, and hand-written kernels based on compiler intrinsics and the like
- The step-by-step approaches taken for adaptation of an existing molecular dynamics trajectory analysis algorithm for OpenACC
- Program and data structure transformations that are beneficial for performance on GPU accelerators and many-core CPUs that employ wide SIMD vector arithmetic units
- Performance tuning techniques that can help OpenACC compilers and runtime systems achieve better performance on target accelerators with typical architecture characteristics

INTRODUCTION

The tremendous performance provided by petascale supercomputers enables scientists to use molecular dynamics (MD) simulations to study in atomic detail the structure and dynamics of large biomolecular complexes, including viruses

Parallel Programming with OpenACC. http://dx.doi.org/10.1016/B978-0-12-410397-9.00011-1

(C. Liu et al., 2016; Perilla, Hadden, Goh, Mayne, & Schulten, 2016; Zhao et al., 2013), the sensory arrays of bacteria (Cassidy et al., 2015), and photosynthetic membranes (Stone et al., 2016), that are otherwise inaccessible to experimental imaging and associated structure determination methods. A decade ago, the required performance of analysis software for MD simulations was just beginning to become a significant consideration for molecular scientists. Today, the long simulation time scales that can be achieved by the combination of state-of-the-art simulation algorithms and leading computing platforms present a formidable challenge for researchers, who must efficiently analyze tens to hundreds of terabytes of trajectory data.

Accelerators such as Graphic Processing Units (GPUs) are a major part of the performance achieved by state-of-the-art supercomputing platforms, so modern simulation and analysis tools have adapted to take advantage of such accelerators for key algorithms. The performance of MD simulation tools is often determined by a few well-known algorithms for computation and time-integration of forces, resulting in only a moderate number of computational kernels that are performance-critical. In contrast, tools for simulation preparation, analysis, and visualization encompass a much larger number of algorithms that are often highly user-customizable to suit the unique needs of a given research project, resulting in a comparatively large number of kernels that need to be optimized to exploit GPUs or other accelerators.

As a representative example, the molecular visualization and analysis tool VMD (Humphrey, Dalke, & Schulten, 1996), developed by the authors, contains roughly half a million lines of code written in C++, and a similar number of lines of code written in high-level scripting languages such as Tcl and Python. The wide range of analysis algorithms that must ultimately support accelerators poses a challenge since it may not be practical to develop and maintain hand-coded accelerator kernels written in high-level single-program multiple-data languages such as CUDA (Nickolls, Buck, Garland, & Skadron, 2008), OpenCL (Stone, Gohara, & Shi, 2010), or ISPC (Pharr & Mark, 2012), nevertheless lower-level hand-coding of Single Instruction Multiple Data (SIMD) vectorized kernels using processor-specific intrinsics such as SSE, AVX, VSX, or similar. In the case of VMD, many existing analysis and visualization algorithms have already been adapted for accelerators (Stone, Hardy, Ufimtsev, & Schulten, 2010; Stone, McGreevy, Isralewitz, & Schulten, 2014; Stone et al., 2016), however many more remain. New algorithms are always being created for accelerators. OpenACC, OpenMP, and other directive-based parallel programming approaches provide an interesting avenue for low-cost adaptation of large portions of existing application codes to heterogeneous computing platforms with GPUs and other accelerators by leveraging the latest advances in compiler technology, parallel runtime systems, and accelerator hardware.

OVERVIEW OF MD CLUSTERING ANALYSIS

MD simulations give rise to a collection of structural snapshots of a molecular system, known as a trajectory, that can be analyzed for interesting patterns (Freddolino,

Harrison, Liu, & Schulten, 2010; Rajan, Freddolino, & Schulten, 2010). Due to the physical principles that govern MD simulations, an ensemble of molecular conformations near a local free-energy minimum is sampled and transitions are commonly observed between nearby low-energy basins (see Fig. 1). Determination of the conformations at the minima of basins is important in the study of protein dynamics and for elucidating the connections between molecular structure and biological function. For instance, during protein folding, multiple intermediate states are observed before reaching the canonical fold. Identification of these intermediates provides important information regarding the misfolding of proteins associated with disorders such as Alzheimer's and mad cow disease (Freddolino et al., 2010). Similarly, in real-space determination of the structure of proteins (Goh et al., 2016), the determination of statistically significant models resulting from a simulation is of utmost importance (Goh et al., 2015).

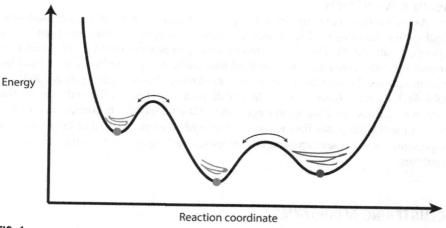

FIG. 1

Schematic of underlying molecular free-energy landscape sampled by an MD simulation. Molecules transition back and forth, as signified by *black arrows*, between local low-energy basins along a reaction coordinate. *Solid circles* denote the representative conformations of each energetic basin.

The structural classification of an MD trajectory using clustering analysis provides a way to systematically determine the conformations associated with separate local free-energy basins. Clustering analysis is an unsupervised machine-learning technique that attempts to meaningfully group data based on the concept of proximity or similarity (Reynolds, Richards, de la Iglesia, & Rayward-Smith, 2006). In the context of MD simulations, molecular conformations are characterized by an array of points in a three-dimensional space, with each point marking the location of an atom in the molecule. Hence, a common method for measuring the dissimilarity between conformations is the root-mean-squared deviation (RMSD) given by

$$\text{RMSD}_{i,j} = \frac{1}{S}\left[\sum_{i}^{S}\left(\bar{x}_i - \bar{x}_j\right)^2\right]^{1/2},$$ (1)

where S is the number of selected atoms in the molecule. Though, RMSD is not a metric in the strict sense (e.g., it does not obey the triangular inequality), it nevertheless succinctly captures the similarity or dissimilarity between structural features of the molecules. In particular, conformations whose structural features are similar yield small RMSD values (<1.5 Å), while dissimilar features are punished severely. Metrics other than RMSD have been proposed to characterize differences between conformations of a molecule. For instance, other commonly used similarity scores involve projections on to principal components (Fraiberg et al., 2015; Han & Schulten, 2014) and their nonlinear variants (Lang, Staudt, Engelhardt, & Hell, 2008; Perilla & Woolf, 2012).

As mentioned above, the immense power of modern petascale supercomputers enables the simulation of large macromolecular complexes over long time scales (Perilla et al., 2015). Thus, it is often necessary to process terabytes of simulation trajectory data, containing hundreds-of-thousands or even millions of molecular conformations. Though the methods for performing clustering analysis are well established, current algorithmic implementations are unable to efficiently handle the massive datasets resulting from large-scale MD simulations. In particular, calculation of the RMSD dissimilarity matrix, as described in more detail in the following, represents an extremely challenging computational aspect of numerous clustering analyses.

CLUSTERING ALGORITHMS

Clustering algorithms principally fall into one of two categories: either hierarchical or partitional, which differ primarily in the way in which clusters are determined (Reynolds et al., 2006). In particular, hierarchical methods organize data into a hierarchical tree of nested clusters using either an agglomerative or divisive scheme (Reynolds et al., 2006). Agglomerative schemes work in a bottom-up fashion, forming larger clusters from smaller ones, while divisive methods use a top-down approach. The decision of whether to merge or divide a given cluster is made according to a so-called linkage criterion that is specified by the user. Partitional methods, on the other hand, organize data into non-overlapping groups. Such methods require the user to specify the number of desired clusters, usually denoted as k. Based on this parameter, an objective function particular to the partitional method in use is iteratively optimized to arrive at a final grouping of k clusters (Reynolds et al., 2006).

Both hierarchical and partitional clustering employ a measure of pairwise proximity or similarity between elements in the input dataset. This information is commonly represented as a similarity (or dissimilarity, or "distance") matrix, in which the ijth-element of the matrix gives the value of the similarity measure between elements i and j in the data. In the case of MD simulations, a trajectory containing S selected atoms and N coordinate frames may be viewed as a $3 \times S \times N$ time-evolving coordinate matrix. Utilizing RMSD to characterize the structural similarity between molecular conformations within a trajectory, an RMSD dissimilarity matrix can be constructed for use in clustering analysis. As depicted in Fig. 2A, the RMSD dissimilarity matrix may be represented as an upper-triangular matrix in which each element $RMSD_{ij}$ gives the pairwise RMSD between structures $\bar{x}_i$ and $\bar{x}_j$. Importantly, during a simulation the molecule of interest diffuses freely, therefore translational degrees of freedom are removed from the resulting trajectories. Similarly, the structures must be aligned in order to remove any rotational degrees of freedom, this alignment is normally accomplished by finding the rotation matrix for which Eq. (1) is minimal (Kabsch, 1976, 1978; P. Liu, Agrafiotis, & Theobald, 2010).

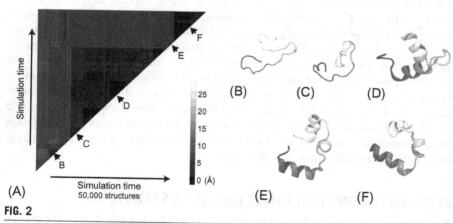

FIG. 2

Computational folding of the villin headpiece protein from an initial random configuration (Freddolino & Schulten, 2009; Rajan et al., 2010). (A) Root-mean-squared deviation (RMSD) matrix between pairwise structures in an MD trajectory. Color-scale ranging from black to white, represents RMSDs between 0 to 25 Å. (B,C) Unfolded structures of the villin headpiece, because of the intrinsic flexibility of unfolded proteins the molecule is able to sample multiple extended states. (D,E) Intermediate states observed during the folding simulations. Structural motifs are present in the form of helices, however, the relative orientation of such helices is different from the canonical fold. (F) Folded structure of the villin headpiece reached after 5 μs of MD simulation (Rajan et al., 2010).

FAST COMPUTATION OF PAIRWISE RMSDs WITH QCP

Widely used approaches for computing RMSDs have typically used one of the well-known structure alignment algorithms to perform pairwise alignment (Kabsch, 1976, 1978), followed by computation of the resulting RMSD using straightforward algorithmic implementations of Eq. (1). This approach is well suited for tasks such as visualization where it is desirable to superimpose the two structures for visual comparison, and for other cases requiring superposition of the two structures for further analyses. However, the determination of the best-fit rotation and subsequent transformation of the atomic coordinates represent unnecessary work in the context of computing the RMSD dissimilarity matrix required for clustering analysis.

Fortunately, there is a higher performance alternative approach based on the use of Theobald's Quaternion Characteristic Polynomial (QCP) method (Theobald, 2005). QCP can be used to compute the minimum RMSD without the need to first determine the optimal rotation and align the pair of structures (Theobald, 2005). It should be noted that QCP is also capable of computing the optimal rotation (P. Liu et al., 2010). The QCP method exploits special properties of the quaternion representation of rotations and of the characteristics polynomial of a 4×4 "key" matrix. To solve for the minimum RMSD, QCP solves for the most positive eigenvalue of the 4×4 key matrix using the Newton-Raphson method to find the largest eigenvalue, which is then used to compute the minimum RMSD. The costliest computation within the QCP algorithm is the calculation of the 4×4 matrix to be solved (Kneller, 2011; P. Liu, Agrafiotis, & Theobald, 2011). Fortunately, with some adaptations we describe in the following, the calculation of the 4×4 matrix is very well suited for fine-grain parallel computing approaches and benefits greatly from the high memory bandwidth of GPUs. The QCP Newton-Raphson solver is well suited for implementation within individual GPU threads or SIMD vector unit lanes. The pseudocode shown in Algorithm 1 summarizes the center of mass determination and translation preprocessing steps and the QCP 4×4 matrix construction loop that we shall target for parallelization with OpenACC directives.

ATOM SELECTIONS AND TRAJECTORY DATA STRUCTURES

A challenge that arises with parallelization of algorithms in any large software application is the need for data to take on a particular layout in memory for most efficient access during computation. Since VMD is heavily used for visualization as well as structure preparation and simulation analysis, its internal data structures are organized to facilitate real-time rendering of large molecular scenes containing hundreds of millions of atoms or other particles. VMD stores atomic coordinate data in an array-of-structures (AOS) format interleaving x, y, and z coordinates, which is the memory organization required by contemporary high-performance graphics APIs such as OpenGL. To achieve the best performance for computation of RMSDs

ALGORITHM 1 QCP CALCULATION OF MINIMUM RMSD FOR A PAIR OF MOLECULAR STRUCTURES

```
 1: for l = 1 to S do {loop over selected atoms in frame A}
 2:    Compute center of mass for trajectory frame A
 3: end for
 4: for l = 1 to S do {loop over selected atoms in frame A}
 5:    Translate atoms so that the center of mass lies at the origin
 6: end for
 7: for l = 1 to S do {loop over selected atoms in frame B}
 8:    Compute center of mass for trajectory frame B
 9: end for
10: for l = 1 to S do {loop over selected atoms in frame B}
11:    Translate atoms so that the center of mass lies at the origin
12: end for
13: for l = 1 to S do {loop over selected atoms in A and B}
14:    Compute ten QCP inner product sums for the Newton-Raphson solver
15: end for
16: QCP Newton-Raphson iteration solves RMSD from inner product sums
17: return RMSD
```

using QCP on SIMD vector units, it is most beneficial to restructure the atomic coordinates in structure-of-arrays (SOA) format, which makes loading and operating on arbitrary-size vectors straightforward.

VMD allows the user to select an arbitrary subset of the atoms in a molecular structure, enabling analysis operations to focus on particular regions of interest. Atom selections used for clustering analysis are typically sparse, often containing only the so-called alpha-carbons that form the backbone of proteins. Alpha-carbons are frequently used to approximate the location of the amino acids in proteins, so they are a natural atom selection to use for clustering analysis. Since molecular modeling tools like VMD typically store molecular structures with atoms ordered according to their chemical structure, alpha-carbons occur within coordinate arrays with an irregular stride with 5–12 atoms between selected alpha-carbons. For the benefit of the performance-intensive loops involved in calculating RMSDs for the dissimilarity matrix, it is best to compact the sparse selection of atomic coordinates into contiguous arrays with unit stride access.

One of the preprocessing steps that must be performed in the QCP algorithm is the translation of each structure so that its center of mass lies at the origin. In cases where this criterion is known to be met, there is no need for further translation. During large-scale dissimilarity matrix calculations, there is a potential for repeated and therefore redundant calculation of center-of-mass and associated translation, since each trajectory frame is involved in up to N QCP RMSD calculations. By performing this step up-front prior to beginning the calculation of the dissimilarity matrix, we can ensure that all structures meet the requirement that their center-of-mass lies at the origin. By migrating these calculations out of QCP and into a preprocessing step, we ensure that no redundant center-of-mass calculations and transformations are performed during the $O(N^2)$ QCP RMSD calculations, and we exploit the performance benefit associated with fusion of the center-of-mass calculation with the atom selection and memory layout optimization operations described in the following.

DISSIMILARITY MATRIX CALCULATION

To streamline the performance of the overall dissimilarity matrix computation, we merged the three preprocessing steps described above so that atom selection compaction, conversion of AOS to SOA memory layout, and calculation of center of mass are all done in a single pass over the molecular structure. The final translation of the center of mass to the origin is done in a second pass by itself, since it cannot be done until the center of mass offset from the origin is known. We also pad the atomic coordinate arrays to an integer multiple of the hardware SIMD vector size to enable the use of a higher performance implementation that requires that all memory loads and stores are vector-aligned. The unified preprocessing approach allows our algorithm to read and write the atomic coordinates only twice prior to the start of the dissimilarity matrix computation.

Although there is a cost associated with optimizing the coordinate data layout in both execution time and memory use, it is $O(N * S)$ with the number of trajectory frames N and the number of selected atoms S. The cost is completely amortized over the large number of trajectory frame accesses during the $O(N^2 * S)$ dissimilarity matrix calculation. The pseudocode shown in Algorithm 2 outlines the key loops and constituent algorithm steps in the overall dissimilarity matrix calculation.

ALGORITHM 2 CALCULATE RMSD DISSIMILARITY MATRIX FOR AN ENTIRE MD TRAJECTORY

```
 1: for i = 1 to N do {loop over trajectory frames}
 2:     Convert sparse atom selection for each frame to compact SOA coordinate array
 3:     Compute center of mass from in-register coordinates values
 4: end for
 5: for i = 1 to N do {loop over trajectory frames}
 6:     Translate each frame so that the center of mass lies at the origin
 7: end for
 8: for j = 1 to N do {loop over trajectory frames}
 9:     for i = 1 to j do {loop over trajectory frames}
10:         for l = 1 to S do {loop over selected atoms}
11:             Sum QCP adjoint matrix components A and E0
12:         end for
13:         Perform Newton-Raphson iteration to solve RMSD from A and E0
14:         RMSDij ⇐ RMSD
15:     end for
16: end for
17: return RMSDij
```

HARDWARE ARCHITECTURE CONSIDERATIONS

State-of-the-art microprocessors, whether CPUs, GPUs, or other accelerators, share a number of macroscopic properties. All major platforms used for High Performance Computing (HPC) consist of processors that contain multiple processor cores and SIMD arithmetic units to provide very high arithmetic throughput that would not be achievable otherwise. This is an area of significant variability among processor designs due to the prevailing classes of workload that were prioritized most highly during their design. Accordingly, programmers must design their algorithms to encompass this hardware variability by exploiting many processor cores, and SIMD vector units of varying width and capability.

Applications must also contend with a significant gap between the performance of arithmetic operations and the performance of memory operations. The commodity CPUs, GPUs, and other accelerators available today all provide arithmetic performance levels that are typically one to two orders of magnitude higher than their achievable memory bandwidth. As an example, the NVIDIA Tesla K20X GPU accelerator used in the Blue Waters (Mendes et al., 2014) and Titan (Joubert et al., 2015) supercomputers provides up to 1.3 TFLOPS double-precision arithmetic throughput, 3.9 TFLOPS single-precision arithmetic throughput, but only up to 250 GB/s memory bandwidth (with ECC disabled). The Tesla K20X arithmetic throughput outpaces its memory bandwidth by roughly a factor of 40 for double-precision, and a factor of 60 for single-precision. In practice real scientific application software contains a lot of integer instructions associated with array indexing and loop control, and there are often opportunities for reuse of values in machine registers. One could reasonably divide those throughput ratios by four or more, but it is clear that even then there is still a very significant gap in the throughput of arithmetic and memory operations.

The main outcome of this observation is that for many scientific codes, particularly those that operate on large data, the primary consideration for performance is often ensuring the optimality of memory operations, with other aspects of algorithm design and performance optimization becoming secondary. In the context of directive-based parallel computing approaches such as OpenMP and OpenACC this typically means that a developer should consider memory locality and memory access performance first and foremost and to leave consideration of arithmetic throughput as something to be optimized only after the throughput of memory operations reaches its peak. In many cases, there are no significant opportunities for increasing performance further after maximizing memory performance. In principle, this is another argument in favor of broader use of directive-based parallel programming systems such as OpenACC; while a compiler may not generate code that runs as fast as purpose-written hand-parallelized code written in lower-level languages such as CUDA, in many cases it is only necessary to achieve performance levels high enough that a kernel's performance becomes memory-bandwidth-bound.

For memory-bandwidth-bound kernels the potential performance gain obtained from the use of OpenACC is limited to the ratio of the memory bandwidth available on the accelerator targeted by OpenACC relative to that of the reference platform.

As an example, the memory bandwidth of the Tesla K20X compares favorably to contemporary x86 CPUs, providing 250 GB/s vs. 64 GB/s or less for a current CPU. Each processor has significantly higher bandwidth for its on-chip caches and registers. For bandwidth-bound algorithms that process large data that is not easily cacheable but for which the working set can fit entirely in on-board GPU DRAM, we can estimate that the Tesla K20X would provide up to a 4× performance improvement vs. the contemporary x86 CPU. In cases where the GPU makes more successful use of its memory system than the CPU does, the speedup would be slightly higher. For datasets that are so large that they cannot be fit entirely in on-board GPU memory, the speedup achieved would very likely be lower, due to overheads incurred in staging and transferring input and output data between the host and the GPU accelerator.

Assuming that the arithmetic throughput of GPUs and other accelerators continues to rise on an exponential curve, and the rate of growth in memory performance remains low as it has been in the past few years, an increasing fraction of software will become memory-bandwidth-bound. This leads to an expectation that over time, more software will become amenable to the use of high-level compiler directives such as OpenACC to achieve required levels of performance.

IMPLEMENTATION

When transforming existing code and adding OpenACC parallelization directives, we have found that as with other parallel programming languages and runtime systems it is desirable to begin the process with a well-written and well-tested reference code, and to incrementally perform code transformations and add compiler directives to achieve effective parallelization while maintaining program correctness. VMD contains extensive built-in Tcl and Python scripting support that make it convenient to extend the program with new features and experimental algorithms that are exposed as new analysis commands. The new analysis commands can then easily be incorporated into scripts for automation of testing, comparison of the performance and results of a new algorithm with an existing one, and so on. The use of parallel scripting interfaces can facilitate testing using large node counts that make short work of large problem sizes that would otherwise take a single workstation an unreasonably long time (Phillips et al., 2014; Stone et al., 2014).

PERFORMANCE EVALUATION TEST CASE

To evaluate the efficacy of our OpenACC implementation, we selected an MD trajectory containing 20,735 atoms per frame, and over 30,000 coordinate frames in total, enabling testing over a range of problem sizes. During initial algorithm development it is convenient to be able to run tests rapidly in an interactive setting where performance impact and correctness of results can be evaluated quickly. For our purposes the choice of a roughly 20,000 atom selection is a representative use case. To obtain a variety of runtimes for convenient testing we simply varied the number of analyzed frames, which impacts runtime significantly due to the quadratic time complexity of the dissimilarity matrix calculation with respect to the number of frames.

MEMORY LAYOUT OPTIMIZATION

Our initial development effort is focused on optimizing the conversion of trajectory frame atomic coordinates between the native AOS memory layout normally used by VMD and an optimized SOA layout. The VMD SOA memory layout interleaves x, y, and z coordinates, with no zero-padding or guarantees of memory alignment other than that required by C/C++ structure alignment. Since the dissimilarity matrix computation accesses each trajectory frame N times, where N is large (on the order of 10,000), the cost of optimizing the memory layout of the atomic coordinates in the trajectory frames is amortized fully. This observation leads to an approach where the trajectory frames are converted from AOS layout to SOA layout well suited for vectorization of the QCP inner product loop on SIMD hardware. We also zero-pad the individual coordinate arrays up to the next multiple of the largest vector size (256 atoms) used by any of our hand-coded kernels. The zero-valued coordinates do not contribute to the sums in the QCP inner product loop. By adding zero-padded elements, we completely eliminate the need for special handling that is otherwise needed for coordinate arrays that are not integer multiples of the host or accelerator vector size.

QCP INNER PRODUCT LOOP

The simplified inner product loop shown in Fig. 3 is generally similar to that found in the reference implementation of QCP made available by Theobald (2005) and P. Liu et al. (2010), except that it implements only the unweighted form of the QCP algorithm, and it uses single-precision atomic coordinates as input, although all of the subsequent arithmetic operations are performed in double-precision. Our implementation uses single-precision input because the vast majority of MD simulation trajectory file formats store atomic coordinates with single-precision floating point numbers, and occasionally with slightly less precision.

Although the QCP inner product loop can be written using single-precision arithmetic, in practice this has either no impact, or a very minor impact on performance since the loop tends toward being memory-bandwidth-bound due to the relatively small number of floating point operations performed per memory reference. This is likely to negate any significant performance benefit from an implementation based on purely single-precision arithmetic. Furthermore, since the QCP inner product loop accumulates the sums of squares, there is a risk of floating point truncation or rounding impacting accuracy for the summation of very large numbers of atomic coordinates. Although techniques such as compensated summation (Kahan, 1965) or recursive summation (Higham, 1993) can be applied to ameliorate this risk, it is difficult to achieve a net performance benefit.

The inner product function uses six 1D SOA coordinate array pointers rather than multidimensional array pointers, simplifying the addition of type specifiers such as

```
// Serial C++ inner product for SOA coordinate storage
double InnerProductSOA(double *A, const int cnt,
                float *crdx1, float *crdy1, float *crdz1,
                float *crdx2, float *crdy2, float *crdz2) {
  double a0, a1, a2, a3, a4, a5, a6, a7, a8;
  double G1=0.0, G2=0.0;
  a0=a1=a2=a3=a4=a5=a6=a7=a8=0.0;

  for (int l=0; l<cnt; l++) {
    double x1, x2, y1, y2, z1, z2;
    x1 = crdx1[l];
    y1 = crdy1[l];
    z1 = crdz1[l];

    G1 += x1*x1 + y1*y1 + z1*z1;

    x2 = crdx2[l];
    y2 = crdy2[l];
    z2 = crdz2[l];

    G2 += x2*x2 + y2*y2 + z2*z2;

    a0 += x1 * x2;
    a1 += x1 * y2;
    a2 += x1 * z2;

    a3 += y1 * x2;
    a4 += y1 * y2;
    a5 += y1 * z2;

    a6 += z1 * x2;
    a7 += z1 * y2;
    a8 += z1 * z2;
  }

  A[0]=a0;  A[1]=a1;  A[2]=a2;
  A[3]=a3;  A[4]=a4;  A[5]=a5;
  A[6]=a6;  A[7]=a7;  A[8]=a8;

  return (G1 + G2) * 0.5;
}
```

FIG. 3

Serial C++ inner product routine for atomic coordinates stored as single-precision
floating point numbers in a structure-of-array (SOA) memory layout suitable for compiler
autovectorization.

const and restrict. The addition of the restrict type specifier informs the compiler that an array is nonoverlapping (not aliased) with other pointer arguments to the function. The use of restrict is particularly important to enable efficient parallelization of code written in C/C++. While compilers are capable of fully automatic alias analysis for Fortran code, the fact that C and C++ allow arbitrary pointer arithmetic means that for reasons of correctness a compiler cannot assume that pointers passed as function arguments are non-overlapping.

To promote exclusive use of machine registers for all summation operations in the inner loop, local variables are used for summation and the final results are written to the array of key matrix components only after completing the loop. In principle, an advanced compiler should do this itself automatically, but by writing our code this way, we are more likely to get a performant loop even with less advanced compilers. This inner loop structure leads directly to the hand-vectorized x86 AVX loop implementation shown in Fig. 4, for comparison.

HAND-VECTORIZED QCP INNER PRODUCT LOOP

One of the key capabilities provided by OpenACC is that it allows the programmer to indicate to the compiler which loops should be profitable targets for vectorization. This is similar to what is available with proprietary compiler directives for programmer guided vectorization, except that it is more broadly applicable across multiple CPUs, accelerator hardware architectures, and compilers by multiple vendors. The use of compiler intrinsics should therefore be viewed primarily as a code vectorization method of last resort, and we included the example here to give an idea of the kind of code that advanced compilers can generate automatically with successful use of OpenACC directives on well-structured loops.

If we count the arithmetic and memory operations in the inner loop in Fig. 3, we see 6 memory loads, 30 floating point operations, and 6 floating point type conversions per loop iteration, as written in plain C++. Observing that contemporary target hardware platforms exhibit ratios of arithmetic vs. memory throughput that typically exceed a factor of 10 or more, we can assume that the algorithm performance is likely to be memory-bandwidth-bound.

The SIMD arithmetic units found in modern microprocessors perform the same operation on a vector of data items simultaneously, thereby enabling higher arithmetic throughput per processor core, and creating a commensurate increase in required memory bandwidth. Vector instructions implicitly reduce the trip count of loops that contain them, with many of the same benefits that are normally associated with manual or automatic loop unrolling, for example, by reducing loop control overheads. Recent x86 CPUs incorporate support for so-called advanced vector extensions (AVX) and fused-multiply-add (FMA) machine instructions. AVX instructions allow vector operations to be performed on four double-precision or eight single-precision values at a time. FMA instructions perform a floating point multiply followed by an add, for example, $a = round(b \times c + d)$ in a single operation, which potentially doubles the arithmetic throughput for this commonly needed operation sequence. On processors that can execute FMA with double the throughput, the effective floating point operation count could be thought of as being almost halved from 36 down to 21, making the code significantly more memory-bandwidth-bound than before. While GPUs have long incorporated FMA machine instructions, they are a much

```
// Hand-coded AVX inner product innermost loop for
// SOA coordinate storage.  Abridged for simplicity.
for (int l=0; l<cnt; l+=4) {
  // load three 4-element single-precision vectors
  __m128 xa4f = _mm_load_ps(crdx1 + l);
  __m128 ya4f = _mm_load_ps(crdy1 + l);
  __m128 za4f = _mm_load_ps(crdz1 + l);

  // convert from single-precision to double-precision
  __m256d xa4 = _mm256_cvtps_pd(xa4f);
  __m256d ya4 = _mm256_cvtps_pd(ya4f);
  __m256d za4 = _mm256_cvtps_pd(za4f);

  vG1 = _mm256_fmadd_pd(xa4, xa4, vG1);
  vG1 = _mm256_fmadd_pd(ya4, ya4, vG1);
  vG1 = _mm256_fmadd_pd(za4, za4, vG1);

  // load three 4-element single-precision vectors
  __m128 xb4f = _mm_load_ps(crdx2 + l);
  __m128 yb4f = _mm_load_ps(crdy2 + l);
  __m128 zb4f = _mm_load_ps(crdz2 + l);

  // convert from single-precision to double-precision
  __m256d xb4 = _mm256_cvtps_pd(xb4f);
  __m256d yb4 = _mm256_cvtps_pd(yb4f);
  __m256d zb4 = _mm256_cvtps_pd(zb4f);

  vG2 = _mm256_fmadd_pd(xb4, xb4, vG2);
  vG2 = _mm256_fmadd_pd(yb4, yb4, vG2);
  vG2 = _mm256_fmadd_pd(zb4, zb4, vG2);

  va0 = _mm256_fmadd_pd(xa4, xb4, va0);
  va1 = _mm256_fmadd_pd(xa4, yb4, va1);
  va2 = _mm256_fmadd_pd(xa4, zb4, va2);

  va3 = _mm256_fmadd_pd(ya4, xb4, va3);
  va4 = _mm256_fmadd_pd(ya4, yb4, va4);
  va5 = _mm256_fmadd_pd(ya4, zb4, va5);

  va6 = _mm256_fmadd_pd(za4, xb4, va6);
  va7 = _mm256_fmadd_pd(za4, yb4, va7);
  va8 = _mm256_fmadd_pd(za4, zb4, va8);
}
```

FIG. 4

Hand-coded AVX inner product loop for SOA coordinate storage, using Intel AVX and
FMA compiler intrinsics that map directly to x86 AVX and FMA SIMD vector machine
instructions.

more recent addition to most commodity CPUs. The loop shown in Fig. 4 has been hand-vectorized using Intel AVX and FMA compiler intrinsics, operating on vectors of four values at a time.

With careful scheduling of the outermost dissimilarity loops it is possible to ensure that one of the structures being compared is reused during consecutive loop iterations. On a CPU with a large L2 cache, we expect that data reuse among consecutive loop iterations reduces the demand for off-chip DRAM memory accesses to half of what is written in the code, significantly improving performance. Even if we assume that only three memory loads in the innermost loop require off-chip memory accesses, we are still likely to have performance that is bound by memory bandwidth. In the specific case of the loop shown in Fig. 4, tests on a dual-socket Intel Xeon E5-2687w v3 compute node demonstrate that the loop is memory bandwidth bound, with peak performance achieved using only 6 out of 20 CPU cores. For the purposes of evaluating OpenACC, we use the hand-coded AVX loop as the baseline performance result for comparison.

Compiler intrinsics have the appearance of a C function, but they are translated by the compiler to low-level machine instructions. Since the compiler handles register assignment and provides type checking, intrinsics are an easier way to write hand-optimized machine-specific code for performance-critical loops than assembly language. The maximum vector length that can be operated on at once is an area of significant hardware variability. While offering the potential for high performance, the major drawback of such low-level approaches is that in most cases the vector data types and intrinsic functions are associated with vectors of a specific size. Thus, adding support for multiple generations of hardware with varying vector sizes usually requires rewriting intrinsics-based code several times which can be a time consuming and therefore costly endeavor.

CODE ADAPTATION AND USE OF OPENACC DIRECTIVES

At this stage, we already implemented efficient routines to copy selected atoms from VMD's internal AOS-layout atomic coordinate arrays from AOS and generate a new linearized and padded SOA-layout coordinate array for use in computing the dissimilarity matrix. We also have clean and performant reference implementations of the QCP inner product loop and the associated RMSD solver function. With these components in hand, we can proceed with final code transformations and addition of OpenACC compiler directives to achieve high performance on GPUs or other accelerators.

In the following, we show several versions of the dissimilarity matrix innermost loops adapted for acceleration with OpenACC. Since OpenACC directives apply to loops, it is important to show as much of the code as possible. To fit the code on a page it is necessary to leave out short code fragments in various places.

In general, the most important steps in adapting an algorithm for parallel execution on an accelerator are to minimize data transfers between the host Central Processing Units (CPUs) and accelerators, and to ensure that the organization of data in accelerator memory is conducive to high-bandwidth data-parallel access, both of which lead to good performance.

Fig. 5 combines the contents of the QCP inner product loop shown in Fig. 3, calls to the QCP Newton-Raphson solver, and the outermost loops over *i* and *j* that compute one triangle of the symmetric matrix of pairwise structure RMSDs—the dissimilarity matrix to be used in subsequent clustering analysis. The first OpenACC directives are added to the key loops as shown in Fig. 5. The most important OpenACC directives to add initially are `kernels`, `copyin`, and `copy`, which have been added to the outermost loops shown in Figs. 5 and 6.

The `copyin` OpenACC directive informs the compiler that it should copy the named host-side array onto the GPU prior to launching the parallel kernel, and that it is not necessary for the data to be copied back after the kernel is complete, for example, the data is either read-only within the GPU kernel, or any modifications made to the data can be discarded and are not needed by the host. The `copy` directive is similar, except that it copies the named array from the host before the GPU kernel executes, and also copies it back to the host after completion. This is necessary for data that are written by the GPU and are ultimately needed on the host. In the case of the dissimilarity matrix calculation, the GPU kernels only write to a triangular region of the array (in the case of a fully symmetric matrix storage scheme), so the matrix is zero-filled on the host and must be copied to and from the GPU so that any unwritten matrix elements are properly set to zero.

The `kernels` directive instructs the compiler that it should automatically analyze the loop nest contained by the *j* loop and look for opportunities to parallelize the loops contained in the loop nest. The `kernels` directive is an easy way to begin parallelizing a code initially, since it pushes the parallelization responsibility entirely onto the compiler, though in many cases the compiler needs to be explicitly informed which loops are independent and therefore safe to parallelize. Similarly, the `loop` directive guides the compiler to attempt to vectorize the loops that are so-labeled, using automatic heuristics to determine appropriate vector sizes, thread block sizes, and so on.

The function `SolveRMSD` called near the bottom of the listing in Fig. 5 refers to the QCP Newton-Raphson solver, which must be annotated with the OpenACC `routine seq` directives, to allow it to be run within a single accelerator thread. The use of the `routine seq` directives for `SolveRMSD` is shown in Fig. 7. The `routine` directive is also used to specify functions that should be parallelized, although that case does not apply to the algorithms involved in this chapter.

The code written in Fig. 5 uses several pointers for access to the coordinate arrays, which can present some difficulties for some OpenACC compilers. To make the code easier for the compiler to autovectorize, indexing arithmetic can be used on a single array pointer, as shown in Fig. 6. The use of indexing arithmetic in place of several pointers can, in some cases, provide a minor performance benefit since on many architectures, pointers are 64-bit quantities. The integer types used for index calculations can sometimes safely use smaller types that consume fewer registers, which can improve GPU thread occupancy (the number of threads that can be scheduled concurrently across the entire GPU). Although the use of a single array pointer simplifies the compiler's task of proving loop independence, further code changes are still needed.

```
    // abridged variable declarations for brevity ...
#pragma acc kernels copyin(crds[0:tsz]), copy(rmsdmat[0:msz])
  for (long j=0; j<framecount; j++) {
    float *crdx1 = crds + (j * 3L * framecrdsz);
    float *crdy1 = crdx1 + framecrdsz;
    float *crdz1 = crdx1 + framecrdsz*2;
#pragma acc loop
    for (long i=0; i<j; i++) {
      float *crdx2 = crds + (i * 3L * framecrdsz);
      float *crdy2 = crdx2 + framecrdsz;
      float *crdz2 = crdx2 + framecrdsz*2;
      // abridged zeroing of accumulators for brevity...
#pragma acc loop
      for (int l=0; l<cnt; l++) {
        x1 = crdx1[l];
        y1 = crdy1[l];
        z1 = crdz1[l];

        G1 += x1*x1 + y1*y1 + z1*z1;

        x2 = crdx2[l];
        y2 = crdy2[l];
        z2 = crdz2[l];

        G2 += x2*x2 + y2*y2 + z2*z2;

        a0 += x1 * x2;
        a1 += x1 * y2;
        a2 += x1 * z2;

        a3 += y1 * x2;
        a4 += y1 * y2;
        a5 += y1 * z2;

        a6 += z1 * x2;
        a7 += z1 * y2;
        a8 += z1 * z2;
      }

      double A[9];  A[0]=a0; /* abridged... */ A[8]=a8;
      double E0 = (G1 + G2) * 0.5;

      float rmsd;
      SolveRMSD(A, &rmsd, E0, cnt);
      rmsdmat[j*framecount + i]=rmsd;
    }
  }
```

FIG. 5

OpenACC kernel version 1 using multiple pointers for access to trajectory coordinates and 1D linearize storage of a 2D rectangular output matrix.

```
      // abridged variable declarations for brevity ...
#pragma acc kernels copyin(crds[0:tsz]), copy(rmsdmat[0:msz])
   for (long j=0; j<framecount; j++) {
      long x1addr = j * 3L * framecrdsz;
#pragma acc loop
      for (long i=0; i<j; i++) {
         long x2addr = i * 3L * framecrdsz;
         // abridged zeroing of accumulators for brevity...
#pragma acc loop
         for (int l=0; l<cnt; l++) {
            x1 = crds[l + x1addr];
            y1 = crds[l + x1addr + framecrdsz];
            z1 = crds[l + x1addr + framecrdsz*2];

            G1 += x1*x1 + y1*y1 + z1*z1;

            x2 = crds[l + x2addr];
            y2 = crds[l + x2addr + framecrdsz];
            z2 = crds[l + x2addr + framecrdsz*2];

            G2 += x2*x2 + y2*y2 + z2*z2;

            a0 += x1 * x2;
            a1 += x1 * y2;
            a2 += x1 * z2;

            a3 += y1 * x2;
            a4 += y1 * y2;
            a5 += y1 * z2;

            a6 += z1 * x2;
            a7 += z1 * y2;
            a8 += z1 * z2;
         }

         double A[9];  A[0]=a0; /* abridged... */ A[8]=a8;
         double E0 = (G1 + G2) * 0.5;

         float rmsd;
         SolveRMSD(A, &rmsd, E0, cnt);
         rmsdmat[j*framecount + i]=rmsd;
      }
   }
```

FIG. 6

OpenACC kernel version 2 using a single pointer but multiple indices for access to trajectory coordinates and 1D linearized storage of a 2D rectangular output matrix.

```
// QCP Newton—Raphson solver to compute the minimum RMSD
// given the ten inner product sums A[] required for
// construction of the 4x4 key matrix.
#pragma acc routine seq
int SolveRMSD(double *A, float *rmsd, double *EO, int cnt) {
  // body of the Newton—Raphson solver ommitted for brevity...
}
```

FIG. 7

OpenACC `routine` directive used to indicate that the QCP Newton-Raphson RMSD solver can be called within an individual thread on a GPU or another accelerator.

The QCP inner product loop *l* ultimately performs data-parallel sum reductions. While the Portland Group (PGI) compilers automatically recognize the existence of the sum reductions and handle them accordingly, some compilers need to be explicitly informed of the need to perform sum reductions on a0 through a8, and G1 and G2. For this purpose, OpenACC provides the `reduction` directive, which can be used to annotate sum reductions as: `reduction(+:a0)`, `reduction(+:a1)`, and so on. We have omitted the explicit annotation of sum reduction directives in the code listings since they are not needed by the PGI compilers. The reduction directives may be required for correct code generation by other compilers.

The output array `rmsdmat` is accessed by computing a linear index from the two *i* and *j* loop variables, but this causes a problem for many compilers that consider such an equation to pose a so-called "loop-carried dependency." If executed in parallel, loop-carried dependencies create a potential for output conflicts among loop iterations. To eliminate the loop-carried dependency we must either reformulate `rmsdmat` to use a two-dimensional array rather than a 1D linearized array, or we can change the loop structure to eliminate the *i* and *j* loops replacing them with a single loop *k* that operates in the linearized index space of `rmsdmat`. For our purposes it turns out to be much simpler to use the second approach, affording the opportunity to convert the code to use a more compact linearized representation of the upper- or lower-triangular portion of the dissimilarity matrix, thereby reducing the memory footprint. The cost of this approach is that *i* and *j* must be computed from the linearized index *k*, which requires a square root and other arithmetic to solve the quadratic equation that relates the indices *i* and *j* to *k* for the triangle of interest. The code shown in Fig. 8 implements this approach, which is the first version of the code that achieves effective parallelization on the GPU.

Although the code modifications and OpenACC directives added in Fig. 8 achieves a high degree of parallelization, there is typically still room for improving performance further by providing the compiler with further guidance on the best vector size to use for a particular target accelerator architecture. In Fig. 9, we explicitly added the `vector` directive and provided guidance to the compiler to use a vector size of 256 by adding `vector(256)` to the existing loop directive. The larger vector size of 256 promotes better hardware utilization on contemporary GPUs, and has the effect

```
void rmsdmat_qcp_acc(int cnt, int padcnt, int framecrdsz,
                     int framecount, const float * restrict crds,
  // abridged function contents for brevity ...
  long i, j, k;
#pragma acc kernels copyin(crds[0:tsz]), copy(rmsdmat[0:msz])
  for (k=0; k<(framecount*(framecount-1))/2; k++) {
    acc_idx2sub_tril(long(framecount-1), k, &i, &j);
    long x1addr = j * 3L * framecrdsz;
    long x2addr = i * 3L * framecrdsz;

#pragma acc loop
    for (long l=0; l<cnt; l++) {
      x1 = crds[l + x1addr];
      y1 = crds[l + x1addr + framecrdsz];
      z1 = crds[l + x1addr + framecrdsz*2];

      G1 += x1*x1 + y1*y1 + z1*z1;

      x2 = crds[l + x2addr];
      y2 = crds[l + x2addr + framecrdsz];
      z2 = crds[l + x2addr + framecrdsz*2];

      G2 += x2*x2 + y2*y2 + z2*z2;

      a0 += x1 * x2;
      a1 += x1 * y2;
      a2 += x1 * z2;

      a3 += y1 * x2;
      a4 += y1 * y2;
      a5 += y1 * z2;

      a6 += z1 * x2;
      a7 += z1 * y2;
      a8 += z1 * z2;
    }

    double A[9];  A[0]=a0; /* abridged... */ A[8]=a8;
    double E0 = (G1 + G2) * 0.5;

    float rmsd;
    SolveRMSD(A, &rmsd, E0, cnt);
    rmsdmat[k]=rmsd; // store linearized triangular matrix
  }
```

FIG. 8

OpenACC kernel version 3 using a loop over the linearized index of the triangular matrix element, with coordinates accessed through a single pointer but multiple indices and 1D linearized storage of a 2D triangular output matrix.

```
void rmsdmat_qcp_acc(int cnt, int padcnt, int framecrdsz,
                     int framecount, const float * restrict crds,
    // abridged function contents for brevity ...
    long i, j, k;
#pragma acc kernels copyin(crds[0:tsz]), copy(rmsdmat[0:msz])
    for (k=0; k<(framecount*(framecount-1))/2; k++) {
      acc_idx2sub_tril(long(framecount-1), k, &i, &j);
      long x1addr = j * 3L * framecrdsz;
      long x2addr = i * 3L * framecrdsz;

#pragma acc loop vector(256)
      for (long l=0; l<cnt; l++) {
      // abridged for brevity ...

      rmsdmat[k]=rmsd; // store linearized triangular matrix
    }
  }
}
```

FIG. 9

OpenACC kernel version 4, identical to version 3 except that the innermost loop has been annotated with the additional vector size directive which can be used to tune performance for a particular problem size or for characteristics of the target accelerator hardware.

of reducing the total number of thread blocks in-flight at once. The larger vector size also reduces the number of memory accesses to disparate coordinate frames competing for very small on-chip caches.

PERFORMANCE RESULTS

The performance of the dissimilarity matrix algorithm was evaluated on multiple hardware platforms in Tables 1 and 2. CPU-based tests were performed on a compute node containing a dual-socket Intel Xeon E5-2687W-v3 at 3.5 GHz and 512GB RAM. The GPU tests were run on the same class of system paired with either an NVIDIA Quadro M6000 (24GB model), or an NVIDIA Tesla K80. The Quadro M6000 achieves 6 TFLOPS single-precision, 0.2 TFLOPS double-precision, and 317GB/s memory bandwidth. The Tesla K80 is a dual-GPU card that achieves an aggregate performance of 8.5 TFLOPS single-precision, 2.9 TFLOPS double-precision, and 480GB/s memory bandwidth. For the single-GPU tests below, the half-K80 performance we expect is 4.25 TFLOPS single-precision, 1.45 TFLOPS double-precision, and 240GB/s memory bandwidth. We chose to include performance data for the two different types of GPUs. The Quadro M6000 strongly emphasizes single-precision arithmetic performance and provides limited double-precision performance, yielding an arithmetic throughput ratio of roughly 30:1 single-precision vs. double-precision. The Tesla K80 is a much more balanced GPU architecture with an arithmetic throughput ratio of roughly 3:1 single-precision vs. double-precision.

Table 1 Comparison of CPU and OpenACC-Based GPU-Accelerated Kernel Performance

Device	Kernel	CPU Cores (Threads)	Runtime (s)	Speedup vs. Dual-Xeon
Xeon E5-2687W-v3	ICC AVX+FMA	20 (1)	54.0	0.38
Xeon E5-2687W-v3	ICC AVX+FMA	20 (2)	29.6	0.69
Xeon E5-2687W-v3	ICC AVX+FMA	20 (4)	22.6	0.91
Xeon E5-2687W-v3	ICC AVX+FMA	20 (6)	21.2	0.97
Xeon E5-2687W-v3	ICC AVX+FMA	20 (40)	20.7	1.00
Xeon E5-2687W-v3	ICC C++	20 (40)	24.2	0.85
Xeon E5-2687W-v3	PGC++ C++	20 (40)	24.2	0.85
Quadro M6000	PGC++ OpenACC	–	10.7	1.93
Tesla K80 (1-GPU)	PGC++ OpenACC	–	6.5	3.18

Kernel timing results include all host-GPU memory transfers and kernel launches required for evaluation of one triangle of a 2001 × 2001 dissimilarity matrix, for a trajectory with 20,000 selected atoms. All speedups are computed relative to the fastest hand-coded AVX and FMA based kernel. The performance data for the Xeon CPU runs using the kernel based on hand-coded AVX and FMA intrinsics demonstrates that the CPU performance is memory-bandwidth-bound even when using a small fraction of the CPU cores. The Tesla K80 result shown used only one of the two GPUs contained on the board.

Table 2 Execution Times Are Reported for Atom Selection Processing (Compaction and Padding of Sparse Selections, AOS to SOA Conversion, and Center-of-Mass Translation Preprocessing Steps), and OpenACC Dissimilarity Matrix Kernels on Multiple Targets for Varying MD Trajectory Sizes (the Side Length of the Dissimilarity Matrix)

Device	Trajectory Frames			
	2001 (s)	4001 (s)	8001 (s)	16001 (s)
Sel. Processing	0.208	0.439	0.869	2.158
Dual Xeon AVX+FMA	20.7	85.8	349.0	–
Quadro M6000	10.7	42.7	171.3	689.9
Tesla K80 (1-GPU)	6.5	25.5	101.5	406.6

The atom selection processing step is identical for all kernels, so there was no need to repeat the test for different targets. CPU and OpenACC-based GPU-accelerated kernel execution times are reported for for varying problem sizes.

The results in Table 1 demonstrate that the Xeon CPU-based kernels are memory-bandwidth-bound as predicted by our earlier analysis. We observe that the dual-Xeon system running hand-coded AVX+FMA kernel achieves 69% of peak performance with only two CPU threads, 91% with four threads, and 97% with six threads. Although the hand-coded AVX+FMA CPU kernel outperforms the best results achieved from compiler autovectorization of C++, we expect that this is because we did not have a way to inform that compiler that the trajectory coordinate memory buffers were guaranteed to be aligned to 16-byte boundaries. Hence, the compilers likely generated memory load/store operations that were slightly less efficient than what was written by hand. We note that the gap in performance between the hand-coded AVX+FMA kernel and either the Intel or PGI compiler-provided autovectorization was under 15%, demonstrative of the fact that in the vast majority of cases it would be unnecessary to write a hand-coded kernel.

The two GPU accelerated kernels handily outperform the best CPU kernels in both cases. This is what we should expect given that the CPU kernels exhibit memory-bandwidth-bound performance with just a few active cores/threads, and given the much higher memory bandwidths provided by GPUs vs. contemporary host CPUs. The K80's significantly higher double-precision arithmetic throughput and larger on-chip register count explain the noteworthy performance gap between the Quadro M6000 and the Tesla K80. The performance results for the half-K80 tests show that despite the superior memory bandwidth of the Quadro M6000 vs. the half-K80 (317 GB/s vs. 240 GB/s), the half-K80's factor of 7× advantage in double-precision arithmetic throughput plays out in its favor. To achieve higher performance on GPUs optimized for single-precision such as the Quadro M6000, one might consider developing a more sophisticated mixed-precision summation scheme or using a variation of a recursive summation approach (Higham, 1993).

The average memory bandwidth (including any benefits from on-chip caches and performance penalties for remote NUMA memory accesses) achieved by the CPU kernel for the 8001 frame test case was 45 GB/s. The average memory bandwidths (including any benefits from on-chip caches) achieved by the GPU kernels for the 8001 frame test case were 92 GB/s for the Quadro M6000 and 157 GB/s for the half-K80. The Quadro M6000 result is below what we would hope for, but this is an outcome of its very low double-precision performance. The half-K80 bandwidth result is a respectable 65% of its 240 GB/s theoretical peak bandwidth, and a good result for a nontrivial kernel with directive-based parallelism. It should be possible to achieve higher performance and a higher fraction of memory bandwidth using a hand-written CUDA kernel that uses advanced hardware features that OpenACC cannot presently exploit (e.g., cross-thread-block reductions), but the achieved results are excellent.

SUMMARY AND CONCLUSION

This chapter demonstrates the use of OpenACC directives to parallelize some of the most costly computations involved in the clustering analysis of MD simulations. Along the way, we provided details about hardware architecture considerations that are important for achieving high performance, particularly those that relate to memory accesses and the layout of data structures in memory. The chapter described methodologies for adapting existing code and data structures to meet the special requirements of massively parallel accelerators such as GPUs, and many-core CPUs. The chapter demonstrated some of the challenges that can arise in the adaptation of existing applications, where compromises must often be made between existing data structure organization and the organization and memory layouts that lead to best performance for other calculations.

We showed what a hand-vectorized CPU kernel looks like using compiler intrinsics for Intel x86 AVX and FMA instructions, and we used it to provide a performance baseline for comparison with compiler-provided autovectorization for CPUs and GPU-accelerated kernels obtained with OpenACC. The OpenACC kernel performance reported here achieves 65% of the theoretical peak GPU memory bandwidth when run on one GPU of the Tesla K80, which is a very respectable outcome. OpenACC kernel performance could be improved further with additional performance tuning and by taking advantage of new features and optimization improvements in upcoming OpenACC compilers, but the results we achieved are representative of what an experienced practitioner can achieve on a very limited time budget. OpenACC directives are well suited to the task of parallelizing legacy codes without the need to maintain a multiplicity of hand-written kernels for different GPUs or other accelerators, and are particularly appropriate when a large amount of code needs to be accelerated in observance of the impacts of Amdahl's law.

ACKNOWLEDGMENTS

The authors acknowledge support from NIH Grants 9P41GM104601 and 5R01GM098243-02, the CUDA Center of Excellence at the University of Illinois, and the Blue Waters sustained-petascale computing project supported by NSF Awards OCI-0725070 and ACI-1238993, the state of Illinois, and "The Computational Microscope" NSF PRAC Awards OCI-0832673 and ACI-1440026, and the Oak Ridge Leadership Computing Facility at Oak Ridge National Laboratory supported by the Office of Science of the Department of Energy under Contract DE-AC05-00OR22725.

REFERENCES

Cassidy, C. K., Himes, B. A., Alvarez, F. J., Ma, J., Zhao, G., Perilla, J. R., ... Zhang, P. (2015). CryoEM and computer simulations reveal a novel kinase conformational switch in bacterial chemotaxis signaling. *eLife*, 10.7554/eLife.08419.

Fraiberg, M., Afanzar, O., Cassidy, C. K., Gabashvili, A., Schulten, K., Levin, Y., & Eisenbach, M. (2015). CheY's acetylation sites responsible for generating clockwise flagellar rotation in *Escherichia coli*. *Molecular Microbiology*, 95, 231–244.

Freddolino, P. L., Harrison, C. B., Liu, Y., & Schulten, K. (2010). Challenges in protein folding simulations. *Nature Physics*, 6, 751–758.

Freddolino, P. L., & Schulten, K. (2009). Common structural transitions in explicit-solvent simulations of villin headpiece folding. *Biophysical Journal*, 97, 2338–2347.

Goh, B. C., Hadden, J. A., Bernardi, R. C., Singharoy, A., McGreevy, R., Rudack, T., ... Schulten, K. (2016). Computational methodologies for real-space structural refinement of large macromolecular complexes. *Annual Review of Biochemistry*, 45, 253–278. http://dx.doi.org/10.1146/annurev-biophys -062215-011113.

Goh, B. C., Perilla, J. R., England, M. R., Heyrana, K. J., Craven, R. C., & Schulten, K. (2015). Atomic modeling of an immature retroviral lattice using molecular dynamics and mutagenesis. *Structure, 23,* 1414–1425.

Han, W., & Schulten, K. (2014). Fibril elongation by $A\beta_{17-42}$: Kinetic network analysis of hybrid-resolution molecular dynamics simulations. *Journal of the American Chemical Society, 136,* 12450–12460.

Higham, N. J. (1993). The accuracy of floating point summation. *SIAM Journal on Scientific Computing, 14*(4), 783–799.

Humphrey, W., Dalke, A., & Schulten, K. (1996). VMD—visual molecular dynamics. *Journal of Molecular Graphics, 14*(1), 33–38.

Joubert, W., Archibald, R., Berrill, M., Brown, W. M., Eisenbach, M., Grout, R., ... Turner, J. (2015). Accelerated application development: The ORNL Titan experience. *Computers and Electrical Engineering, 46,* 123–138.

Kabsch, W. (1976). A solution for the best rotation to relate two sets of vectors. *Acta Crystallographica. Section A, 32,* 922–923.

Kabsch, W. (1978). A discussion of the solution for the best rotation to relate two sets of vectors. *Acta Crystallographica. Section A, 34,* 827–828.

Kahan, W. (1965). Pracniques: Further remarks on reducing truncation errors. *Communications of the ACM, 8*(1), 40.

Kneller, G. R. (2011). Comment on "Fast determination of the optimal rotational matrix for macromolecular superpositions" [J. Comp. Chem. 31, 1561 (2010)]. *Journal of Computational Chemistry, 32*(1), 183–184.

Lang, M. C., Staudt, T., Engelhardt, J., & Hell, S. W. (2008). 4Pi microscopy with negligible sidelobes. *New Journal of Physics, 10,* 043041.

Liu, C., Perilla, J. R., Ning, J., Lu, M., Hou, G., Ramalho, R., ... Zhang, P. (2016). Cyclophilin A stabilizes HIV-1 capsid through a novel non-canonical binding site. *Nature Communications, 7,* 10714.

Liu, P., Agrafiotis, D. K., & Theobald, D. L. (2010). Fast determination of the optimal rotational matrix for macromolecular superpositions. *Journal of Computational Chemistry, 31*(7), 1561–1563.

Liu, P., Agrafiotis, D. K., & Theobald, D. L. (2011). Rapid communication reply to comment on: "Fast determination of the optimal rotational matrix for macromolecular superpositions". *Journal of Computational Chemistry, 32*(1), 185–186.

Mendes, C. L., Bode, B., Bauer, G. H., Enos, J., Beldica, C., & Kramer, W. T. (2014). Deploying a large petascale system: The Blue Waters experience. *Procedia Computer Science, 29,* 198–209.

Nickolls, J., Buck, I., Garland, M., & Skadron, K. (2008). Scalable parallel programming with CUDA. *ACM Queue, 6*(2), 40–53.

Perilla, J. R., Goh, B. C., Cassidy, C. K., Liu, B., Bernardi, R. C., Rudack, T., ... Schulten, K. (2015). Molecular dynamics simulations of large macromolecular complexes. *Current Opinion in Structural Biology, 31,* 64–74.

Perilla, J. R., Hadden, J. A., Goh, B. C., Mayne, C. G., & Schulten, K. (2016). All-atom molecular dynamics of virus capsids as drug targets. *Journal of Physical Chemistry Letters, 7*(10), 1836–1844. http://dx.doi.org/10.1021/acs.jpclett.6b00517.

Perilla, J. R., & Woolf, T. B. (2012). Towards the prediction of order parameters from molecular dynamics simulations in proteins. *The Journal of Chemical Physics, 136,* 164101.

Pharr, M., & Mark, W. R. (2012). *ISPC: A SPMD compiler for high-performance CPU programming.* In *Innovative parallel computing (InPar), 2012.* (pp. 1–13).

Phillips, J. C., Stone, J. E., Vandivort, K. L., Armstrong, T. G., Wozniak, J. M., Wilde, M., & Schulten, K. (2014). *Petascale Tcl with NAMD, VMD, and Swift/T*. In *SC'14 workshop on high performance technical computing in dynamic languages, sc '14* (pp. 6–17). IEEE Press.

Rajan, A., Freddolino, P. L., & Schulten, K. (2010). Going beyond clustering in MD trajectory analysis: An application to villin headpiece folding. *PLoS One, 5*, e9890.

Reynolds, A. P., Richards, G., de la Iglesia, B., & Rayward-Smith, V. J. (2006). Clustering rules: A comparison of partitioning and hierarchical clustering algorithms. *Journal of Mathematical Modelling and Algorithms, 5*(4), 475–504.

Stone, J. E., Gohara, D., & Shi, G. (2010). OpenCL: A parallel programming standard for heterogeneous computing systems. *Computing in Science and Engineering, 12*, 66–73.

Stone, J. E., Hardy, D. J., Ufimtsev, I. S., & Schulten, K. (2010). GPU-accelerated molecular modeling coming of age. *Journal of Molecular Graphics and Modelling, 29*, 116–125.

Stone, J. E., McGreevy, R., Isralewitz, B., & Schulten, K. (2014). GPU-accelerated analysis and visualization of large structures solved by molecular dynamics flexible fitting. *Faraday Discussions, 169*, 265–283.

Stone, J. E., Sener, M., Vandivort, K. L., Barragan, A., Singharoy, A., Teo, I., ... Schulten, K. (2016). Atomic detail visualization of photosynthetic membranes with GPU-accelerated ray tracing. *Parallel Computing, 55*, 17–27.

Theobald, D. L. (2005). Rapid calculation of RMSDs using a quaternion-based characteristic polynomial. *Acta Crystallographica. Section A, 61*(4), 478–480.

Zhao, G., Perilla, J. R., Yufenyuy, E. L., Meng, X., Chen, B., Ning, J., ... Zhang, P. (2013). Mature HIV-1 capsid structure by cryo-electron microscopy and all-atom molecular dynamics. *Nature, 497*, 643–646.

Incrementally accelerating the RI-MP2 correlated method of electronic structure theory using OpenACC compiler directives

12

Janus Juul Eriksen[a]

qLEAP Center for Theoretical Chemistry, Department of Chemistry, Aarhus University,
Aarhus C, Denmark

The purpose of this chapter is to demonstrate how electronic structure many-body theories may be incrementally accelerated in an efficient and portable manner by means of OpenACC compiler directives, with an illustrative application to the RI-MP2 method. The efficiency of the implementation (using six K40 GPUs) is illustrated through a series of test calculations, for which the accelerated code is capable of reducing the total time-to-solution by at least an order of magnitude over an optimized CPU-only reference implementation.

At the end of this chapter the reader will have an understanding of:

- The use of accelerator offloading in quantum chemistry
- Asynchronous pipelining of computations and data transfers
- Hybrid CPU/GPU computing using OpenMP compiler directives
- Fortran interoperability with CUBLAS
- Pinning of memory in CUDA Fortran

INTRODUCTION

In electronic structure theory, both coupled cluster (CC) (Čížek, 1966, 1969; Paldus, Čížek, & Shavitt, 1972) and many-body perturbation theory (MBPT) (Shavitt &

[a]Present address: Institut für Physikalische Chemie, Johannes Gutenberg-Universität Mainz, Mainz, Germany.

Parallel Programming with OpenACC. http://dx.doi.org/10.1016/B978-0-12-410397-9.00012-3

Bartlett, 2009) offer a systematic approach toward the full configuration interaction (FCI) (Helgaker, Jørgensen, & Olsen, 2000) wave function—the exact solution to the time-independent, nonrelativistic electronic Schrödinger equation—within a given one-electron basis set. In both hierarchies of methods, the Hartree-Fock (HF) solution, in which each electron of a molecular system is treated in a mean-field bath of all other electrons, is the reference to which correlated corrections are made by including excited configurations into the wave function. Moving beyond the HF approximation, not only the effects that prevent two electrons with parallel spin from being found at the same point in space are considered (so-called exchange (or Fermi) correlation, which is fully described by HF theory), but also the corresponding Coulombic repulsion between electrons start being described. This implies that upon traversing up through either of the CC or MBPT hierarchies, increasingly more of such (so-called dynamical) correlation is included in the wave function, with a complete description met at the target FCI limit.

In the MBPT series, the lowest-order perturbative correction to the HF energy for the isolated effect of connected double excitations is that of the noniterative second-order Møller-Plesset (MP2) model (Møller & Plesset, 1934). As an improvement, the CC hierarchy offers the iterative CC singles and doubles (CCSD) model (Purvis & Bartlett, 1982), which accounts not only for connected double excitations, but does so to infinite order in the space of all single and double excitations out of the HF reference. However, the additional accuracy of the CCSD model over the MP2 model comes at a price, as not only is the energy now evaluated iteratively, but each iteration cycle is also significantly more expensive than the simple noniterative evaluation of the MP2 energy, scaling as $\mathcal{O}(N^6)$ as opposed to $\mathcal{O}(N^5)$ (where N is a composite measure of the total system size). Thus, whereas both methods have nowadays become standard tools to computational quantum chemists, the current application range of the MP2 model considerably exceeds that of the CCSD model, due to the practical difference in associated computational cost.

Nevertheless, the time-to-solution for an average MP2 calculation is still substantial when targeting increasingly larger systems, for example, in comparison with cheaper, albeit less rigorous, and less systematic tools such as those of semiempirical nature or those that calculate the energy from a functional of the one-electron density. For this reason, most efficient implementations of the MP2 model invoke what is known as the resolution-of-the-identity (RI) approximation for reducing the computational cost (the prefactor) as well as lowering the memory constraints (Feyereisen, Fitzgerald, & Komornicki, 1993; Vahtras, Almlöf, & Feyereisen, 1993; Weigend & Häser, 1997; Whitten, 1973). Despite being an approximation to the MP2 model, the development of optimized auxiliary basis sets has managed to significantly reduce the inherent RI error, and for most reasonable choices of the intrinsic thresholds of a modern implementation, the error affiliated with the actual approximation will be negligible. However, while the computational cost is notably reduced in an RI-MP2 calculation with respect to its MP2 counterpart, its formal $\mathcal{O}(N^5)$ scaling with the size of the system will often still make it demanding if no fundamental algorithmic changes are made (Almlöf, 1991; Ayala & Scuseria,

1999; Doser, Lambrecht, Kussmann, & Ochsenfeld, 2009; Doser, Zienau, Clin, Lambrecht, & Ochsenfeld, 2010; Werner, Manby, & Knowles, 2003). One way in which this challenging issue may be addressed is by attempting to accelerate the rate-determining step in the evaluation of the RI-MP2 energy. However, it should be noted how the clear majority of all electronic structure programs being developed today are primarily written and maintained by domain scientists, many of which hold temporary positions working (simultaneously) on various theoretical and/or application-oriented projects. Thus, while said scientists might decide to implement a given accelerated method from scratch (presumably using some low-level approach unrelated to the language in which the actual code base is written), they might not be responsible for extending it with new features and capabilities nor for the routine maintenance required with the emergence of novel future architectures. Add to that the typical requirements of a single code base and, in particular, platform-independence, which most codes are subject to in the sense that any addition of accelerated code must not interfere with the standard compilation process, and one will potentially arrive at more reasons against investing the necessary efforts than reasons in favor of doing so.

In the present chapter, it will be demonstrated how to incrementally accelerate many-body theories in an efficient and portable manner by means of OpenACC compiler directives, with an illustrative application to the RI-MP2 method. As with OpenMP worksharing directives for Single-Instruction Multiple-Data (SIMD) instructions on multicore Central Processing Units (CPUs), these are treated as mere comments to a nonaccelerating compiler, and the resulting accelerated code will hence be based on the original source, which, in turn, makes the implementation portable, intuitively transparent, and easier to extend and maintain.

The target architecture, onto which we shall offload parts of the computational workload, will in the present study be Graphics Processing Units (GPUs). The evaluation of the RI-MP2 energy has previously been ported to GPUs in the group of Alán Aspuru-Guzik (Olivares-Amaya et al., 2010; Vogt et al., 2008; Watson, Olivares-Amaya, Edgar, & Aspuru-Guzik, 2010), as, for example, reviewed in a recent contribution to a book devoted to the subject of electronic structure calculations on GPUs (Olivares-Amaya, Jinich, Watson, & Aspuru-Guzik, 2016). However, whereas that implementation made use of the GPU-specific and low-level CUDA compute platform in addition to optimized GPU libraries, the present implementation(s) will not be limited to execution on GPUs; for instance, the current OpenACC standard (version 2.5) offers support for multicore CPUs as well as many-core processors, such as, for example, the Intel Xeon Phi products, but whereas some compiler vendors (e.g., PGI) have started to experiment with OpenACC as an alternative to OpenMP for multicore (host) architectures, no optimizations for many-core x86 processors have been released by any vendor as of yet (mid-2016). Such optimizations are, however, scheduled for future releases. Thus, OpenACC has the potential to offer a single programming model that may encompass host node SIMD execution as well as offloading of compute-intensive code regions to a variety of accelerators, which might make for cleaner, more transparent, and considerably more portable code, also with respect to performance. The present author will leave it to the reader to judge whether or not this is indeed the case for the RI-MP2 case study presented here.

THEORY

In the closed-shell (canonical) MP2 model (Møller & Plesset, 1934), the correlation energy is given by the following expression

$$E_{\mathrm{MP2}} = -\sum_{ijab} \frac{g_{aibj}(2g_{aibj} - g_{ajbi})}{\epsilon_{ij}^{ab}} \qquad (1)$$

in terms of two-electron electron repulsion integrals (ERIs), g_{aibj} (Mulliken notation), over spatial (spin-free) HF virtual orbitals a, b and occupied orbitals i, j

$$g_{aibj} = \iint \frac{\phi_a^*(\mathbf{r}_1)\phi_b^*(\mathbf{r}_2)\phi_i(\mathbf{r}_1)\phi_j(\mathbf{r}_2)}{|\mathbf{r}_1 - \mathbf{r}_2|} d\mathbf{r}_1 d\mathbf{r}_2 \qquad (2)$$

as well as the difference in energy between these, $\epsilon_{ij}^{ab} = \epsilon_a + \epsilon_b - (\epsilon_i + \epsilon_j)$. Besides the final evaluation of the MP2 energy in Eq. (1), the dominant part of an MP2 calculation is the construction of the four-index ERIs. In the so-called resolution-of-the-identity MP2 (RI-MP2) method (Feyereisen et al., 1993; Vahtras et al., 1993; Weigend & Häser, 1997), these are approximated by products of two-, $V_{\alpha\gamma}$, and three-index, W_{aia}, integrals by using the following symmetric decomposition

$$g_{aibj} \approx \sum_{\gamma} C_{ai}^{\gamma} C_{bj}^{\gamma}. \qquad (3)$$

In Eq. (3), Greek indices denote atomic orbitals within an auxiliary fitting basis set used for spanning the RI, and the fitting coefficients, C_{ai}^{γ}, are defined as

$$C_{ai}^{\gamma} = \sum_{\alpha} W_{ai\alpha}[\mathrm{V}^{-1/2}]_{\alpha\gamma}. \qquad (4)$$

In terms of computational cost, the evaluation of two- and three-index integrals and/or the calculation of the fitting coefficients will dominate the overall calculation for small systems ($\mathcal{O}(N^3)$- and $\mathcal{O}(N^4)$-scaling processes, respectively). However, upon an increase in system size, the final $\mathcal{O}(N^5)$-scaling assembly of the two-electron integrals in Eq. (3) will start to dominate, and this process is thus the ideal candidate for accelerating the RI-MP2 model. If the permutational symmetry of the two-electron integrals in Eq. (3) is taken into consideration, the evaluation of Eqs. (1) and (3) may be collectively expressed as in the pseudocode Fig. 1. Here, nocc, nvirt, and naux denote the number of occupied orbitals, virtual orbitals, and auxiliary basis functions, respectively, while EpsOcc, EpsVirt, and eps denote the corresponding occupied and virtual orbital energies as well as the difference between these. How large the involved dimensions grow for a given calculation depends very much on the size of

```
[...]
do j = 1,nocc
   do i = j,nocc
      call dgemm ( 't','n',nvirt,nvirt,naux,1.0d0,Calpha(:,:,j),naux,&
            & Calpha(:,:,i),naux,0.0d0,g_ij,nvirt )
      eps_ij = EpsOcc(i) + EpsOcc(j)
!$omp parallel do default(none) shared(g_ij,EpsVirt,nvirt) &
!$omp& firstprivate(eps_ij,i,j) private(a,b,eps_ijb,eps,pre) &
!$omp& reduction(+:rimp2_energy)
      do b = 1,nvirt
         eps_ijb = eps_ij - EpsVirt(b)
         do a = b,nvirt
            eps = eps_ijb - EpsVirt(a)
            rimp2_energy += pre * (g_ij(a,b)**2 + g_ij(b,a)**2 &
                           & - g_ij(a,b)*g_ij(b,a)) / eps
         enddo
      enddo
!$omp end parallel do
   enddo
enddo
[...]
```

FIG. 1

The RI-MP2 kernel.

the actual system as well as the quality of the one-electron basis set used, but for now it suffices to note that typically $nocc \ll nvirt \ll naux$, see also the "Computational Details" section. Finally, the prefactor pre handles the permutational symmetry of the integrals, that is, it is equal to 1.0d0 for coinciding occupied and virtual indices, 2.0d0 when either of these coincide, and a default value of 4.0d0 (Fig. 1).

IMPLEMENTATION

In all versions of the code (GPU-1 through GPU-8; see the "GPU-1" and "GPU-8" sections), the orbital energies (EpsOcc and EpsVirt) as well as the tensor containing the fitting coefficients (Calpha) are initialized with unique, yet arbitrary single and/or double precision numbers (depending on the context), as the calculation of these are not the objective of the present study. The different codes may be found in full online (Gitlab, 2016), and a short summary of the incremental optimizations occurring in each of the different code versions is provided in Table 1.

GPU-1

In the first optimization of the kernel, the matrix multiplications (MMs) are offloaded to the GPU, as these BLAS3 library operations are among those that are capable of exploiting the power of the accelerator most optimally (Leang, Rendell, & Gordon, 2014). Here, the compute (CUBLAS) stream is set equal to the default acc_async_sync intrinsic handle (with PGI, by linking with '-Mcuda'), and the logical gpu

Table 1 Summary of the Accelerated RI-MP2 Implementations in the "GPU-1" through "GPU-8" Sections

Code Version	Summary
GPU-1	Offload the matrix multiplication (dgemm)
GPU-2	Perform the energy summation on the device
GPU-3	Use multiple devices
GPU-4	Hybrid CPU/GPU implementation
GPU-5	Tiling of the Calpha tensor
GPU-6	Asynchronous pipelining
GPU-7	Pinning of Calpha into page-locked memory
GPU-8	Use single-precision arithmetics (sgemm)

(.true. if a device is present) determines whether to call the CUBLAS or CPU-optimized (e.g., MKL) dgemm routine through the interface. Thus, in a CPU-only run, both the MM and the subsequent energy summation are performed on the host, whereas in the present GPU-1 scheme, the former of these is performed on the device and the latter on the host (Fig. 2).

```
[...]
!$acc data copyin(Calpha) create(g_ij) if(gpu)
do j = 1,nocc
   do i = j,nocc
      call dgemm_interface ( 't','n',nvirt,nvirt,naux,1.0d0,&
              & Calpha(:,:,j),naux,Calpha(:,:,i),naux,0.0d0,g_ij,nvirt,&
              & acc_async_sync,cublas_handle,gpu )
!$acc update self(g_ij) if(gpu)
      eps_ij = EpsOcc(i) + EpsOcc(j)
!$omp parallel do default(none) shared(g_ij,EpsVirt,nvirt) &
!$omp& firstprivate(eps_ij,i,j) private(a,b,eps_ijb,eps,pre) &
!$omp& reduction(+:rimp2_energy)
      do b = 1,nvirt
         eps_ijb = eps_ij - EpsVirt(b)
         do a = b,nvirt
            eps = eps_ijb - EpsVirt(a)
            rimp2_energy += pre * (g_ij(a,b)**2 + g_ij(b,a)**2 &
                          & - g_ij(a,b)*g_ij(b,a)) / eps
         enddo
      enddo
!$omp end parallel do
   enddo
enddo
!$acc end data
[...]
```

FIG. 2

The GPU-1 scheme.

GPU-2

In the first optimization of the GPU code, the copyout (host update) of the `g_ij` intermediate is avoided by performing the worksharing energy summation on the device instead. By avoiding the (redundant) data transfer of `g_ij`, the entire kernel has effectively been ported to the device. As such, the implementation will take full advantage of the accelerator, but we note how the host is now completely idle during the computation, an issue which we shall attend to later in the "GPU-4" section. For now, we note that both the `EpsOcc` and `EpsVirt` vectors have been declared as present in the OpenACC parallel region in order to avoid excessive data movement, so these have to join the `Calpha` tensor in the copyin clause of the outer data region directive. The two relevant tensor elements of the `EpsOcc` vector have furthermore been explicitly fetched into the highest level of the cache, even though most, if not all, compilers would do this automatically. However, verbosity is used here not only for pedagogical purposes; rather, it is used to aid the compiler in the analysis of the nested loop, in the same way as the `independent` clause has been added (loop iterations are explicitly data-independent) and the GPU parallelization of the energy summation has been explicitly mapped to thread gangs (thread blocks) and vectors (individual threads), although the compiler might decide upon this partitioning even in the absence of the clauses. In general, while an initial OpenACC port can, and perhaps should be overly implicit, it is good practice to enforce the final implementation to be verbose, not only to make it more transparent to the present and future developers of the code, but also to guarantee comparable execution with compilers from different vendors. However, we have here abstained from explicitly mapping the loops to x number of thread blocks (`num_gangs(x)`) of length y (`vector_length(y)`), as this would make the code less general in case it should also be able to target other types of architectures, cf. the "Introduction" section (Fig. 3).

GPU-3

Having succeeded in porting the kernel to a single device, as opposed to a host-only execution, the next obvious step is to port it to multiple devices. In doing so, one has the option between (at least) two different strategies, namely: using (1) message passing (MPI); or (2) worksharing compiler directives (OpenMP). For option (1), each MPI rank has to create its own context, and sharing the host main memory among the individual ranks is thus nontrivial (although indeed possible). Furthermore, one would have to create an additional layer of communication on top of a possible existing MPI intra-node parallelization of the kernel. For option (2), on the other hand, the individual devices are mapped to individual OpenMP threads, which among them share a common shared memory context. For memory-intensive many-body methods in electronic structure theory, this is an attractive feature as the individual tensors often grow very large in size. Thus, by embedding the OpenACC implementation of the "GPU-2" section within an OpenMP parallel region, we can extend the accelerated code from one to multiple devices (Fig. 4).

```
[...]
!$acc data copyin(Calpha,EpsOcc,EpsVirt) copy(rimp2_energy) create(g_ij)
[...]
!$acc parallel loop gang independent &
!$acc& present(g_ij,EpsOcc,EpsVirt,rimp2_energy) &
!$acc& firstprivate(nvirt,j,i) private(b,a,pre,eps_ijb,eps) &
!$acc& reduction(+:rimp2_energy)
      do b = 1,nvirt
!$acc cache(EpsOcc(i),EpsOcc(j))
         eps_ijb = EpsOcc(i) + EpsOcc(j) - EpsVirt(b)
!$acc loop vector independent reduction(+:rimp2_energy)
         do a = b,nvirt
            eps = eps_ijb - EpsVirt(a)
            rimp2_energy += pre * (g_ij(a,b)**2 + g_ij(b,a)**2 &
                                 & - g_ij(a,b)*g_ij(b,a)) / eps
         enddo
!$acc end loop
      enddo
!$acc end parallel loop
[...]
!$acc end data
[...]
```

FIG. 3

The GPU-2 scheme.

```
[...]
!$omp parallel num_threads(acc_num_devices) default(none) &
!$omp& shared(nocc,nvirt,EpsOcc,EpsVirt,naux,Calpha,g_ij,cublas_handle) &
!$omp& private(j,i,b,a,pre,eps_ij,eps_ijb,eps,gpu_id) &
!$omp& firstprivate(acc_device_type) reduction(+:rimp2_energy)
gpu_id = omp_get_thread_num()
call acc_set_device_num ( int(gpu_id,kind=4) , acc_device_type )
!$acc data copyin(Calpha,EpsOcc,EpsVirt) copy(rimp2_energy) create(g_ij)
!$omp do schedule(dynamic,1)
do j = 1,nocc
   do i = j,nocc
      call dgemm_interface ( 't','n',nvirt,nvirt,naux,1.0d0,&
                  & Calpha(:,:,j),naux,Calpha(:,:,i),naux,0.0d0,g_ij,nvirt,&
                  & acc_async_sync,cublas_handle(gpu_id+1),.true. )
      [...]
   enddo
enddo
!$omp end do
!$acc end data
!$omp end parallel
[...]
```

FIG. 4

The GPU-3 scheme.

Here, a total of `acc_num_devices` threads is spanned in the parallel region (queried from the `acc_get_num_devices(acc_device_type)` API function) and each individual host thread (`gpu_id`) gets assigned its own device through a call to the `acc_set_device_num()` API routine. The individual CUBLAS handles are stored in a vector (`cublas_handle`) of length `n_threads`. Finally, we note how the loop scheduling has been explicitly declared in the worksharing over the outermost j-loop, as this is heavily load-imbalanced; however, the additional overhead introduced by the dynamic scheduling is negligible compared to the idle time which would be introduced with the default static schedule.

GPU-4

In the GPU-3 version of the code in the "GPU-3" section, only the devices attached to the compute node take part in the workload, while the node stays idle throughout the evaluation of the RI-MP2 energy. In order to alleviate this waste of resources, one might consider increasing the number of OpenMP threads in the parallel region from `acc_num_devices` to, for example, the number of CPU cores or, more generally, the `OMP_NUM_THREADS` environment variable. However, by doing so, the load imbalance of the j-loop would be exposed due to the heterogeneity in architecture. Thus, instead one needs to flatten (or collapse) the two outer loops into one large, composite outer loop with loop cycles of identical size. This way, the host cores might be regarded as accelerators on their own, although some that are operating at a significantly lower processing power than the device(s) (Fig. 5).

In the present version of the code, the default value of the `gpu` logical (prior to the parallel region) is `.false.`, and the loop scheduling is now decided upon at runtime; more specifically, a static schedule (with default chunk size) is chosen if accelerators are absent (the computational resources amount to the `OMP_NUM_THREADS` host cores), while in the heterogeneous case of hybrid host/device execution ([`OMP_NUM_THREADS` − `acc_num_devices`] host cores and `acc_num_devices` devices), the same dynamic schedule (with a chunk size of 1) as for the GPU-3 code is chosen. It should be noted—as is often the case when optimizing the code for accelerator offloading—that the present CPU-only version of the code even marks an improvement over the original code in the "GPU-1" section, in particular for small, although less so for large matrix dimensions, as running `n_threads` single-threaded MMs concurrently will generally be more efficient than running a single multithreaded MM (over `n_thread` threads) sequentially `n_thread` times. However, this performance improvement occurs at the expense of having to store multiple private copies of the `g_ij` tensor (of size `nvirt**2`), but in the grander scheme of things, for example, considering that the `Calpha` tensor is of size `naux*nvirt*nocc`, cf. the "Computational Details" section, this is next to negligible.

GPU-5

As mentioned at the end of the "GPU-4" section, the involved tensors—in particular that containing the fitting coefficients, `Calpha`—grow large upon moving to larger

```
[...]
!$omp parallel
n_threads = omp_get_num_threads()
!$omp end parallel
[...]
if (acc_num_devices .eq. 0) then
    call omp_set_schedule(omp_sched_static,0)
else
    call omp_set_schedule(omp_sched_dynamic,1)
endif
[...]
!$omp parallel num_threads(n_threads) default(none) &
!$omp& shared(nocc,nvirt,EpsOcc,EpsVirt,naux,Calpha,cublas_handle) &
!$omp& private(ji,j,i,b,a,g_ij,pre,eps_ijb,eps,gpu_id) &
!$omp& firstprivate(gpu,acc_num_devices,acc_device_type) &
!$omp& reduction(+:rimp2_energy)
gpu_id = omp_get_thread_num()
if (gpu_id .le. (acc_num_devices-1)) then
    gpu = .true.
    call acc_set_device_num ( int(gpu_id,kind=4) , acc_device_type )
endif
!$acc data copyin(Calpha,EpsOcc,EpsVirt) copy(rimp2_energy) &
!$acc& create(g_ij) if(gpu)
!$omp do schedule(runtime)
do ji = 1,(nocc**2+nocc)/2
    call calc_i_geq_j ( ji,nocc,j,i )
    [...]
enddo
!$omp end do
!$acc end data
!$omp end parallel
[...]
```

FIG. 5

The GPU-4 scheme.

system sizes and/or larger basis sets (collectively referred to herein as a transition to increasingly larger *problem sizes*). For instance, even for moderate-sized problems (cf. the "Results" section), the memory constraints may be in excess of what is feasible on a Kepler K20X card (6 GB), and for increasingly larger problem sizes, the total device memory requirements can grow well beyond what is possible on a Kepler K40 card (12 GB). However, since the entire premise for the RI-MP2 model is that it should be able to target larger problem sizes than the regular MP2 model (which, of course, is the regime where acceleration of the kernel is most needed), these constraints, in combination with the fact that only two tiles of the fitting coefficient tensor are required to be residing on the device in each loop cycle (i.e., Calpha(:,:,j) and Calpha(:,:,i)), give motivation to a tiled implementation (Fig. 6).

```
[...]
!$acc data copyin(EpsOcc,EpsVirt) copy(rimp2_energy) create(g_ij) if(gpu)
!$omp do schedule(dynamic,1)
do ji = 1,(nocc**2+nocc)/2
   call calc_i_geq_j ( ji,nocc,j,i )
!$acc data pcopyin(Calpha(:,:,j),Calpha(:,:,i)) if(gpu)
   [...]
!$acc end data
enddo
!$omp end do
!$acc end data
!$omp end parallel
[...]
```

FIG. 6

The GPU-5 scheme.

Obviously, the increased data movement (the (potential) copyin of the i-th and j-th tile in each loop cycle) in the present version of the code over the single, but considerably larger data transfer in the previous implementations introduces a net slow-down. However, by separating the kernel into individual data transfers, we shall now see how this enables a pipelining of operations, while lowering the memory requirements dramatically, cf. the "Results" section.

GPU-6

In the GPU-5 version of the code, the requirements on the size of the device main memory were markedly reduced, but since the data movement and computations became synchronized at the same time, as these occur on the same stream (that corresponding to the default acc_async_sync handle), the implementation is significantly slower than the GPU-4 version in the "GPU-4" section. If, however, the available device main memory offers the storage of more than two tiles of size naux*nvirt, the copyin of the tile(s) required for the next loop cycle may be scheduled to occur concurrently with the current computations without the need for any immediate synchronization. This sort of pipelining can be achieved by making only a few small modifications to the GPU-5 version of the code (Fig. 7).

In this asynchronous version of the code, the data transfers are done on the streams corresponding to handles 0 and 1 (i.e., the possible values of mod(inc,2)), while the computations—that is, the MMs and the energy summation—are carried out on the stream mapped to handle 2. Note how the loop index, which might usually be used for pipelining, is not a valid choice in the present context due to the dynamic OpenMP scheduling. Instead, a thread-private incremental counter (inc) is introduced. Furthermore, the CUBLAS stream is now not the default one (acc_async_sync), but rather explicitly mapped to async handle 2, and the data dependencies are controlled through the use of (async) wait directives. In particular, two streams

```
[...]
!$omp do schedule(dynamic,1)
do ji = 1,(nocc**2+nocc)/2
    call calc_i_geq_j ( ji,nocc,j,i )
    inc = inc + 1
!$acc data pcopyin(Calpha(:,:,j),Calpha(:,:,i)) async(mod(inc,2)) if(gpu)
!$acc wait(mod(inc,2)) async(2) if(gpu)
    call dgemm_interface ( 't','n',nvirt,nvirt,naux,1.0d0,&
             & Calpha(:,:,j),naux,Calpha(:,:,i),naux,0.0d0,g_ij,nvirt,&
             & 2,cublas_handle(gpu_id+1),gpu )
!$acc wait(2) async(mod(inc,2)) if(gpu)
!$acc parallel loop gang independent &
!$acc& present(g_ij,EpsOcc,EpsVirt,rimp2_energy) &
!$acc& firstprivate(nvirt,j,i) private(b,a,pre,eps_ijb,eps) &
!$acc& reduction(+:rimp2_energy) async(2) if(gpu)
    do b = 1,nvirt
        [...]
    enddo
!$acc end parallel loop
!$acc end data
enddo
!$omp end do
!$acc wait
!$acc end data
!$omp end parallel
[...]
```

FIG. 7

The GPU-6 scheme.

are used for data transfers such that the waits within the ji-loop are made asynchronous as well. However, despite pipelining the data transfers and computations, the former of these two operations will still dominate whenever the (potential) copyins of the two tiles of Calpha take longer than the CUBLAS dgemm. As we shall see in the "Results" section, this is indeed the case; hence, whereas the present code is a clear improvement over the synchronous GPU-5 version, it is still significantly slower than the native, memory-intensive GPU-4 version. To understand why, and to see how to remedy this, we shall need to revisit how (a)synchronous device data transfers are done with CUDA/OpenACC.

GPU-7

Whenever memory is allocated on the host through, for example, an allocate statement, it is stored in so-called nonlocked pages such that the memory might potentially be swapped out to disk if need be. However, GPU devices cannot access data directly from nonlocked (or *pageable*) host main memory, so at the time when the data transfer is invoked, the driver needs to access every single page of the nonlocked memory, copy it into a page-locked (or *pinned*) memory buffer (which needs to be allocated beforehand), followed next by the actual transfer, the wait for completion, and finally the deletion of said page-locked buffer. Although the size of these buffers can be altered (in the PGI OpenACC runtime, for instance, this is done through the `PGI_ACC_BUFFERSIZE` environment variable), it is not intuitive what buffer size will be most suitable for a given problem size (Fig. 8).

```
[...]
! fitting coefficients
#ifdef PGI
real(8), allocatable, dimension(:,:,:), pinned :: Calpha
#else
real(8), allocatable, dimension(:,:,:) :: Calpha
#endif
[...]
! allocate the Calpha tensor
allocate ( Calpha(naux,nvirt,nocc),stat = alloc_stat,pinned = pinned_stat )
if (alloc_stat .ne. 0) stop " insufficient memory (Calpha) "
if (.not. pinned_stat) print *," pinned allocation of Calpha failed "
[...]
```

FIG. 8

The GPU-7 scheme.

Now, instead of using pinned memory as merely a staging area for transfers between the device and the host, one might instead choose to directly allocate host variables in pinned memory. Traditionally, this is done by allocating/deallocating host main memory with the `cudaHostAlloc` / `cudaFreeHost` routines of the CUDA API and subsequently pinning/unpinning the allocation by calling `cudaHostRegister` / `cudaHostUnregister`. In the PGI-specific CUDA Fortran extension, however, the use of pinned memory may be enforced simply by applying the `pinned` variable attribute on the declaration of an allocatable tensor. Besides the allocation of `Calpha` in pinned rather than pageable memory, no further changes are made with respect to the GPU-6 version of the code in the "GPU-6" section. However, since some operating systems and installations may restrict the use, availability, or size of page-locked memory, the allocation has been augmented by a third argument, which, if it fails (`pinned_stat` is `.false.`) makes the user aware that the allocation has defaulted to a regular allocation in paged memory.

As we shall see in the "Results" section, this simple change to the declaration of the `Calpha` tensor now makes the calculations for all relevant problem sizes completely compute-bound in the same way as the native GPU-4 version of code. Thus, as the present version of the code uses vastly less device memory than the GPU-4 version, it will in principle scale to as large dimensions of `Calpha` as may fit into host main memory. Furthermore, as the initial copyin of the entire `Calpha` is avoided, the present version of the code will actually scale better than the GPU-4 version for all but the smallest problem sizes, cf. the "Scaling With Number of Devices" section.

GPU-8

In standard RI-MP2 implementations, all involved steps (evaluation of ERIs, construction of fitting coefficients, and the final energy assembly) are performed using double precision arithmetics. However, motivated by two recent papers (Knizia, Li, Simon, & Werner, 2011; Vysotskiy & Cederbaum, 2011), which both claim that single precision arithmetics can be applied for the construction of the four-index ERIs in Eq. (3) (since this step is being performed in an orthogonal basis), we shall now, as a final optimization step, do exactly this by substituting the `dgemm` by a corresponding `sgemm` in the code. Here, the interface to `sgemm` is formulated in precisely the same way as the interface to `dgemm`. Not only is the performance bound to improve from the use of single precision arithmetics, but also the storage requirements on the tiles of the `Calpha` tensor and the `g_ij` intermediate are further lowered by a factor of two (Fig. 9).

```
[...]
do ji = 1,(nocc**2+nocc)/2
    [...]
    call sgemm_interface ( 't','n',nvirt,nvirt,naux,1.0d0,&
                    & Calpha(:,:,j),naux,Calpha(:,:,i),naux,0.0d0,g_ij,nvirt,&
                    & 2,cublas_handle(gpu_id+1),gpu )
    [...]
    do b = 1,nvirt
        eps_ijb = EpsOcc(i) + EpsOcc(j) - EpsVirt(b)
        do a = b,nvirt
            rimp2_energy += pre * (dble(g_ij(a,b))**2 + dble(g_ij(b,a))**2 &
                            & - dble(g_ij(a,b))*dble(g_ij(b,a))) / eps
        enddo
    enddo
    [...]
enddo
[...]
```

FIG. 9

The GPU-8 scheme.

RESULTS

In the present section, we shall numerically compare the different versions of the RI-MP2 kernel discussed in the "Implementation" section. Following some initial details in the "Computational Details" section on the calculations to follow, we first compare the various codes on an equal footing for execution on a single accelerator device in the "Scaling With Problem Size" section, while in the "Scaling With Number of Devices" section, we shall look at the scaling with the number of available devices. The accumulated performance against CPU-only calculations is reported for the best among the proposed schemes in the "Total Performance" section.

COMPUTATIONAL DETAILS

For the purpose of evaluating the various GPU schemes of the "Implementation" section, we shall conduct performance tests on four problems of increasing size, namely the [ala]-5 system (five alanine amino acids in an α-helix arrangement) in the cc-pVXZ (X = D, T, Q, and 5) basis sets (Dunning Jr., 1989) and corresponding cc-pVXZ-RI auxiliary basis sets (Hättig, 2005; Weigend, Köhn, & Hättig, 2002), which are of double-, triple-, quadruple-, and pentuple-ζ quality. Denoting the four problems as DZ, TZ, QZ, and 5Z, respectively, the problem sizes are defined in terms of the number of occupied orbitals, virtual orbitals, auxiliary basis functions, and size of `Calpha` in GB (`mem`) as:

- DZ: `nocc` = 100; `nvirt` = 399; `naux` = 1834; `mem` = 0.6
- TZ: `nocc` = 100; `nvirt` = 1058; `naux` = 2916; `mem` = 2.5
- QZ: `nocc` = 100; `nvirt` = 2140; `naux` = 4917; `mem` = 8.4
- 5Z: `nocc` = 100; `nvirt` = 3751; `naux` = 7475; `mem` = 22.4

In terms of computational hardware, the accelerators used are NVIDIA Kepler K40 GPUs (2880 processor cores @ 745 MHz (GPU Boost @ 875 MHz enabled, cf. the "GPU boost" section) and 12 GB main memory) and the host nodes are Intel Ivy Bridge E5-2690 v2, dual socket 10-core CPUs (20 cores @ 3.00 GHz and 128 GB main memory). The (single- or multi-threaded, depending on the version of the code) host math library is Intel MKL (version 11.2) and the corresponding device math library is CUBLAS (CUDA 7.5). All calculations are serial (non-MPI), and the OpenMP- and OpenACC-compatible Fortran compiler used is that of the PGI compiler suite (version 16.4).

GPU boost

On the K40 GPUs, the base core clock rate is 745 MHz. However, provided that the power and thermal budgets allow for it, e.g., for small problem sizes in the current context, the GPU offers the possibility of boosting the application performance by increasing the GPU core (and memory) clock rates. Since the GPU will dynamically reset the clock rates to the default values whenever it cannot safely run at the selected clocks, the use of GPU Boost is an additional (free) way of enabling even more performance gain from the accelerator. From the results in Fig. 10, we note how for the double- and triple-ζ calculations in double precision (scheme GPU-7), the net increase amounts to 7–13%, while the effect of the increased application clock rates diminishes for the larger QZ problem. For the corresponding calculations in single precision, however, the increase in performance comes close to matching the theoretical increase in moving from 745 MHz over 810 MHz (9%) to 875 MHz (17%), and the results in Fig. 10 hence mirror the intrinsic difference between the performance of single and double precision math library routines as well as the possible gain of using the former of these whenever possible.

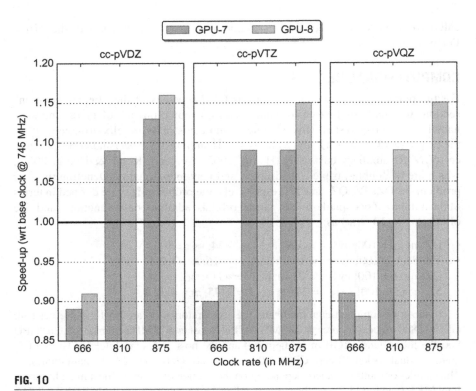

FIG. 10

The performance of the GPU-7 and GPU-8 schemes with the selected graphics clock rate for the three problem sizes, XZ (X = D, T, and Q).

SCALING WITH PROBLEM SIZE

In Fig. 11, results are presented for the relative speed-up against a CPU-only run for the eight different GPU schemes of the "Implementation" section. Schemes 1–3 are compared against the CPU-only version of scheme 1 (note that schemes 2 and 3 are identical for execution on a single GPU, cf. the "GPU-3" section), whereas schemes 4–7 are compared against the CPU-only version of scheme 4, which, itself, gives speed-ups of 48% (cc-pVDZ), 27% (cc-pVTZ), 14% (cc-pVQZ), and 7% (cc-pV5Z) over scheme 1 for the four different problem sizes. Finally, scheme 8 is compared against a CPU-only single precision version of scheme 4, which gives speed-ups of 89% (cc-pVDZ), 101% (cc-pVTZ), 100% (cc-pVQZ), and 106% (cc-pV5Z) over scheme 4 in double precision. For the largest of the four problem sizes (5Z), only the CPU-only versions of schemes 1 and 4 as well as the OpenACC-accelerated schemes 5–8 were possible to run due to the large memory requirements, cf. the discussion in the "GPU-5" section.

As is clear from Fig. 11, the performance gained from exclusively using the GPU is not as good as that gained from using both the CPU and the GPU simultaneously. Focusing further on the hybrid schemes (4–8), we note how the optimal speed-up for

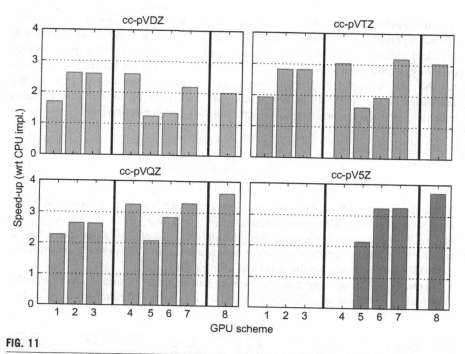

FIG. 11

Single-GPU scaling with problem size for the eight different GPU schemes. For details, please see the text.

the schemes using double precision arithmetics is met (on a K40 card) for problem sizes somewhere in-between that of the TZ and QZ problems of the present test, while for scheme 8, which uses single precision arithmetics, a small improvement is still observed in moving from the QZ to the 5Z problem. By comparing the tiled schemes 5 and 6 with the full scheme 4, it appears that the performance of the former schemes suffers from the increased amount of data transfers for problems DZ, TZ, and QZ, whereas for the pinned scheme 7, this is only the case for the smallest DZ problem. For the largest of the problem sizes (5Z), the tiled schemes cannot be compared to the full scheme 4, but from profiling runs using `nvprof`, it is confirmed that the total compute time for schemes 6 and 7 is equal to the time spent in the `dgemm` and the OpenACC parallel region. For scheme 8, profiling runs too confirm that the calculations are compute-bound, but now also for the smallest DZ problem, as a result of the smaller tiles that need to be copied to the device in each loop cycle.

SCALING WITH NUMBER OF DEVICES

With the results in the "Scaling With Problem Size" section illustrating how the different schemes perform on a single accelerator device, we now turn to the scaling with the number of devices. In Fig. 12, the scaling with the number of GPUs is presented, reported in terms of the relative deviation from ideal behavior. For scheme 3, the ideal scaling is a simple proportionality with the number of GPUs (performance doubling, tripling, etc., on two, three, etc., GPUs), whereas for schemes 4–8, this is not the case, as each CPU core is now treated as an accelerator on its own, cf. the discussion in the "GPU-4" section. Thus, the ideal speed-up for the homogeneous scheme 3 (R_1) and the heterogeneous schemes 4–8 (R_2) are defined as

$$R_1 = N_{\text{GPUs}}, \tag{5a}$$

$$R_2 = \frac{(N_{\text{threads}} - N_{\text{GPUs}}) + N_{\text{GPUs}}S}{(N_{\text{threads}} - 1) + S}. \tag{5b}$$

In the definition of R_2 in Eq. (5b), the constant factor $S = N_{\text{threads}}K$, where K is the time ratio between a CPU-only calculation ($N_{\text{threads}} = $ OMP_NUM_THREADS; $N_{\text{GPUs}} = 0$) and a GPU-only calculation using a single GPU ($N_{\text{threads}} = N_{\text{GPUs}} = 1$), accounts for the relative difference in processing power between a single CPU core (assuming ideal OpenMP parallelization on the host) and a single GPU.

From Fig. 12, we note how the scalings of schemes 3 and 4 are practically identical, as are those of schemes 7 and 8; for all of the different schemes, a clear

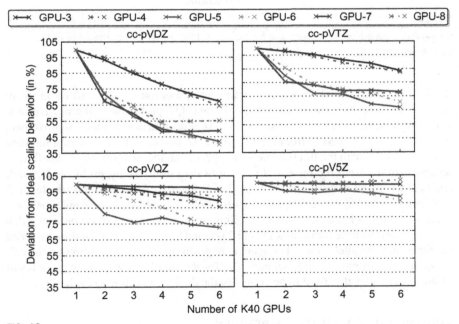

FIG. 12

Deviation from ideal scaling with the number of GPUs for schemes 3–8. For details, please see the text.

improvement in the scaling is observed in moving to larger problem sizes, but this improvement is somewhat less prominent for the asynchronous tiled scheme 6 and again much less for the synchronous scheme 5. While schemes 3 and 4, which store the full `Calpha` tensor in device main memory, scale the best for small problem sizes, the picture is shifted in favor of the tiled schemes (in particular the pinned schemes 7 and 8) upon moving to larger problem sizes, since the large copyin of `Calpha` prior to the actual energy evaluation is avoided in these.

Finally, by noting that for the hybrid schemes 4–8 there is a total of `(nocc(1+nocc))/2` tasks that need to be distributed among the CPU cores and accelerator devices, we may complement the scaling results in Fig. 12 by corresponding results for the relative GPU workload. These results are presented in Fig. 13 for schemes 6–8; for all of the four problem sizes, the utilization of the GPUs is better for the pinned schemes 7 and 8—as a result of the faster data transfers—but less so upon moving to increasingly larger problems. Also, we note how for the present problem sizes and CPU/GPU hardware, the actual utilization of the host node is minor (less than 10%) when, say, three or more GPUs are attached to said node. Still, the hybrid schemes, with the exception of the synchronous scheme 5, are always faster than the corresponding GPU-only scheme 3.

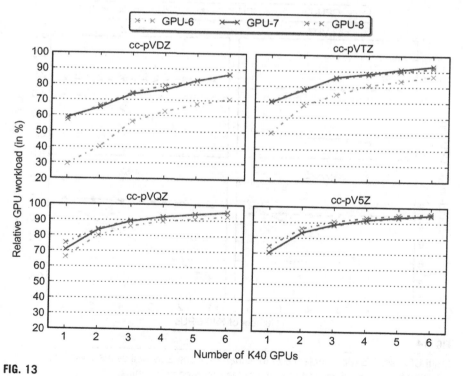

FIG. 13

Relative GPU workload with number of GPUs for schemes 6–8.

TOTAL PERFORMANCE

Having assessed how each of the proposed schemes accelerate the RI-MP2 energy evaluation for execution on a single GPU, as well as how the schemes that may utilize more than one GPU scale with the available resources, we now combine the results of Figs. 11 and 12 in Fig. 14, which reports the multi-GPU speed-up of schemes 7 and 8 over the double and single precision CPU-only versions of scheme 4. In Fig. 14, the speed-up resulting from using single rather than double precision arithmetics has also been indicated. From the results, it is obvious that both schemes perform well with the number of GPUs, but that scheme 8 generally scales better than scheme 7. In fact, using six K40 GPUs, as in the present study, is seen to reduce the total time-to-solution over the CPU-only versions of either scheme 7 or 8 by more than an order of magnitude for all but the smallest possible problem sizes, as is visible from the total timings plotted in Fig. 15. This is indeed a noteworthy acceleration of the RI-MP2 kernel, since the use of compiler directives—as long as the complete fitting coefficients fit into main memory on the host—makes it somewhat unnecessary to explicitly MPI parallelize the code.

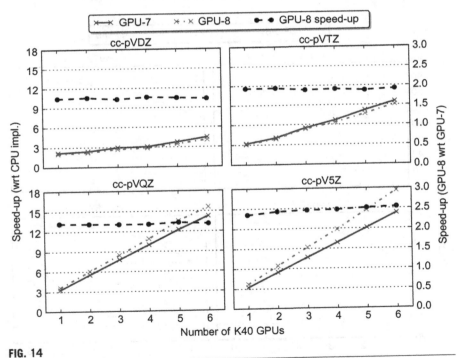

FIG. 14

Multi-GPU scaling with problem size for schemes 7 and 8 as well as the speed-up resulting from using single rather than double precision arithmetics.

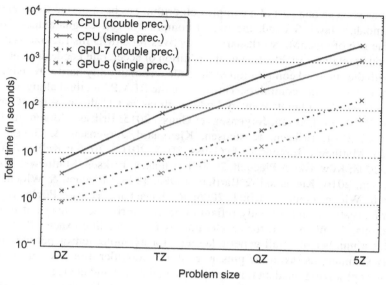

FIG. 15

Total time-to-solution for the CPU-only and hybrid CPU/GPU versions of schemes 7 and 8 (using six K40 GPUs).

SUMMARY AND CONCLUSION

In the present chapter, OpenACC compiler directives have been used to compactly and efficiently accelerate the $\mathcal{O}(N^5)$-scaling rate-determining step of the RI-MP2 method. Through a total of eight steps, the computations have been incrementally offloaded to the accelerators (GPUs in the present context), followed by a subsequent optimization of the involved data transfers. In the final versions of the code, computations and data traffic have been asynchronously pipelined, and an explicit pinning of the involved tensors in page-locked host memory has been introduced in order to make the tiled GPU schemes compute-bound on par with the more memory-intensive schemes. Due to their minimal memory footprints and efficient dependence on optimized math libraries, the two final versions of the code using either double or single precision arithmetics are capable of scaling to as large systems as allowed for by the capacity of the host main memory.

The evaluation of the RI-MP2 energy has been accelerated using a high-level approach through the use of compiler directives rather than a more low-level, albeit possibly more efficient approach through a recasting of the code using the CUDA compute platform. This has been a deliberate choice, based on a number of reasonings. First and foremost, it is the opinion of the present author that accelerated code needs to be relatively easy and fast to implement, as new bottlenecks are bound to appear as soon as one part of a complex algorithm has been ported to accelerators (cf. Amdahl's law). Second, the use of compiler directives guarantees—on par with the use of OpenMP worksharing directives for SIMD instructions—that the final code remains portable, that is, the addition of accelerated code does not interfere with the standard compilation of the code on commodity hardware using standard nonaccelerating compilers. Third, since the RI-MP2 method alongside other, more advanced noniterative many-body methods in CC theory alike (Crawford & Stanton, 1998; Eriksen, Jørgensen, & Gauss, 2015; Eriksen, Jørgensen, Olsen, & Gauss, 2014; Eriksen, Kristensen, Kjærgaard, Jørgensen, & Gauss, 2014; Eriksen, Matthews, Jørgensen, & Gauss, 2015, 2016a, 2016b; Kállay & Gauss, 2005, 2008; Kowalski & Piecuch, 2000; Kristensen, Eriksen, Matthews, Olsen, & Jørgensen, 2016; Kucharski & Bartlett, 1998a, 1998b; Piecuch & Wloch, 2005; Piecuch, Wloch, Gour, & Kinal, 2006; Raghavachari, Trucks, Pople, & Head-Gordon, 1989) are intrinsically reliant on large matrix-vector and matrix-matrix operations, the main need for accelerators is for offloading exactly these. Thus, besides a number of small generic kernels, for example, tensor permutations or energy summations (as in the present context), compiler directives are primarily used for optimizing the data transfers between the host and device(s), for instance by overlapping these with device computations. Hopefully, the generality of the discussion in the present chapter will encourage and help others to accelerate similar codes of their own.

Finally, one particular potential area of application for the present implementation deserves a dedicated mentioning. While the discussion of the RI-MP2 method herein has been exclusively concerned with its standard canonical formulation for full molecular systems, we note how the method has also been formulated within a number of so-called local correlation schemes, of which one branch relies on either a physical (Ishikawa & Kuwata, 2009; Kobayashi, Imamura, & Nakai, 2007; Mochizuki et al., 2008) or orbital-based (Baudin, Ettenhuber, Reine, Kristensen, & Kjærgaard, 2016; Eriksen, Baudin, et al., 2015; Friedrich, 2007; Friedrich & Dolg, 2009; Guo, Li, & Li, 2014; Guo, Li, Yuan, & Li, 2014; Kristensen, Ziółkowski, Jansík, Kjærgaard, & Jørgensen, 2011; Ziółkowski, Jansík, Kjærgaard, & Jørgensen, 2010) fragmentation of the molecular system. In these schemes, standard canonical calculations are performed for each of the fragments before the energy for the full system is reduced at the end of the total calculation. Thus, by accelerating each of the individual fragment (and possible pair fragment) calculations, the total calculation will be accelerated as well without the need for investing additional efforts, and the resulting reduction in time-to-solution hence has the potential to help increase the range of application for these various schemes.

ACKNOWLEDGMENTS

This work was supported by the European Research Council under the European Union's Seventh Framework Programme (FP/2007-2013)/ERC Grant Agreement

No. 291371 and the developments which led to the final production code used resources of the Oak Ridge Leadership Computing Facility (OLCF) at Oak Ridge National Laboratory, TN, USA, which is supported by the Office of Science of the Department of Energy under Contract DE-AC05-00OR22725. The actual production runs were performed on an NVIDIA test cluster, the access to which is gratefully acknowledged. Finally, the author wishes to thank Thomas Kjærgaard of Aarhus University, Tjerk Straatsma and Dmitry Liakh of OLCF, Luiz DeRose, Aaron Vose, and John Levesque of Cray Inc., as well as Mark Berger, Jeff Larkin, Roberto Gomperts, Michael Wolfe, and Brent Leback of the NVIDIA Corporation.

REFERENCES

Almlöf, J. (1991). *Chemical Physics Letters, 181*, 319.

Ayala, P. Y., & Scuseria, G. E. (1999). *The Journal of Chemical Physics, 110*, 3660.

Baudin, P., Ettenhuber, P., Reine, S., Kristensen, K., & Kjærgaard, T. (2016). *The Journal of Chemical Physics, 144*, 54102.

Čížek, J. (1966). *The Journal of Chemical Physics, 45*, 4256.

Čížek, J. (1969). *Advances in Chemical Physics, 14*, 35.

Crawford, T. D., & Stanton, J. F. (1998). *International Journal of Quantum Chemistry, 70*, 601.

Doser, B., Lambrecht, D. S., Kussmann, J., & Ochsenfeld, C. (2009). *The Journal of Chemical Physics, 130*, 64107.

Doser, B., Zienau, J., Clin, L., Lambrecht, D. S., & Ochsenfeld, C. Z. (2010). *Physical Chemistry, 224*, 397.

Dunning, T. H., Jr. (1989). *The Journal of Chemical Physics, 90*, 1007.

Eriksen, J. J., Baudin, P., Ettenhuber, P., Kristensen, K., Kjærgaard, T., & Jørgensen, P. (2015). *Journal of Chemical Theory and Computation, 11*, 2984.

Eriksen, J. J., Jørgensen, P., & Gauss, J. (2015). *The Journal of Chemical Physics, 142*, 14102.

Eriksen, J. J., Jørgensen, P., Olsen, J., & Gauss, J. (2014). *The Journal of Chemical Physics, 140*, 174114.

Eriksen, J. J., Kristensen, K., Kjærgaard, T., Jørgensen, P., & Gauss, J. (2014). *The Journal of Chemical Physics, 140*, 64108.

Eriksen, J. J., Matthews, D. A., Jørgensen, P., & Gauss, J. (2015). *The Journal of Chemical Physics, 143*, 41101.

Eriksen, J. J., Matthews, D. A., Jørgensen, P., & Gauss, J. (2016a). *The Journal of Chemical Physics, 144*, 194102.

Eriksen, J. J., Matthews, D. A., Jørgensen, P., & Gauss, J. (2016b). *The Journal of Chemical Physics, 144*, 194103.

Feyereisen, M. W., Fitzgerald, G., & Komornicki, A. (1993). *Chemical Physics Letters, 208*, 359.

Friedrich, J. (2007). *The Journal of Chemical Physics, 126*, 154110.

Friedrich, J., & Dolg, M. (2009). *Journal of Chemical Theory and Computation, 5*, 287.

Gitlab.. (2016). https://gitlab.com/januseriksen/openacc-rimp2.

Guo, Y., Li, W., & Li, S. (2014). *The Journal of Physical Chemistry. A, 118*, 8996.

Guo, Y., Li, W., Yuan, D., & Li, S. (2014). *Science China: Chemistry, 57,* 1393.

Hättig, C. (2005). *Physical Chemistry Chemical Physics, 7,* 59.

Helgaker, T., Jørgensen, P., & Olsen, J. (2000). *Molecular electronic-structure theory.* West Sussex, UK: Wiley & Sons, Ltd.

Ishikawa, T., & Kuwata, K. (2009). *Chemical Physics Letters, 474,* 195.

Kállay, M., & Gauss, J. (2005). *The Journal of Chemical Physics, 123,* 214105.

Kállay, M., & Gauss, J. (2008). *The Journal of Chemical Physics, 129,* 144101.

Knizia, G., Li, W., Simon, S., & Werner, H.-J. (2011). *Journal of Chemical Theory and Computation, 7,* 2387.

Kobayashi, M., Imamura, Y., & Nakai, H. (2007). *The Journal of Chemical Physics, 127,* 74103.

Kowalski, K., & Piecuch, P. (2000). *The Journal of Chemical Physics, 113,* 18.

Kristensen, K., Eriksen, J. J., Matthews, D. A., Olsen, J., & Jørgensen, P. (2016). *The Journal of Chemical Physics, 144,* 64103.

Kristensen, K., Ziółkowski, M., Jansík, B., Kjærgaard, T., & Jørgensen, P. (2011). *Journal of Chemical Theory and Computation, 7,* 1677.

Kucharski, S. A., & Bartlett, R. J. (1998a). *The Journal of Chemical Physics, 108,* 5243.

Kucharski, S. A., & Bartlett, R. J. (1998b). *The Journal of Chemical Physics, 108,* 9221.

Leang, S. S., Rendell, A. P., & Gordon, M. S. (2014). *Journal of Chemical Theory and Computation, 10,* 908.

Mochizuki, Y., Yamashita, K., Murase, T., Nakano, T., Fukuzawa, K., Takematsu, K.…Tanaka, S. (2008). *Chemical Physics Letters, 457,* 396.

Møller, C., & Plesset, M. S. (1934). *Physical Review, 46,* 618.

Olivares-Amaya, R., Jinich, A., Watson, M. A., & Aspuru-Guzik, A. (2016). In R. C. Walker & A. W. Götz (Eds.), *Electronic structure calculations on graphics processing units: from quantum chemistry to condensed matter physics.* Chichester, UK: John Wiley & Sons, Ltd.

Olivares-Amaya, R., Watson, M. A., Edgar, R. G., Vogt, L., Shao, Y., & Aspuru-Guzik, A. (2010). *Journal of Chemical Theory and Computation, 6,* 135.

Paldus, J., Čížek, J., & Shavitt, I. (1972). *Physical Review A, 5,* 50.

Piecuch, P., & Wloch, M. (2005). *The Journal of Chemical Physics, 123,* 224105.

Piecuch, P., Wloch, M., Gour, J. R., & Kinal, A. (2006). *Chemical Physics Letters, 418,* 467.

Purvis, G. D., & Bartlett, R. J. (1982). *The Journal of Chemical Physics, 76,* 1910.

Raghavachari, K., Trucks, G. W., Pople, J. A., & Head-Gordon, M. (1989). *Chemical Physics Letters, 157,* 479.

Shavitt, I., & Bartlett, R. J. (2009). *Many-body methods in chemistry and physics: many-body perturbation theory and coupled-cluster theory.* Cambridge, UK: Cambridge University Press.

Vahtras, O., Almlöf, J., & Feyereisen, M. W. (1993). *Chemical Physics Letters, 213,* 514.

Vogt, L., Olivares-Amaya, R., Kermes, S., Shao, Y., Amador-Bedolla, C., & Aspuru-Guzik, A. (2008). *The Journal of Physical Chemistry. A, 112,* 2049.

Vysotskiy, V. P., & Cederbaum, L. S. (2011). *Journal of Chemical Theory and Computation, 7,* 320.

Watson, M. A., Olivares-Amaya, R., Edgar, R. G., & Aspuru-Guzik, A. (2010). *Computing in Science and Engineering, 12,* 40.

Weigend, F., & Häser, M. (1997). *Theoretical Chemistry Accounts, 97,* 331.

Weigend, F., Köhn, A., & Hättig, C. (2002). *The Journal of Chemical Physics, 116*, 3175.

Werner, H.-J., Manby, F. R., & Knowles, P. J. (2003). *The Journal of Chemical Physics, 118*, 8149.

Whitten, J. L. (1973). *The Journal of Chemical Physics, 58*, 4496.

Ziółkowski, M., Jansík, B., Kjærgaard, T., & Jørgensen, P. (2010). *The Journal of Chemical Physics, 133*, 14107.

Using OpenACC to port large legacy climate and weather modeling code to GPUs

13

Xavier Lapillonne*, Katherine Osterried†, Oliver Fuhrer*

Federal Office of Meteorology and Climatology MeteoSwiss, Zurich, Switzerland* Center for Climate Systems Modeling (C2SM), ETH Zurich, Zurich, Switzerland†

The purpose of this chapter is to describe a step-by-step porting approach for weather and climate model Fortran code to run on GPUs using CUDA and OpenACC.

At the end of this chapter, the reader will have a basic understanding of:

- How to use OpenACC to port components of a production weather and climate model achieving a gain of about a factor of 2.3× in terms of time to solution and about a factor of 3× in terms of energy to solution
- The step-by-step approach to port large sections weather and climate model code with OpenACC
- Optimizations that may be introduced to enhance performance further on GPU when using OpenACC

INTRODUCTION

Weather and climate models typically encompass a large codebase maintained by an international developer community of weather and climate researchers. Since the life-cycle of weather and climate models is often in the order of 30 years, they tend to contain a significant fraction of legacy Fortran code. Furthermore, many code sections of these models have a low compute intensity, so the speedup achieved by executing individual code sections on accelerators may not be sufficient to compensate for the extra cost of the data transfers between the Central Processing Unit (CPU) and the accelerator. As a consequence, a significant fraction of the legacy code has to be ported to accelerators in order to avoid costly data transfers as much as possible. Since the effort of a complete rewrite—for example, in CUDA—may be excessive, porting the code to accelerators using compiler directives is an attractive and time-efficient alternative.

The material presented here is inspired by our experience in porting the full COSMO (Consortium for Small Scale Modeling) weather and climate model. When beginning the effort to port and optimize the COSMO model to run on Graphic Processing Units (GPUs), the first step taken was to profile the model carefully. The goal of porting the code to GPU and optimizing it is to reduce run-time. It is therefore fundamental to have a good understanding of not only which subroutines are taking the most computational time in the program, but also where the large data transfers may occur between the CPU and GPU. Several profiling tools have been used during the porting and optimization process of the COSMO model. The profiler from Nvidia is useful to understand the performance of in-dividual kernels, while internal timers have been used to get a global overview of the different model components when running the model at scale on a distrib-uted system. Fig. 1 shows the runtime of different sections of the model in the production environment at the Federal Office of Meteorology and Climatology MeteoSwiss (in Switzerland).

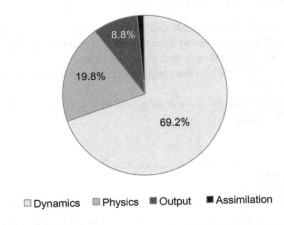

FIG. 1

Operational COSMO runtime distribution.

Clearly, the dynamics—the part of the model solving the governing equations of flow motion—is the most time-consuming portion of the model run. However, the dynamics section was ported with a different strategy directly using CUDA (Fuhrer et al., 2014), and is therefore not discussed here. The porting and optimization work with OpenACC directives was applied to the physics parameterizations and the data assimilation sections of the code, which are the second and fourth most costly components of the model, respectively.

The COSMO model code that was ported to GPU using the mixed approach with CUDA and OpenACC is now used for the production of weather forecasts on a hybrid multi-GPU Cray CS-Storm system at the Federal Office of Meteorology and Climatology MeteoSwiss. Comparison with a CPU only system of equivalent generation has shown that for the weather forecast production, a gain of approximately a factor of 2.3× is achieved in terms of time to solution, and a factor of approximately 3× in terms of energy to solution.

In this chapter, we shall focus on the porting of the so-called *physical parameterizations* (sometimes also simply referred to as the "physics") of the model which was achieved with OpenACC in COSMO. The physical parameterizations refer to the code components that handle processes that are not explicitly resolved on the computational grid: for example, subgrid scale turbulence. A weather and climate model will contain several physical parameterizations, each one responsible for representing a specific physical process important for modeling the atmosphere. In the source code they will be integrated as separate source code modules, as they are often shared between weather and climate models.

Weather and climate models typically employ a computational grid on which the main governing equations of air mass flow are computed. In COSMO, a structured, three-dimensional grid is employed. The three dimensions (denoted by the indices i,j,k in the source code) correspond to the three space dimensions (latitude, longitude, height above ground). On this computational grid, the main prognostic variables describing the state of the atmosphere at a specific instant in time are defined. For example, the air temperature would be defined as a three-dimensional array t(i,j,k) describing the atmospheric temperature at each gridpoint of the computational grid. Such three-dimensional arrays are often also referred to as *fields*. The outermost loop in any weather and climate model will then be a loop over time, integrating forward in time the state of the atmosphere described by the prognostic variables. As a consequence, the physical parameterizations will both read and modify these variables by looping over all gridpoints on every timestep. One special characteristic of the physical parameterizations is that the algorithms employed are almost exclusively column based, meaning that the result of a computation for a specific gridpoint (i,j,k) only depends on information from neighboring gridpoints in the k-direction (and not in the i/j-directions). This fact will be leveraged for the parallel execution on the accelerator.

PORTING APPROACH: STEP BY STEP

The purpose of this section is to provide a concrete step-by-step approach and discuss some of the key OpenACC constructs which have been used for the GPU port of the COSMO model. To this end, we provide a simplified toy model example which contains the key components and structure, e.g., the physical parameterizations and output, of a typical community "atmospheric" model.

SIMPLIFIED ATMOSPHERIC MODEL

The example is written in Fortran 90 in a functional programing style and is available for download. In the downloaded source, the base serial simplified atmospheric model is contained in the `example_serial` directory. Fig. 2 shows the body of the main driver code (`main.f90`). It contains a call to the `initialize` subroutine which allocates and initializes two global fields: t and qv. The "time loop" where the physical parameterizations and output are called is then executed for nstop iterations. After the time loop, the `cleanup` subroutine deallocates the global variables.

```
CALL initialize()

  !------------------------------------------------------------
  ! time loop

  DO ntstep = 1, nstop

    ! call the physical parameterizations
    CALL physics()

    ! call outputs
    CALL write_output( ntstep )

  END DO
  !------------------------------------------------------------

CALL cleanup()
```

FIG. 2

Main driver code showing the initialization of the time loop, which contains the calls to the physical parameterizations, outputs, and model clean-up.

The physics subroutine, shown in Fig. 3, calls the two physical parameterizations `saturation_adjustment` and `microphysics`. The global fields t and qv are passed by argument to the parameterization together with an intermediate automatic Fortran array qc. The `saturation_adjustment` and `microphysics` are doing some compute intensive operations over the horizontal i,j- and vertical k-directions.

```
! driving routine for the physical parameterizations
SUBROUTINE physics()

   IMPLICIT NONE

   ! local variables
   REAL*8 :: qc(nx,ny,nz)    ! temporary variable used    in the physics

   ! call a first physical parameterization
   CALL saturation_adjustment(nx, ny, nz, t, qc, qv)

   ! call a second physical parameterization
   CALL microphysics(nx, ny, nz, t, qc, qv)

END SUBROUTINE physics
```

FIG. 3

Physics driving routine calling two parameterizations: saturation adjustment
and microphysics.

In the following, unless otherwise stated, we only focus on the execution time
of the main time loop and neglect initialization and clean-up time. The execution
times reported in this chapter are averaged over 10 runs. The "model" configuration
(problem size) is fixed to $128 \times 128 \times 60$ grid points, which is representative of a
typical number of points per subdomain when running a real atmospheric model on
a distributed system and 100 time iteration steps.

As a baseline reference, execution time on CPU is obtained with an OpenMP
version of the code (in the `example_openmp` directory) run on a 12-core Intel Xeon
E5-2690 v3 (Haswell) CPU. The code is compiled with the Cray CCE compiler with
optimization flags "-O3 -homp" and gives a time of 240 ms.

STEP 1: ADDING PARALLEL REGIONS

The first step in the porting of the physics parameterizations to GPU using OpenACC directives is simply to add parallel regions to the code using the directives `$acc parallel`/`$acc
end parallel` and `$acc loop`. The parallel/end parallel directive pair tells the compiler
that the specified region has code which should be parallelized, and the loop directive tells
the compiler the specific location of the loops to be executed in parallel.

In the example presented here, we begin by porting the nested `i,j,k` loops in the
`m_parameterizations.f90` file to GPU. There are two physics parameterizations in
separate subroutines in this file, `saturation_adjustment` and `microphysics`, each
of which contains a nested `i,j,k` loop that can be executed on the GPU. First, the
`$acc parallel` and `$acc end parallel` directives are placed around the nested do
loops, as shown in Fig. 4.

```
!$acc parallel
  DO k = 1, nlev
    DO j = 1, npy
      DO i = 1, npx
        qv(i,j,k) = qv(i,j,k) + cs1*EXP(cs2*( t(i,j,k)-t0 )/( t(i,j,k)-cs3) )
        qc(i,j,k) = cs4*qv(i,j,k)
      END DO
    END DO
  END DO
  !$acc end parallel
```

FIG. 4

Add a parallel region to the loops in the saturation_adjustment routine.

Next, $acc loop directives are added at the beginning of each of the do loops. Note that the k loop in the microphysics subroutine has a dependency on (k-1). Therefore, the $acc loop seq directive is used to declare explicitly that this loop must be run sequentially, while the other two loops in the nesting can be run in parallel with only the $acc loop directive, as shown in Fig. 5.

```
!$acc parallel
  !$acc loop seq
  DO k = 2, nlev
    !$acc loop
    DO j = 1, npy
      !$acc loop
      DO i = 1, npx
        qv(i, j, k) = qv(i,j,k-1) + cm1*(t(i,j,k)-cm2)**cm3
        t(i, j, k)  = t(i, j, k)*( 1.0D0 - cm4*qc(i,j,k)+qv(i,j,k) )
      END DO
    END DO
  END DO
  !$acc end parallel
```

FIG. 5

Add the $acc loop directive to the loops in the microphysics subroutine.

The code is then compiled with only these small modifications and run on GPU. Once the code is running on GPU, it is important to validate systematically the output of the calculations. In the atmospheric model example presented here, this is accomplished by examining the mean of the qv variable every 20 time steps (which is printed in the standard output). The output of the GPU run is checked against the CPU reference to verify that the results are within rounding errors.

In the downloaded source, the corresponding code can be found in the example_ openacc_step1 directory. The code compiled with both the Portland Group, Inc. (PGI) and Cray compilers with optimization flags, "-O3 -ta=nvidia" and "-O3 -hacc," respectively, is now run on a NVIDIA Tesla K80 dual GPU accelerator card and the results for the main time loop are shown in Fig. 6. Note that for simplicity, the example GPU code is only parallelized with OpenACC; this means we are only able to use one of the two GK210 GPUs of the K80.

Run	Duration of time loop (PGI; ms)	Duration of time loop (Cray; ms)
Step 1: add parallel regions	1406	1014

FIG. 6

Runtimes for step 1.

Although the code is now running on the GPU at the end of the first porting step, it is actually much slower than the reference CPU OpenMP version of 240 ms. This issue will be addressed in the next porting step. The different timings between the two compilers for this first example is here mostly due to a different behavior regarding the so-called pinned memory. By using the flag "-ta=nvidia,pinned" with PGI the time goes down to 1024 ms similar to what is obtained with the Cray compiler. The "pinned" flag however has also negative impact for some of the later examples, and we therefore keep "-O3 -ta=nvidia" for PGI for the remainder.

In general, the timing of the main time loop is the main concern for porting of an atmospheric model to GPU, because the initialization and clean-up time is much smaller compared to the time stepping portion of the actual atmospheric model. However, it should also be noted here that initialization time for the code compiled with PGI (not shown on the table) has increased when the OpenACC directives were added to the code. This is because, depending on the OpenACC implementation, the device is generally initialized when encountering the first parallel region, which adds some time cost. In the example code presented here, an OpenACC parallel region is used in the m_setup.f90 code to initialize the GPU, and the initialization time is therefore not accounted for in the time reported for the execution of the main time loop. It is good to be aware of this additional time required for the initialization of the GPU, as the first OpenACC parallel region in your code may be within the main time loop.

STEP 2: MANAGING DATA TRANSFERS

In the first porting step, OpenACC parallel regions were added to the code and successfully used to run part of the code on GPU. However, this resulted in a slowdown of the code, instead of a speedup. The reason for this is the lack of data management in the code. At the beginning of each OpenACC parallel region, the variables needed for calculation are copied from the CPU to the GPU at the beginning of the region, and then back again at the end of the parallel region. This results in a significant amount of time being spent transferring data, as there are now two OpenACC parallel regions being executed during each time loop—see Fig. 7.

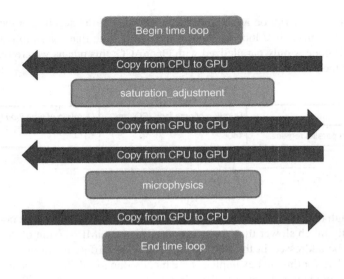

FIG. 7

Schematic of data transfers at the beginning of step 2.

To mitigate this problem, in step 2 more OpenACC directives are added to eliminate the unnecessary data transfers between the CPU and the GPU. First, an unstructured data region is created for the global variables t and qv in m_setup. f90. The data are first allocated on the GPU using the $acc data enter cre- ate statement, and then copied from the CPU to the GPU using the $acc update device statement during the initialize subroutine. The $acc data enter state- ment requires a matching $acc exit data statement, which is placed right before deallocation of the global variables in the cleanup subroutine in m_setup.f90, as shown in Fig. 8.

These OpenACC data directives ensure that the t and qv variables are allocated and copied to the GPU before the time loop instead of being copied back and forth between OpenACC parallel regions—see Fig. 9.

Next, a data region is created for the local variable qc in m_physics.f90 using the $acc data create and $acc end data statement, shown in Fig. 10. The $acc data create directive allocates memory on the GPU, but does not copy data from host to GPU when entering a region or copy data to the host when exiting a region. The data region spans the two calls to the parameterization subroutines and thus ensures that the qc variable is not copied back and forth between the CPU and the GPU between the calls to the saturation_adjustment and microphysics subroutines.

Data regions are also needed in the subroutines in the m_parameterization.f90 file to indicate that the variables t, qv, and qc are now already located on the GPU (from another containing data region). Therefore, $acc data present and $acc end data statements are added at the beginning and end of the saturation_adjustment and microphysics subroutines, as shown in Fig. 11.

```
SUBROUTINE initialize()
- - - - - - - - - - - - - - - - - - - - - - - - - - - - - - - - - - - - - - - - - -
! allocate memory
    ALLOCATE( t(nx,ny,nz), qv(nx,ny,nz) )

    ! allocate on the GPU
    !$acc enter data create(t,qv)

    ! initialize global fields
    DO k =1, nz
- - - - - - - - - - - - - - - - - - - - - - - - - - - - - - - - - - - - - - -
    END DO

    ! initialize fields on the GPU
    !$acc update device(t,qv)
- - - - - - - - - - - - - - - - - - - - - - - - - - - - - - - - - - - - - - -

SUBROUTINE cleanup()
    IMPLICIT NONE
    ! deallocate on the GPU
    !$acc exit data delete(t,qv)
    DEALLOCATE( t, qv )
  END SUBROUTINE cleanup
```

FIG. 8

Allocate, initialize, and deallocate the global variables on GPU during the initialize
and clean-up subroutines in m_setup.f90.

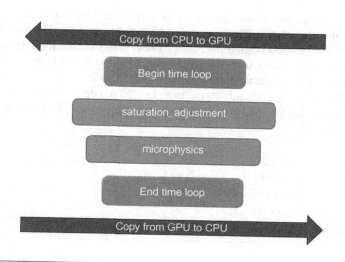

FIG. 9

Schematic diagram showing data transfers after step 2.

```
!$acc data create(qc)
    ! call a first physical parameterization
    CALL saturation_adjustment(nx, ny, nz, t, qc, qv)

    ! call a second physical parameterization
    CALL microphysics(nx, ny, nz, t, qc, qv)
    !$acc end data
```

FIG. 10

Add a data region for the local physics variable.

```
!$acc data present(t,qv,qc)
    ! do the computation
    !$acc parallel
    !$acc loop
    DO k = 1, nlev
..............................
    END DO
    !$acc end parallel
    !$acc end data
```

FIG. 11

Add data regions in the physics subroutines.

While the code would compile and run with these OpenACC data regions in place, it would not validate. This is because the variable qv is used by the CPU in the write_output subroutine called from main.f90 during the time loop. However, this variable is not copied back from the GPU to the CPU, so the CPU does not have the correct values for this variable during the time loop. An $acc update host statement is used in the write_output subroutine in m_io.f90 to copy only that variable back from the GPU to the CPU during an output time step so that it can be output by the CPU—see Fig. 12.

```
IF (MOD(ntstep, nout) /= 0) RETURN
    !$acc update host(qc)
    ! compute mean of variable qv
    qv_mean = 0.0D0
```

FIG. 12

Add update host directive before output.

Once all of these modifications are made, the code is compiled with the PGI and Cray compilers, run on GPU, and validated (by checking the mean values of qv every 20 time steps in the standard output against the reference CPU run). In the downloaded source, the corresponding code can be found in the `example_openacc_step2` directory. Fig. 13 shows the resulting timings.

Run	Duration of time loop (PGI; ms)	Duration of time loop (Cray; ms)
Step 1: add parallel regions	1406	1014
Step 2: managing data transfers	87	82

FIG. 13

Runtimes after step 2.

By applying the OpenACC data directives and eliminating unnecessary data transfers between the CPU and the GPU, speedups of about 2.8× have been achieved compared to the reference CPU version.

STEP 3: BASIC OPTIMIZATIONS

The third step in the OpenACC porting of the simple atmospheric model is to perform some basic optimizations. These are small changes to the code which bring an additional speedup that is not expected to be as large as the initial speedup that was achieved in steps 1 and 2 of the porting approach. There are three separate basic optimizations that are applied here to the simple atmospheric model code.

Fine-grain control of parallelism

The first optimization is to add some clauses to the `$acc loop` directives in the physics parameterization subroutines `saturation_adjustment` and `microphysics`. Because the loops in the `saturation_adjustment` subroutine are tightly nested, a collapse(3) clause is added to the `$acc loop` directive on the outer loop. This means that the three loops are collapsed together and treated as one large loop. All three loops in the `microphysics` subroutine cannot be collapsed together because of the dependency in the k loop. However, the i and j loops could be collapsed together if desired.

Gang and vector clauses are also added to the `$acc loop` directives in the physics subroutines. The gang and vector clauses are used to distribute the iterations of the loops among the gangs or in vector mode, respectively. In the `saturation_adjustment` subroutine, both the gang and vector clauses are added to the single `$acc loop` directive, as shown in Fig. 14.

In the `microphysics` subroutine, the vector clause is added to the i loop, because the vector clause should be associated with the loop of the stride-1 index in the arrays (left most index in Fortran, in this case the i loop). The gang clause is added to the j loop, and the k loop must still be run sequentially because of the dependency in k (see Fig. 15).

```
!$acc data present(t,qv,qc)
    ! do the computation
    !$acc parallel
    !$acc loop gang vector collapse(3)
    DO k = 1, nlev
       DO j = 1, npy
```

FIG. 14

Add clauses to the $acc loop directive in the saturation_adjustment subroutine.

```
!$acc parallel
  !$acc loop seq
  DO k = 2, nlev
     !$acc loop gang
     DO j = 1, npy
        !$acc loop vector
        DO i = 1, npx
```

FIG. 15

Add clauses to the $acc loop directive in the microphysics subroutine.

Ideal placement of the gang, vector, and collapse clauses on the $acc loop directives is architecture dependent, and therefore requires testing on the target accelerator to be effective as an optimization tool.

Porting the output/reductions

The next optimization that is applied to the code involves the addition of a parallel region. In the write_output subroutine in the m_io.f90 file, there is another nested i,j,k loop that is a good candidate for parallelization. This loop nest requires some additional care as it involves the reduction of the array variable qv to a scalar, namely the computation of the mean of qv. The reduction clause of the $acc loop directive is introduced here to specify that the nested i,j,k loop involves the calculation of a scalar value from an array of values. In this case, it is an addition operation on the qv_mean scalar, so the reduction clause is as follows: reduction(+:qv_mean).

To port the nested loop in the write_output subroutine, OpenACC parallel and data regions are added as in step 1. In addition, the reduction clause for the $acc loop directive is applied. To optimize the parallelism of the loops further, the gang, vector, and collapse clauses are also applied to the $acc loop directive, as shown in Fig. 16.

Note that because the variable qv is now used on the GPU, the $acc update host statement introduced in step 2 of the porting can be removed.

```
!$acc data present(qv)
 ! compute mean of variable qv
 qv_mean = 0.0D0
 !$acc parallel
 !$acc loop gang vector collapse(3) reduction(+:qv_mean)
 DO k = 1, nz
   DO j = 1, ny
     DO i = 1, nx
```

FIG. 16

Add the $acc loop directive with clauses to the write_output subroutine.

Removal of automatic arrays

The final optimization step involves replacing the local automatic array qc from the m_physics.f90 file with an allocatable array. This is another data management technique that allows the qc variable to be allocated and deallocated on the GPU outside the time loop, instead of during the time loop. Memory allocation and deallocation on the GPU is a time-consuming operation, and it is best done ahead of time and not when immediately needed.

To implement this change, qc is added to the fields in the m_fields.f90 file. Then, subroutines are added to the m_physics.f90 file to allocate (init_physics) and deallocate (finalize_physics) the qc variable on both the CPU and GPU (see Fig. 17). Calls to these subroutines are then added to the m_setup.f90 file, outside of the time loop.

```
SUBROUTINE init_physics()
    IMPLICIT NONE
    ! allocate memory
    ALLOCATE( qc(nx,ny,nz) )
    !$acc enter data create(qc)
 END SUBROUTINE init_physics
 !--------------------------------------------------------
 ! Finalize the local physics array
 SUBROUTINE finalize_physics()
    IMPLICIT NONE
    ! deallocate memory
    !$acc exit data delete(qc)
    DEALLOCATE(qc)
 END SUBROUTINE finalize_physics
```

FIG. 17

Add subroutines to allocate and deallocate the local physics variable on GPU and CPU.

Once these three optimizations are applied to the code, it is compiled with the PGI and Cray compilers and then run again, resulting in the timings found in Fig. 18 after validation of the code. In the downloaded source, the corresponding code can be found in the `example_openacc_step3` directory.

Run	Duration of time loop (PGI; ms)	Duration of time loop (Cray; ms)
Step 1: add parallel regions	1406	1014
Step 2: managing data transfers	87	82
Step 3: basic optimizations	72	61

FIG. 18

Runtime after step 3.

By applying the basic optimizations, speedups of 3.3× (PGI) and 3.9× (Cray) from the reference CPU run are achieved.

PARALLEL LOOP CONTAINING SUBROUTINE CALLS

In the previous sections, a three-step approach for porting the simple atmospheric model has been described. However, the example code is somewhat simplistic and only contains subroutines with purely nested loops. In a real application, the call tree may be more complex and may in particular contain subroutine calls within the parallel loops. This case can be handled by using the `$acc routine` clause.

The purpose of this section is to show an example where this OpenACC construct is required. To this end we assume the code is structured differently, with the horizontal loop i and j directly in the `physics` and a modified version of the `saturation_adjustment` and `microphysics` subroutines being called for each iterations of the i,j loop. An OpenACC data region and a parallel region are added around these new nested do loops in the `physics` subroutine (see Fig. 19).

The OpenACC data region outside the main time loop that was described in step 2 of the previous section is also implemented, so that the main variables are copied to and from the GPU outside of the main time loop.

The `$acc routine seq` directives are added to the `saturation_adjustment` and `microphysics` subroutines. The `seq` clause tells the compiler that there will be no further parallelization inside the routine. This clause is required for the microphysics subroutine because the k loop inside must be run sequentially as a result of the dependency on k-1. The `saturation_adjustment` routine must also be run sequentially, because the i loop in the `physics` subroutine has the `vector` clause, which is the lowest level of parallelization that can be applied.

```
!$acc data present(t,qc,qv)
 !$acc parallel
 !$acc loop gang
DO j = 1,ny
   !$acc loop vector
   DO i = 1,nx
. . . . . . . . . . . . . . . . . . . . . . . . . . . . . . .
   END DO
END DO
!$acc end parallel
!$acc end data
```

FIG. 19

Add OpenACC parallel and data regions to the physics subroutine.

The OpenACC parallel region that was described in step 3 in the previous section in the `write_output` subroutine is also implemented here, again using the reduction clause for the `$acc loop` directive.

There is one final directive that must be added before the code will compile. In OpenACC any module variables in the same module as a subroutine containing an `$acc routine` directive must be explicitly declared using the `$acc declare` directive, so an `$acc declare` directive is added in the `m_parameterizations.f90` file to declare and copy the module variables to the GPU (see Fig. 20).

```
MODULE m_parameterizations
  IMPLICIT NONE
  ! module constants
  REAL*8 ::  cs1 = 1.0D-6, cs2 = 0.02D0, cs3 = 7.2D0, cs4=0.1D0, t0=273.0D0
  REAL*8 ::   cm1 = 1.0D-6, cm2=25.0D0, cm3=0.2D0, cm4=100.0D0

  !$acc declare copyin(cs1, cs2, cs3, cs4, t0)
  !$acc declare copyin(cm1, cm2, cm3, cm4)
CONTAINS
```

FIG. 20

Add `$acc declare` statements for the module variables in m_parameterizations.f90.

Once all of these directives have been added, the code is compiled with the PGI and Cray compilers and is run. In the downloaded source, the corresponding code can be found in the `example_openacc_alt1` directory. After validation, the timings shown in Fig. 21 are obtained. It can be seen that the timings for the code with the `$acc routine` directives are comparable to those from step 2 (Cray compiler) and step 3 (PGI compiler).

Run	Duration of time loop (PGI; ms)	Duration of time loop (Cray; ms)
Step 1: add parallel regions	1406	1014
Step 2: managing data transfers	87	82
Step 3: basic optimizations	72	61
Alternate code 1 (acc routine)	76	99

FIG. 21

Alternate code runtime.

INTERFACING WITH CUDA

Another important OpenACC feature is the ability to interface Fortran OpenACC code with CUDA code. This was in particular useful in the COSMO project to interface the dynamics section, which was ported with CUDA, to the rest of the model which was ported with OpenACC. Here, we provide an interfacing example where the saturation adjustment is implemented as a CUDA kernel. A proper interoperability between the Fortran and C/CUDA part is ensured thanks to the BIND(C) attribute and the ISO_C_BINDING module (introduced with the Fortran 2003 standard). In order to avoid data transfers between the CPU and the GPU, we directly pass the addresses of the data, allocated on the GPU in the Fortran part, to the CUDA code. This is achieved by using the `host_data use_device` OpenACC construct around the call to the CUDA routine together with the C_LOC inquiry function, as illustrated in Fig. 22.

The CUDA version of the `saturation_adjustment` routine is shown in Fig. 23. We note that there are no `cudamalloc` nor any data transfers required, because the addresses of the arrays allocated in the Fortran part are directly passed to the kernel. This CUDA implementation is comparable in performance to the implementation in step 3; on running the CUDA version on the GPU, we obtained a run time of 58 ms with the Cray compiled version and 61 ms with the PGI compiled version (see Fig. 24). In the downloaded source, the corresponding code can be found in the `example_openacc_alt2` directory.

```
! Interface to CUDA function using iso_c_binding
 INTERFACE
   ! Pass pointer and dimensions of ijk fields to dycore
   SUBROUTINE saturation_adjustment_cuda( ntot, t, qc, qv,  &
                       cs1, cs2, cs3, cs4, t0  ) &
       BIND(c, name='saturation_adjustment_cuda')
    USE, INTRINSIC :: iso_c_binding
    INTEGER(C_INT), value       :: ntot
    TYPE(C_PTR), value          :: t,qc,qv
    REAL(KIND=C_DOUBLE), value :: cs1,cs2,cs3,cs4,t0
   END SUBROUTINE saturation_adjustment_cuda
 END INTERFACE


 ! Call the CUDA wrapper routine
 !$acc data present(t,qv,qc)
 !$acc host_data use_device(t,qv,qc)
 call saturation_adjustment_cuda(npx*npy*nlev,        &
               C_LOC(t(1,1,1)),             &
               C_LOC(qc(1,1,1)),            &
               C_LOC(qv(1,1,1)),            &
               cs1, cs2, cs3, cs4, t0 )
 !$acc end host_data
 !$acc end data
```

FIG. 22

The routine `saturation_adjustment` is adapted to call the CUDA function `saturation_adjustment_CUDA`. Addresses to the GPU memory are passed as arguments using the `host_data use_device` construct.

PERFORMANCE OPTIMIZATION
ADVANCED OPTIMIZATION TECHNIQUES

In step 3 of the step-by-step porting approach in the previous section, some basic OpenACC optimization techniques were introduced. In this section, further techniques for optimizing OpenACC ported code are described, including loop fusion, scalar replacement, caching, and on-the-fly computation.

Loop fusion and reordering

Because the COSMO model is a code that was initially designed to be optimized with compiler auto-vectorization for Single Instruction, Multiple Data (SIMD) architectures, there are many loops in the physics parameterization subroutines that have a form similar to that found in Fig. 25.

```
//----------------------------------------
// saturation adjustment kernel
__global__  void saturation_adjustment_kernel(int ntot,
                              double *t, double *qc, double *qv,
                              double cs1, double cs2, double cs3, double cs4,
double t0)
{
    int tid = blockIdx.x * blockDim.x + threadIdx.x;
    if ( tid < ntot ) {
        qv[tid] = qv[tid] + cs1*exp(cs2*( t[tid]-t0 )/( t[tid]-cs3) );
        qc[tid] = cs4*qv[tid];
    }
}


//----------------------------------------
// Cuda function calling the saturation adjustment kernel
    void saturation_adjustment_cuda(int ntot,
                              double *t, double *qc, double *qv,
                              double cs1, double cs2, double cs3, double cs4, double t0)
{
    // Set cuda grid dimensions
    const int THREADS_PER_BLOCK = 128; //number of gpu threads per block
    const int NUMBER_OF_BLOCKS = ceil(ntot/THREADS_PER_BLOCK);

    // Calling CUDA kernel
    saturation_adjustment_kernel<<<NUMBER_OF_BLOCKS,
THREADS_PER_BLOCK>>>(ntot,t,qc,qv,
                              cs1,cs2,cs3,cs4,t0);

}

};
```

FIG. 23

CUDA version of the saturation adjustment subroutine.

Run	Duration of time loop (PGI; ms)	Duration of time loop (Cray; ms)
Step 1: add parallel regions	1406	1014
Step 2: managing data transfers	87	82
Step 3: basic optimizations	72	61
Alternate code 1 (acc routine)	76	99
Alternate code 2 (CUDA)	58	61

FIG. 24

Alternate code runtime.

```
do k=2,nk
do i=1,ni
        some code 1 ...
        c(i) = D*exp(a(i,k-1))
end do
do i=1,ni
        a(i,k)=c(i)*a(i,k)
        some code 2 ...
end do
end do
```

FIG. 25

Pseudocode of the physics parameterizations in COSMO.

Each loop in the example pseudocode contains a short number of calculations, and variables that are calculated in one loop are then used in a different loop calculation. This code form works well with systems taking advantage of compiler auto-vectorization for generating SIMD instructions, but is typically not ideal for GPUs. On GPUs, if parallel regions are applied to each loop in the pseudocode, we have numerous individual GPU kernels, often with the same variables in them. Furthermore, a lot of variables require explicit data management between GPU kernels. Applying OpenACC directives as in the step-by-step approach presented above would result in the pseudocode shown in Fig. 26.

The first optimization that can be applied here is a so-called *loop fusion and loop reordering*. With this technique, a sequence of loops with the same loop index is fused into a single loop containing a larger amount of computation. This reduces the number of kernels that the GPU needs to launch (i.e., removes the associated kernel launch overhead) and results in simpler data management. We additionally swap the i and k loop, which is also beneficial for the scalar replacement optimization described in the next section. Applying loop fusion and reordering to the pseudocode would result in the pseudocode shown in Fig. 27.

Scalar replacement

The second optimization technique that can be applied here is *scalar replacement*. After combining the loops in the loop fusion step, the variable $c(i)$ is first calculated from some other variables, and then used in a calculation of a final variable. Because the variable c is only used as an intermediate variable, it does not need to be stored in an array, but can be stored as a scalar. The main advantage here is that this variable

```
do k=2,nk
!$acc parallel
!$acc loop gang vector
do i=1,ni
        some code 1 ...
        c(i) = D*exp(a(i,k-1))
end do
!$acc end parallel
!$acc parallel
!$acc loop gang vector
do i=1,ni
        a(i,k)=c(i)*a(i,k)
        some code 2 ...
end do
!$acc end parallel
end do
```

FIG. 26

Add $acc parallel and loop directives to the pseudocode.

```
!$acc parallel
!$acc loop gang vector
do i=1,ni
!$acc loop seq
  do k=2,nk
    some code 1 ...
    c(i)=D*exp(a(I,k-1))
    a(I,k)=c(i)*a(I,k)
    some code 2 ...
  end do
end do
!$acc end parallel
```

FIG. 27

Apply loop fusion and reordering technique to the pseudocode.

may simply be stored in a register and does not need to be stored in the main memory of the device. Fig. 28 shows the pseudocode with the loop fusion and scalar replacement optimizations applied.

```
!$acc parallel
!$acc loop gang vector
do i=1,ni
!$acc loop seq
  do k=2,nk
     some code 1 ...
     zc=D*exp(a(I,k-1))
     a(I,k)=zc*a(I,k)
     some code 2 ...
  end do
end do
!$acc end parallel
```

FIG. 28

Apply loop refactoring and scalar replacement to the pseudocode.

Caching

In the physics, as shown in the example code, and in the above described pseudocode, there are some dependencies between the vertical levels. It may be beneficial to save those variables which are reused at the next level as scalars, as illustrated in Fig. 29. This technique, which we refer to here as caching, has the benefit (similar to scalar replacement) that the cached variables may be stored in a register and can be read again directly without accessing the main memory. Although this type of optimization could sometimes be done automatically by the compiler, we have seen in practice that such manual optimizations are often beneficial.

On-the-fly computation

When a computation is done multiple times, it is often beneficial for the CPU to store the result and reuse it at several places. On the GPU, however, the ratio between FLOP/s and memory bandwidth is such that in most cases it is better to avoid the additional memory accesses required to read the precomputed values, and simply to recompute the values "on the fly" every time they are needed.

```
!$acc parallel
!$acc loop gang vector
do i=1,ni
a_km1=a(i,1)
  do k=2,nk
     some code 1 ...
     zc=D*exp(a_km1)
     a_km1=zc*a(i,k) ! save value in scalar
     a(i,k)=a_km1
     some code 2 ...
  end do
end do
!$acc end parallel
```

FIG. 29

Manual caching in a scalar variable.

RESULTS FOR THE RADIATION PARAMETERIZATION

In order to illustrate the impact that the advanced optimizations described in the previous section can have on a working Fortran code that has been accelerated with OpenACC directives, we present in this section results for the radiation parameterization used in the COSMO model. The radiation parameterization is one of the physics modules in COSMO, and is used to calculate the radiative equilibrium in the atmosphere (e.g., the solar radiation or cloud radiation). Here, the so-called Ritter-Geleyn radiation parameterization (Ritter & Geleyn, 1992) is considered. This parameterization in the COSMO model is composed of about 18 subroutines and corresponds to approximately 10,000 lines of Fortran code. The entire radiation code, except the initialization, is ported with OpenACC. For the majority of the code, OpenACC directives are simply added without any further optimizations (that is, no loop fusion or reordering, scalar replacement, on-the-fly computation, or caching techniques are applied). Profiling of the radiation code indicated that one component, namely the radiative equilibrium solver, accounts for about 80% of the radiation runtime, and is therefore a good candidate for optimization. The radiative equilibrium solver corresponds to about 1500 lines of code, i.e., 15% of the total radiation code, and is split over four subroutines. The base code is well optimized for CPU execution, and in particular is written in a friendly way for compiler auto-vectorization. The more advanced optimizations, as discussed in the previous section, are therefore applied to this component of the radiation code (Lapillonne & Fuhrer, 2014) to make it more suitable for running on GPUs.

In the results from this optimization effort described here, the BASE version is the original "optimized for CPU" code where OpenACC parallel and data regions have simply been added. In the OPT1 version, the loops have been restructured to be more GPU friendly (see Fig. 27). Finally, in the OPT2 version, some precomputed arrays are replaced with on-the-fly computations and caching using scalar variables is introduced in the vertical direction. The code is parallelized employing the Message Passing Interface (MPI), using a domain decomposition method in the two horizontal directions. The reference CPU results are obtained on a 12-core Intel Xeon E5-2690 (Haswell) CPU using the Cray compiler and 12 MPI-threads. The CPU results are compared to those obtained on a NVIDIA Tesla K80 GPU card using both the Cray and PGI compilers in Fig. 30. Note that the K80 is a so-called dual GPU card, the GPU results are obtained using 2 MPI ranks so as to use both GPUs. The compiler version are Cray cce 8.4.0 with optimization flags "-O3 -hacc" and PGI 16.3 with "-O3 -ta=tesla:O0,cc35." For this version of the PGI compiler, the best results are obtained with "-ta=tesla:O0" as compared to higher optimization, e.g., "-ta=tesla:O3," due to some conflict between optimizations in the PGI tool chain. As in the section with the simplified atmospheric code, we again consider a domain size of $128 \times 128 \times 60$ grid points.

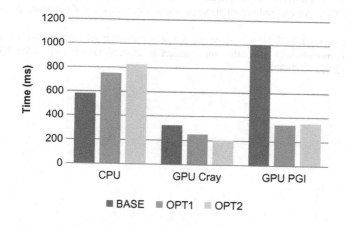

FIG. 30

COSMO radiation timing for a $128 \times 128 \times 60$ domain using the Cray and PGI compiler. CPU, 12-core Intel Xeon E5-2690 v3 (Haswell); GPU, Nvidia Tesla K80 card.

Looking first at the GPU results, we can see significant improvement when going from the base to the GPU-optimized code which stresses the importance of such optimizations. For the Cray compiler the time is reduced by 40% and by about a factor of 3× for PGI. We also notice that there are some differences between the compilers, in particular for the base code case, which result from different internal compiler optimizations. Another interesting point to note is that the GPU optimizations degrade performance on CPU, mostly because the final OPT2 code is less favorable for auto-vectorization. Additionally, the on-the-fly computations are less favorable on CPU in this part of the code, as the execution is compute-bound on CPU while it is memory-bound on the GPU. For community codes like COSMO, which should run with high performance on both CPU and GPU architectures, this lack of performance portability is a problem. One must either find an acceptable trade-off between the performance on different architectures, or, when the amount of code is limited in size as for the radiative solver, keep two separate versions: one for CPU and one for GPU. Finally, comparing the best CPU results (BASE) to the best GPU results (OPT2 with Cray), we achieved a speedup of about a factor of 2.9× on the GPU.

REFERENCES

Consortium for Small-Scale Modelling. The COSMO model. www.cosmo-model.org.
Fuhrer, O., Osuna, C., Lapillonne, X., Gysi, T., Cumming, B., Bianco, M., et al. (2014). Towards a performance portable, architecture agnostic implementation strategy for weather and climate models. *Supercomputing Frontiers and Innovations*, 2313-8734. *1*(1), 45–62.
Lapillonne, X., & Fuhrer, O. (2014). Using compiler directives to port large scientific applications to GPUs: An example from atmospheric science. *Parallel Processing Letters*, *24*(1), 1450003.
Ritter, B., & Geleyn, J.-F. (1992). A comprehensive radiation scheme for numerical weather prediction models with potential applications in climate simulations. *Monthly Weather Review*, *120*(2), 303–325.

Index

Note: Page numbers followed by *b* indicates boxes, *f* indicates figures and *t* indicates tables.

Printed in the United States
By Bookmasters